# Praise for *Poised for Ex...* P9-APM-925

"Karima Mariama-Arthur's *Poised for Excellence* shines new light on a path to personal and professional excellence. Its strategies capture ageless truths uniquely presented for our times. The breadth of her experience is beautifully woven into a guide that inspires the reader toward excellence. In a time of social chaos and information overload, *Poised for Excellence* helps to position the next generation of leaders to guide us out of the morass."
—Kamau Bobb *STEM Director, Constellations Center for Equity in Computing, Georgia Institute of Technology*

"Rarely is a leadership book equally practical and inspiring. Mariama-Arthur approaches leadership as self-actualization, providing a clear methodology while igniting the desire to take the prescribed actions to achieve a leadership personal best."
—Hayley Foster *Short Talk Expert® and Author,* Don't Tank Your TED Talk

"'Effective leadership' is a scarce commodity on which successful organizations, policies, and social interactions as well as education and academic work highly depends. Based on such rightful argument, the author of this inspiring book shows, in accessible style, how complex but 'effective leadership' can be learned practiced and developed. If your interests or professional needs require better understanding or enhancement of leadership skills … read this book."
—Jan Sadlak *President, IREG Observatory on Academic Ranking and Excellence*

"*Poised for Excellence* is a perfect training tool for rising and aspiring cadets at the United States Military Academy at West Point. Relevant for anyone in the military or civilian sector who endeavors to become the best leader they can possibly be, its insights will inspire you to rethink your path to leadership and empower you to become a better one."
—Andre Rush, Master Sergeant (MSG) *Senior Enlisted Aide/Advisor to the Superintendent, United States Military Academy at West Point*

"Karima Mariama-Arthur generously, graciously and expertly shares invaluable perspectives and experiences for personal and professional leadership excellence. Her insights are practical, accessible and implementable. Considerably more than a self-help book, Karima's offering is a bright light illuminating the path of those who are indeed poised for excellence."
—Patrina Clark, *CEO, Pivotal Practices Consulting*

"Bypassing the tendency of traditional leadership development models that simply categorize existent characteristics of perceived effective leadership traits, Karima Mariama-Arthur utilizes her extensive experience in nurturing human potential to cultivate the leadership development process. Karima's work not only provides the tools needed to develop the core leadership skills addressed by traditional models, but also those outside of them, while simultaneously utilizing personal reflection as a means of developing the interpersonal sensitivities needed to connect with the self at a deeper level. This perspective provides important context for understanding individual and group dynamics, which invariably helps organizations to achieve their strategic objectives."

—Malik R. Watkins, *Principal, Taking Ownership Public Service Associate, Strategic Operations and Planning Assistance Carl Vinson Institute of Government, University of Georgia*

"Turbulent times, such as those we live in now, demand the insights and guidance of "true leaders." *Poised for Excellence* is an exceptional guidebook, chock-full of key strategies for harnessing true leadership acumen. It speaks to my innermost conviction that leadership faculty is not merely hereditary, but is also acquired through a lifelong process of learning, focus and practice. I hope you enjoy reading it and applying its thought-provoking principles as much as I have."

—Amal Daraghmeh Masri, *CEO, Middle East Business Magazine and News*

Karima Mariama-Arthur

# Poised for Excellence

## Fundamental Principles of Effective Leadership in the Boardroom and Beyond

palgrave
macmillan

Karima Mariama-Arthur
WordSmithRapport
Washington, District of Columbia, USA

ISBN 978-3-319-87824-9          ISBN 978-3-319-64574-2   (eBook)
DOI 10.1007/978-3-319-64574-2

Cover illustration: © JohnDWilliams / Getty Images

Printed on acid-free paper

This Palgrave Macmillan imprint is published by Springer Nature
The registered company is Springer International Publishing AG
The registered company address is: Gewerbestrasse 11, 6330 Cham, Switzerland

# Foreword

Leadership always has been a topic of significant interest to me. For 32 years, I have taught leadership development to civilians in the academic, government, business, and corporate sectors. I also have had the privilege of leading Marines throughout my career with the exceptional Corps. My experience confirms that there is no such thing as a "born leader." No fairy dust lands on the shoulders of a newly promoted leader and magically provides direction on what the person should do. Everyone, without exception, must *learn* to lead. Experienced executives understand this concept and prioritize developing sound leaders in every area of an organization for its success. The most successful corporations in the world have this thread in common.

You are fortunate to have this copy of *Poised for Excellence*. Karima's unique professional insights, skills, and experience all have been brought to bear in this authoritative book on leadership. There are three reasons why you not only should read this book but also make it required reading for all leaders in your organization.

First, it makes the critical and, often overlooked, connection between soft skills, such as emotional intelligence, and leadership. Based on my more than 30 years of experience as a Marine officer, I can attest to the need for a high EQ.

Second, Karima's writing style makes it an enjoyable read. Any reader would want to devour it cover to cover, and use it as a "go-to" manual for leadership excellence. The fact remains that, there are numerous leadership books on the market, some better than others and some that readers put down almost as quickly as they pick them up. This one stands out.

Third, all leaders must do one thing above everything else—accomplish the mission or task at hand. Failure is not an option. Experienced and successful executives and leaders across industries know that their success depends on the ability to work through others—that is, those they lead—to accomplish the tasks. This book provides leaders with the fundamental tools that will ensure success and advance their leadership missions in the boardroom and beyond.

Karima has successfully compiled, in one book, a tour de force on leadership. Topics, such as emotional intelligence, owning mistakes, decision making, and challenging the status quo, are just a few of the key areas that reflect her expertise and, more importantly, provide readers with guidance on building competence across the panoply of leadership. Additionally, she has provided emerging as well as seasoned leaders with a clear path to success, chock-full of valuable takeaways that, when applied, will help able leaders to guide their organization into an optimistic and prosperous future.

Finally, I have always pointed out to all who listen: Women make extraordinary leaders. Karima, an exceptional and greatly admired leader in her own right, continues to make my point. This book is a testament to the remarkable ability of women to wield expertise and influence in a space that traditionally has been dominated by men. I am humbled to have been asked to write the Foreword to *Poised for Excellence—Principles of Effective Leadership in the Boardroom and Beyond*.

Enjoy the read and put what you learn into practice!

Colonel, U.S. Marine Corps (Ret.)                    John T. Boggs
President, Fortitude Consulting, LLC

# Preface

I have devoted my career to engaging and developing leaders at all levels, within traditional organizational hierarchies and outside of them. As the CEO of a boutique consulting firm specializing in professional development and a trusted advisor to accomplished individuals around the globe, I advocate for lifelong learning and the enthusiastic development of human potential.

As a burgeoning professional, I committed to developing core leadership skills and sought the advice of seasoned leaders who provided clear direction on navigating the often treacherous waters of leadership. These pivotal mentoring relationships helped me stretch and grow, and I resolved to embrace leadership development for the long haul.

Each leadership crucible required me to dig deeper to discover new possibilities, and each new discovery was a catalyst for my evolution. The challenges, considered individually and collectively, affirmed the powerful connection among self-examination, self-actualization, and self-mastery: The trio that has inspired my leadership ambitions in the courtroom, the boardroom, and beyond. Each challenge also taught me that the path toward effective leadership is lifelong, and, more importantly, requires an earnest commitment to excellence.

For leaders, individual achievement is not the only measure of success. Success also includes the interrelated processes and performance benchmarks of the institutions and organizations that they serve. That said, discerning leaders realize that they must cultivate personal effectiveness, because collective success necessarily depends on individual performance. As numerous studies make clear, excellent leaders are key to successful organizations.[1]

A compelling aspect of leadership is its evolutionary nature. It is a skill, rather a *skillset*, that can be developed through learning and practice. The argument, which holds that great leaders are born and not made, is specious at best. The Great Man theory of leadership was debunked long ago.

The pathway to effective leadership is contextual and collaborative, and it requires mastery of certain knowledge, skills, and abilities. Trial and error, risk management, adaptation, and increased perception are some of the tools of the trade that must be picked up along the path. Effective leadership demands mental and behavioral acuity; grit; creativity; innovation; and, of course, the ability to apply all this spectacular learning in real time.

Although some leaders seek positions of authority, others stumble into leadership roles. Another type of leader only rises to the occasion out of compulsion, when no one else is willing or able to step up to the plate. Regardless of how a leader arrives at the reins of power, the success of an endeavor is contingent on effective leadership.

This book presents a cross-section of fundamental leadership principles gleaned from my research, observations, and experiential learning as an advisor to high-level corporate, academic, government, and nonprofit business leaders. The pages ahead will introduce readers to selected core principles and walk them through the stages of the internalization process, which will help them develop leadership skills. All leaders, emerging or seasoned, can benefit from the perspectives and exercises contained herein.

My advice to readers is to fully explore each principle to understand how it contributes to effectiveness. Try to apply the Core Strategies. Then, after completing each of the Journal Questions in the chapter, reflect on any new perspectives gained. Finally, implement each Leadership Challenge. Follow the recommendations and observe your acumen grow exponentially. Thoroughly examining the principles and strategies in each chapter presents a unique opportunity to rethink the way leadership is viewed. Strive to achieve a personal best.

We all are works in progress.

At our best, though, we are poised for excellence!

Washington, DC                                          Karima Mariama-Arthur
September 2017

# Note

Abbatiello, A., Knight, M., Philpot, S., & Roy, I. (2017 February 28). Leadership Disrupted: Pushing the Boundaries. *Global Human Capital Trends*. Retrieved March 3, 2017 from https://dupress.deloitte.com/dup-us-en/focus/human-capital-trends/2017/developing-digital-leaders.html? id=us:2el:3dc:du p3822:awa:cons:hct17.

# Acknowledgments

To my amazing son, Khalil, who constantly inspires me to stand taller, to lead fearlessly, and to continue to spread my wings. I would not have written this book but for your sweet inspiration. To my remarkable family and friends who believed in me and kept pushing me to commit my best efforts to this book project. Your support reflects an enduring abundance of love, respect, and accommodation that continue to invigorate my spirit daily. I am proud to be in the arena, fighting for excellence, with you by my side.

Thanks to the Honorable John Boggs, Marine Corps Colonel; my incredibly talented team of editors; and the remarkable team at Palgrave. Without all your unique and considerable contributions, this book would not have come to fruition. I am sincerely grateful for the outpouring of love, support, insight, and graciousness that you have each given so willingly and without reservation.

# Contents

# Part I

## Principles that Foster Leadership Excellence Through Focused Introspection

# 1

# Exceptional Leaders Are Lifelong Learners

*Learning is a lifelong vocation inspired by unique opportunities to explore the unknown. Leaders who embrace this principle can maximize their own success and provide the tools that encourage others to follow their examples.*

Our world is changing at breakneck speed. Advances in technology have opened new vistas, streamlined operations, and increased opportunities for businesses and individuals alike. Not surprisingly, geographical boundaries that once divided us now seem insignificant.

The demands of this ever-evolving global ecosystem require leaders to pivot quickly and adapt to change decisively. The crux of this coveted skill set is what psychologist Howard Gardner identified and refers to as searchlight intelligence, one of several distinct theories of multiple intelligences.[1] It is the ability to "connect the dots between people and ideas, where others see no possible connection."[2] Searchlight intelligence is not an innate trait. It can be developed by virtually anyone with enough time, the right tools, and proper motivation.

As noted in the Introduction, exceptional leaders are not born. They are lifelong learners who have committed themselves to articulating a vision and to inspiring and motivating others. As their frame of reference gets broader because of their comprehensive learning experiences, they do not hold their knowledge back, but instead look for ways to transmit it to the next generation. Improvements in their leadership abilities occur in stages. Great leaders are persistent and never stop trying to learn. They intentionally cultivate growth and focus on incorporating lessons from their experiences in the hope of expanding their vision and refining their unique leadership techniques.

© The Author(s) 2018
K. Mariama-Arthur, *Poised for Excellence*, DOI 10.1007/978-3-319-64574-2_1

Although our educational system provides a formal structure and a foundation for learning, it rarely instills a love for perpetual learning. An effective leader must enjoy evolving through learning because, as today's variables change, yesterday's information quickly becomes obsolete. To close the gap between what we know and what is relevant, smart leaders must consciously seek out new opportunities to learn, develop, and advance. It is this unquenchable thirst for knowledge and evolution that separates exceptional leaders from the pack.

Even still, standout leaders are not merely self-interested knowledge seekers. They are also determined advocates who actively encourage leaders at all levels to stake a bold claim to their success. By demonstrating the power of incessant learning in their own lives, they inspire others to follow their examples enthusiastically. Their earnest commitment to helping others achieve greater purpose is a glowing testament to the value of effective leadership.

In an eye-opening Deloitte study described in *Global Human Capital Trends 2014*, effective leadership is the "No. 1 talent issue facing organizations around the world." To increase efficacy, organizations cite the need for increasing learning opportunities. More specifically, they need to "develop new leaders faster, globalize leadership programs, and build deeper bench strength."

Even though a focused strategy is a key step in addressing this global crisis, organizations also must acknowledge that continual learning and professional development need to go "hand in glove" to create effective leaders. Organizations embracing this principle create a compelling dynamic that inspires proactive learning in their workforce. Such a climate fosters greater collaboration and a spirit of teamwork. In addition, when specific performance and financial incentives are inserted into the mix, organizations usually thrive and advance to new levels of success.

The observations of an oil and gas industry CEO whom I previously advised add relevant context. Acknowledging her enthusiasm for persistent learning and development, she explained why she chose executive coaching to sharpen her skillset. She delved into her philosophy and summed it up by saying that no matter how much she earned or which new Fortune 100 client joined her roster, she always felt the need for continual learning. Perpetually improving her skillset provided unlimited opportunities to exhibit her best professional facet and to maximize the value for every client.

The CEO further clarified it this way: "Once you stop learning, you forfeit the right to teach others. You become stagnant and wed to best practices instead of innovating. At that point you will find that your clients outgrow you." She noted that her clients were always pleased by the powerful insights and unique market strategies she brought to the table. "They always walk away feeling full," she said: "Lifelong learning is a gift, not only to ourselves, but to others as well." Touché!

# Core Strategies

The strategies outlined in the following sections offer guidance for cultivating your skill and insight as a lifelong learner. They are distilled from the lessons I have learned from exceptional leaders across various industries.

## Pursue relevant, high-caliber knowledge sources

Expanding your knowledge base is not simply about increasing consumption. It requires identifying the most relevant and quality sources that can best enhance understanding of an industry, problem, or challenge. If someone reads a hundred books on quantum physics hoping to become an effective litigator, rest assured that time has been squandered. By the same token, even a relevant source might not enrich knowledge at the requisite levels. Start by identifying the leading experts who address the issue that needs to be explored. Then build a foundation of primary sources comprised of 5 to 10 books and scholarly articles. Half of these should discuss the broad background. The rest might zero in on a more specific dimension. Make sure the sources selected address contrasting viewpoints because there is always more than one way to view anything.

## Cultivate "deep smarts"

Lifelong learning is not an exercise in fact gathering. Although it does require mastering the fundamentals (competence) and continually expanding one's knowledge base to more advanced levels, there is also a greater end: "*deep smarts.*" What one *thinks* about and what one *does* with her or his knowledge repertoire impacts the ability to understand it fully and apply it in broader contexts. To develop an expert-level skillset, delve beyond the surface and engage learning and its application holistically. Deep smarts are cultivated by homing in on the unique combination of an individual's "particular mindset, education and experience."[3] Leveraging these components enhances the ability to problem solve, innovate, and deliver greater value to others.

Consider the neurosurgeon who uses a Harvard medical degree, extensive research, writings, and surgical experience to successfully navigate high-risk brain tumors. Not only is this knowledge reservoir remarkable, but it carries the potential to transform the practice of medicine. Think about your own unique blend of education, experience, and mindset and how it can be leveraged to make more valuable contributions in your field. Cultivating deep smarts can revolutionize your industry, inspire greater trust in supporters, and advance the overall goal of lifelong learning at a high level.

## Secure "high-touch" experiences with best-of-breed advisors

It is impossible to be all-knowing, no matter how smart or experienced a professional you may be. Everyone has knowledge gaps and dabbling—or worse, bluffing—that usually ends in disaster. The higher one climbs up the ladder of success, the greater the likelihood of encountering unchartered territory. Whenever your own knowledge reserves become exhausted while trying to steer through an unfamiliar scenario, consider seeking the one-on-one advice of someone more knowledgeable. Even the most accomplished leaders consistently strive to secure "high-touch" experiences with industry experts, and leaders at all levels can gain new perspective by engaging with able advisors.

Experts with specialized knowledge can offer practical advice on any number of substantive or procedural matters. Soliciting their wisdom can only enrich your understanding. Your accountant, for example, provides you with nuanced financial advice all year long. You use that advice to make critical tax-related decisions. If you could make these decisions on your own, you would, right?

Experts exist for a reason and having bona fide access to them when needed matters. No two professionals are alike in the real sense of the term. All experts have unique experiences, thinking, and communication styles, which effectively means a higher likelihood of you benefitting from the advice of more than one expert. Receiving another person's input only adds value and, more often than not, has a multiplier effect.

## Engage in observation and introspection

Observation and introspection are straightforward methods of advancing learning, regardless of discipline. Observing something directly helps you gain information about it. Think about the first time you watched someone bake a cake. If you wanted to recreate it afterward, chances are that you could, as long as you recalled the ingredients and instructions. A desire to learn more about one's self requires an inward journey to a deeper level. Introspection provides an opportunity to explore thoughts and feelings up close. Too often, we delay these exercises until something goes awry.

A better approach is to be proactive and set aside time for self-contemplation on a regular basis. Think about your decisions, progress, and missteps. Assess where more critical thinking and better decision making could have better served you. When you become conscious of detrimental thinking or behavior, abandon it and course correct. Above all, be honest with yourself. Hard truth is the best compass for navigating the path to self-actualization. For example, if working grueling, 14-hour shifts prevented you from properly studying for a critical exam, acknowledge it. Then determine two or three new possible avenues of approach. Neither observation nor introspection will work absent the willingness to confront the truth, stretch, or improve. So, prepare to do it with an open mind in advance.

## Step outside your comfort zone

Anything that becomes routine is at the risk of falling into a rut. Comfort is, well, comforting, and change can be difficult; however, learning is a lot like building muscle. Growth always causes some degree of temporary discomfort; embrace it and forge ahead. Commit to success for the long haul to see results. There are no shortcuts for lifelong learners: Broadening one's knowledge base requires real work.

Be willing to show up enthusiastically and try something new. If you want to get fit, and your current routine is not delivering, you may need to step outside your comfort zone. Tweaking your diet and turbocharging your exercise routine may be necessary to boost your results. It may be difficult at first; however, focused effort and consistency eventually help you to move past the hardship into a sweet spot. Just continue to visualize the desired outcome and trade what is familiar for what can enlarge your possibilities.

## Journal Questions

1. Identify any personal or professional development programs that you have previously completed and describe how each helped you achieve specific goals. Additionally, list any books that you have read during the past 12 months. For each book, describe any specific insights gained and how its application has advanced your knowledge and/or skill base.
2. Describe at least three missed opportunities resulting from a lack of qualifications or inexperience. What kinds of targeted learning might have changed those outcomes?

3. List five ways you can encourage lifelong learning within your organization.
4. How did this principle help you better understand your leadership role? How will its mastery enable you to cultivate greater effectiveness?
5. How will you use the preceding strategies to advance a personal commitment to lifelong learning?

## Leadership Challenge

What have you *always* wanted to learn to do, but never actively pursued? Maybe it is learning to cook, swim, or fly an airplane. Make a list of three dreamed-about pursuits that you have postponed to date. Which factors have prevented you from pursuing them? Next, determine the necessary steps required to pursue each activity, prioritizing them by importance. Establish a timeline of execution and a budget. Finally, write a statement pledging to complete each activity according to the terms stipulated. After each pledge, sign your name. How do you feel after having done this?

## Notes

1. Gardner, H. (2006). Multiple intelligences: New horizons (Completely revised and updated.). New York: Basic Books.
2. Mikkelsen. K., & Jarche, H. (2015, October 16). The Best Leaders Are Constant Learners. Harvard Business Review 93 (10). Retrieved June 10, 2016 from https://hbr.org/2015/10/the-best-leaders-are-constant-learners.
3. Leonard, D., Barton, G., & Barton, M. (2013). Make Yourself an Expert. *Harvard Business Review*, 91(4), 127–132.

# 2

# Emotional Intelligence Drives Leadership Success

*Cognitive intelligence and technical expertise account for a mere fraction of what leaders need to be successful. The mastery of soft skills, specifically the ability to perceive and influence our own emotions and the emotions of others, is critical to negotiating day-to-day interactions and to leading others.*

Intelligence is an intriguing concept that includes a wide range of knowledge, skills, and abilities. Not limited merely to cognitive ability or technical expertise, it includes key skillsets that relate to human engineering—namely, the ability to communicate, negotiate, and lead.[1] To execute and perform skillfully at high levels, a successful leader must govern with emotional intelligence.

This is especially true of experienced business leaders. Although cognitive intelligence and technical expertise help leaders carry out the basic functions of their work, the other side of leadership—the ability to create a compelling vision and to inspire others to embrace it—is more difficult to quantify. This is because developing emotional intelligence routinely is subordinated to the mastery of hard skills. Consequently, emotional incompetence is often identified as the primary cause of executive derailment.[2] In addition to performing the primary responsibilities within their areas of expertise, leaders must effectively manage human relationships, leverage influence, and cultivate thriving cultures that foster organizational success. Without emotional intelligence, these tasks are difficult, if not impossible, to accomplish.

© The Author(s) 2018
K. Mariama-Arthur, *Poised for Excellence*, DOI 10.1007/978-3-319-64574-2_2

# But What Exactly Is Emotional Intelligence?

The term "emotional intelligence" was coined by Professors Peter Salovey and John D. Mayer in 1990. They describe it as "a form of social intelligence that involves the ability to monitor one's own and others' feelings and emotions, to discriminate among them, and to use this information to guide one's thinking and action."[3] In other words, it is the ability to be aware of, to influence, and to express one's own emotions, as well as the ability to perceive and to influence those of others in the context of interpersonal relationships. Emotional intelligence helps leaders navigate the world around them successfully, especially in a socioemotional context.

Dr. Daniel Goleman later adopted the term and expanded the research on the subject. He discovered that, whereas cognitive intelligence (IQ) and technical expertise are important factors in determining competence, emotional intelligence (EQ) might be more important in predicting performance. Goleman's pivotal study examined factors contributing to the overall success of top executives. He found that emotional intelligence made a 90 percent difference in the success of the top performers.[4]

According to Goleman, emotional intelligence consists of five basic components: self-awareness, self-regulation, motivation, empathy, and social skills.[5] The following sections provide a closer look at each.

## Self-Awareness

We have a universe of emotions to draw from, and the ability to identify and connect with them—*to understand the self as an object*—is what helps one become self-aware. Emotions are visceral reactions to internal and external stimuli; these reactions become habits. To use these "habits" effectively, we must be intentional about the ones that we create, as well as those we eliminate. This requires observation and introspection to increase mindfulness and a greater understanding of one's character, emotions, motivations, and drive.

Knowing *why* we feel what we feel is equally as important as knowledge of the emotion itself. Do you understand your emotional triggers? Can you see them coming? Do you recognize the emotional triggers in others? Your ability to comprehend emotions in yourself and others is the first step toward developing the skills needed to influence your own emotions in the future.

## Self-Regulation

Although the ability to identify and understand emotions is critical to becoming more self-aware, exercising influence and control over them—in other words, self-regulating—is sometimes challenging. We all experience emotional highs and lows, but the ability to redirect and control them is what distinguishes effective leaders from those who fall victim to unbridled passions. Those who constantly blurt out angry words during a heated argument know the pain of regret. Similarly, chances are that those who have ever reacted negatively to constructive feedback not only missed the point of the exercise, but also experienced consequences because of their knee-jerk reaction.

Our ability to exercise control over emotions is critical to maturing personally and professionally as well as developing quality interpersonal relationships and influencing how others perceive us. We all know that mood swings are natural. Humans are not machines personified. We have emotions that usually overflow spontaneously. In professional life, however, they need to be controlled to avoid creating "ripples" that could potentially damage our standing within the workplace.

## Motivation

Do you have a vision for your success, fueled by an internal passion that keeps you focused and excited about achieving it? Or, are you dependent on outside forces to prod you toward milestones along the way? Optimistic drive and persistence, coupled with the ability to overcome odds with courage in the face of adversity, can make the difference in your ability to accomplish long-term goals and achieve the ultimate vision of success. Developing this trait puts one in the driver's seat and keeps one fully accountable for his or her success. Motivation is a constant reminder of why we do what we do. In times of doubt and distress, it can provide renewed energy and focus for completing the task at hand. Even when faced with slim odds, motivation fuels purpose and encourages one to find new and better ways of achieving a desired outcome. Self-motivation is also a prerequisite to inspiring others to champion change because your drive can be contagious.

## Empathy

A strong sense of compassion and sensitivity toward others are essential in developing trust, rapport, and overall quality relationships. They are also the building blocks of empathy. Humans are a social species with a congenital desire to connect with each other. That desire emits vibes, which define and structure interpersonal relationships. It can also help create connections that generate warmth and encourage reciprocity in your personal and professional circles.

Considerate leaders never hesitate to exhibit genuine empathy with others. Of equal significance, though, is the ability to suppress biases. Are you able to identify yours when examining another person's viewpoints or unique circumstances? The ability to appreciate diverse perspectives and experiences is especially important for those in a leadership role. Holding narrow points of view often leads to shortsightedness. In an ever-changing and increasingly heterogeneous global society, enlarging your frames of reference and developing a more comprehensive worldview are vital to creating the context for embracing the concepts of tolerance, diversity, collaboration, and innovation.

## Social Skills

As humans, we are drawn instinctively to relationships in nearly every facet of life. The very nature of leadership requires that people interact to collaborate and to achieve common goals. Thus, developing social skills should be a top priority for anyone in a leadership role. In high-stakes business endeavors, social currency is just as important as the terms of any negotiated agreement. Successfully navigating these specialized interactions requires the ability to perceive nuance, marshal etiquette, and persuade minds. These skills also help manage everyday situations (e.g., standard communication, social networking, and conflict resolution.)

A leader devoid of well-honed social skills will quickly learn that an impressive IQ and related technical expertise are often insufficient for negotiating the socio-professional waters. Developing these components of emotional intelligence provides leaders with essential career-advancing skills that have an immediate impact on day-to-day interactions.

I cannot help but recall an incident that will further elaborate the point. An attorney was referred to me as an executive coaching client. His human resources department had advised him of its concerns over his poor temperament and emotional outbursts, but the episodes were becoming more frequent and affecting his work as well as his relationships inside and outside of the firm. Although an extremely accomplished attorney, he found it difficult more often than not to reign in his temper. Conscious of this anomaly, he was worried that he would lose his job if he did not quickly improve his disposition.

Cognizant of the need to immediately address the situation, we drew up a strategy to help him develop greater emotional intelligence, which involved recognizing and controlling feelings and situations that triggered negative internal reactions. During our time together, he learned to positively respond rather than be impulsive. This helped him not only to keep his job but also to create and maintain healthier professional relationships.

# Core Strategies

The strategies outlined in the following sections offer guidance for cultivating the skill and insight required of an emotionally intelligent leader. They are distilled from the lessons I have learned from exceptional leaders across various industries.

## Increase the Range of Your Emotions

Challenging yourself to identify and experience a more diverse range of emotions on a daily basis can increase self-awareness. You can escalate this process simply by being more sensitive to your emotions. When they arise, identify them individually by name and think about why you are experiencing them. For example, if you notice that you are feeling "sad," ask yourself why and note what specific events may be contributing to this feeling. Also, ask yourself to identify "sad" on a continuum so that you can arrive at a more precise feeling.

What you are feeling may be more accurately described as "disappointed" or "heartbroken" rather than sad. Over time, you will discover key distinctions that will help you expand and take control of your emotional wheelhouse. Although it might seem counterintuitive, becoming more skilled in identifying and understanding the emotions of others will also increase self-awareness. Insight into emotional influences that shape others' thoughts and actions also promotes insight into the self, which allows you to influence others' thoughts and actions.

## Exercise Greater Control Over Thinking and Behavior

Learning to control thinking and behavior takes work, but it is doable with discipline and consistent effort. Instead of habitually reacting to stimuli, decide to respond on your own terms. In other words, be proactive rather than reactive. When faced with a decision, consider the possible options and their consequences. When you fear an uncontrollable outburst of innate anger coming on, take a deep breath, change the track of thoughts, sip a bit of water, or simply smile. The feelings of anger will eventually subside.

Knowing that uncontrolled anger can damage your health, relationships, and professional standing is impetus enough to control it with constructive actions that may appear trivial like those described previously. Similarly, if you notice you are becoming irritated by a coworker's incessant talking (especially while you are trying to concentrate on your work and a deadline), instead of aggressively "popping off," be assertive and let the person know that the talking is interfering with your ability to work. Chances are they will be considerate and stop.

Handling the situation this way not only helps one regain sanity, but prevents the unnecessary drama associated with allowing emotions to take control. By focusing on producing the best outcomes through clarity of thought and intentional behavior, you can completely transform your state of mind and achieve positive results.

## Thoughtfully Engage Others to Develop Empathy

Developing empathy is vital to improving every interaction, and it requires intentional engagement with others. Embracing perspectives other than yours, being less judgmental, and giving others the benefit of doubt are ways to cultivate empathy through thoughtful engagement. When someone expresses a difference of opinion, get curious instead of shooting him or her down. Think of it as an opportunity to learn from someone who might have had different experiences.

Learn to be a good listener, too. An active listener establishes good eye contact, uses engaging body language, and asks substantive follow-up questions. Try out these techniques during your next 1:1 conversation and notice how differently interpersonal dynamics develop. These strategies enhance the ability to establish rapport and understanding, which are the basis for trust, high-quality interactions, and long-term relationships.

## Ramp Up Intrinsic Motivation

If you are serious about making progress in any area of life, start by determining whether you are driven by the carrot or the stick. Do you find the promise of reward more motivating or the fear of punishment? Let me explain. Are you more connected to your fitness goal when you imagine donning flattering beachwear with newfound confidence? Alternatively, are you simply eager to avoid the negative consequences associated with being overweight?

Adopt whichever mindset is more compelling and then formulate a strategy broken down into individual tasks. This will move your goals forward and decrease the anxiety of tackling them all together. Finally, execute the plan. Remember, consistent focus and drive are key to sustaining long-term motivation.

## Increase Social Competence

Because we are *social beings*, it is nearly impossible to avoid human contact. Therefore, it makes sense to embrace relationships and make them work to your advantage. Learning social competence is a multifaceted process that involves basic conversation, complex communication, networking, collaborating, social etiquette, and conflict resolution. Honing a skill promotes its use in other areas, so expect some degree of crossover. To get started, move out of your comfort zone and practice active listening, engaging in meaningful conversations, collaborating, negotiating, and exercising common courtesies whenever possible.

A perfect opportunity to try these strategies is at the next networking event that you attend. Instead of simply hoping to walk away with a few new business cards and an opportunity to reconnect, aim at increasing social competence. Go in focused on improving a single skillset, such as thoughtfully introducing yourself or maintaining a good eye contact—skills you can practice repeatedly throughout the event. You may think these suggestions are common sense, but experience teaches that they are anything but.

## Journal Questions

1. Identify a situation where you used emotional intelligence to achieve a desired outcome. What specific component(s) did you use and how did it (they) impact the outcome?
2. Recall a situation where you observed someone utilizing emotional intelligence. What did you notice about the person's demeanor, communication skills, and overall behavior?
3. Which components of emotional intelligence are most important to you? Which are the least important? Explain.
4. How did this principle help you better understand your role as a leader? How will its mastery enable you to cultivate greater effectiveness?
5. How will you use the preceding strategies to advance your commitment to becoming a more emotionally intelligent leader?

## Leadership Challenge

List the emotions that you experience regularly. Do you like them? Why or why not? Now, write down three ways that can increase the influx of positive emotions you experience daily. Try out these strategies for a week and track your progress. Make a note in your journal every time you experience a positive emotion, specifically identifying it by name. How do you feel being more aware of your emotions? Next, write down three ways in which the regular experience of these emotions can make you a better leader. Strive to implement the techniques daily and record any improvement in your interactions and performance.

## Notes

1. Deutschendorf, H. (2015 October). Why Emotionally Intelligent People Are More Successful. *Fast Company*. Retrieved October 14, 2016 from https://www.fastcompany.com/3047455/why-emotionally-intelligent-people-are-more-successful.
2. Deutschendorf, H. (2015 October). Why Emotionally Intelligent People Are More Successful. *Fast Company*. Retrieved October 14, 2016 from https://www.fastcompany.com/3047455/why-emotionally-intelligent-people-are-more-successful.
3. Salovey, P., Brackett, M.A.P., & Mayer, J. (2004). Emotional Intelligence: Key Readings on the Mayer and Salovey Model. New York: National Professional Resources.
4. Goleman, D. (1995). Emotional Intelligence: Why It Can Matter More Than IQ. New York: Bantam Books.
5. Goleman, D. (1995). Emotional Intelligence: Why It Can Matter More Than IQ. New York: Bantam Books.

# 3

# Get Out of Your Way and Stop Sabotaging Your Success

*We repeatedly frustrate our success by standing in our way. As leaders, we must recognize the roadblocks to our success and remove them.*

Because the path to success begins with your self-concept, *you* are often the biggest obstacle to your achievement. If you are positive, you usually find that your dreams flourish and your endeavors thrive. If you are negative, you might find yourself plagued by self-limiting beliefs. Falling victim to such beliefs, however, can be a self-fulfilling prophecy, eroding your self-esteem, drive, and the ability to take action toward achieving dreams. If you reinforce these beliefs by engaging in self-limiting behaviors, you are likely to sabotage yourself.

Getting in your way represents one of the most common and formidable personal challenges on the road to attaining long-term success. It manifests itself as a relentless loop of self-deprecation, doubt, disillusionment, and fear, all of which negatively impact your performance. Even though most people are focused on external threats to their well-being and success, the greatest menace usually lies within. That said, it is critical to shift your perspective and carefully examine the role you play in enabling your own outcomes.

It can be difficult to recognize the threat that you pose to yourself, and it is nearly impossible to deal with a problem that you cannot see or, worse, refuse to acknowledge. Leaders must be honest with themselves to discover and confront their demons. Being vulnerable and surrendering your ego facilitates the process: When humility guides introspection, there is no limit to what you can discover and improve. The world then becomes your oyster and you are free to mine for its pearls.

© The Author(s) 2018
K. Mariama-Arthur, *Poised for Excellence*, DOI 10.1007/978-3-319-64574-2_3

There are four core elements that impede or facilitate success in eradicating self-sabotage: Thoughts, feelings, emotions, and behavior. *Thoughts* are based on cognition, a conscious intellectual act designed to help one acquire knowledge and understanding. *Feelings* "originate in the neocortical regions of the brain and are mental associations and reactions to emotions, and are subject to being influenced by personal experience, beliefs and memories."[1] *Emotions* "are lower level responses occurring in the subcortical regions of the brain, the amygdala and the ventromedial prefrontal cortices, creating biochemical reactions in your body altering your physical state."[2] Moreover, "emotions play out in the theater of the body. Feelings play out in the theater of the mind," notes renowned neuroscientist Antonio Damasio.[3] *Behavior* is a physical manifestation of thoughts, emotions, and feelings.

Knowing how the emotive reactions manifest themselves allows you to confront and influence them. First, one filters emotions through feelings, which are influenced by what is most familiar. Feelings help one to identify frames of reference that color our experiences and create deeper meaning through context. Next, one tries to make sense of it all and strives to acquire greater knowledge and understanding through thinking (cognition). Finally, individuals act, and behavior is shaped by all the preceding components.

By confronting the core elements in order—feelings, emotions, thinking and behavior—you can map out a deliberate plan for getting out of your way and ending self-sabotage once and for all. Being candid with yourself is an essential stepping stone for making this important leap. If you deny the truth, it will only hinder your ability to get out of your way.

Once the self is no longer an internal obstacle to success, it becomes easier to confront external obstacles, which often pale in comparison to the internal ones. Effective leaders dive deep into their psyches to discover any threats they pose to themselves and eradicate them. They are eager to become their very best and to own their roles in the process of personal transformation, so they set out to eliminate each threat, one by one and brick by brick. Their goal is to clear the landscape of mental debris so that they can think clearly and function at a high level without interference from the internal roadblocks that lead to self-sabotage and frustrate opportunities for greater success. Instead of defending their circumstances and surrendering to their demons, they take charge: They get out of their way and stop sabotaging their success.

I once worked with a university professor who failed to understand how she was consistently getting in her way despite receiving straightforward and constructive feedback from others. The university required that she fulfill certain requirements before she could receive a salary increase. Incident to this, she would often complain about her financial circumstances and how a raise would help her get ahead. Even still, she refused to take the appropriate steps to secure her financial future, arguing that it was unnecessary and too much work. To make matters worse, her poor grooming habits and routine violations of the university's dress code further exacerbated her predicament. Because of her demeanor, the students did not respect her authority, which was reflected in their interactions. This dilemma reinforced her lack of confidence and made it extremely difficult for her to develop rapport with other professors and to advocate for herself.

When I shared my observations with her, in hopes of opening the door for important dialogue, she said they were irrelevant. She made excuses, arguing that the university was out to get her because she was a maverick. She also claimed that the students and other professors were simply disrespectful and self-absorbed. This professor could not see how she was contributing to her problems and refused to acknowledge any evidence that pointed in that direction. Unfortunately, she became an obvious obstacle to her own success and additional self-sabotage was imminent.

## Core Strategies

The strategies outlined in the following sections offer guidance for cultivating the skill and insight necessary to eliminate self-sabotage. They are distilled from the lessons I have learned from exceptional leaders across various industries.

### Do Not Make Excuses

Rationalizing nonperformance will not improve your circumstances. It will only make matters worse. Explaining away your responsibility and accountability may feel temporarily freeing; however, it also makes for a slippery slope, increasing the likelihood of you doing it again and, thus, creating a persistent cycle of dereliction. This poignant cycle can frustrate your progress and tear at your self-esteem. A client's decision not to rehire you based on your frequent tardiness is valid.

Resist the urge to justify your behavior. Shun excuses, own up to your behavior, and assess where you may have gone wrong before blaming others. Instead of complaining, be constructive and take the necessary steps to course-correct and steer your life in a new direction. Overcoming the tendency to make excuses is an integral step in getting out of *your* way.

## Jettison Fear

Fear can be a paralyzing force that sways your thoughts and behavior, as well as taxes your capabilities. The way to overcome it is by confronting it head on. That is the true definition of courage, but it is also where most people fall down. The next time fear creeps in, encourage yourself to act by focusing on what you will achieve by exercising courage, no matter how small the victory may seem. Perspective is a powerful force when facing fear; use it to your advantage. Having a positive frame of reference helps to build intestinal fortitude, which can be leveraged in the future. Although fear may be challenging from time to time, confronting it with conviction helps you to move past it and build the confidence necessary to succeed.

## Refuse to Procrastinate

Procrastination causes stress and forces work to flow through a choke-point. More often than not, procrastination leads to substandard work and a marked decrease in overall performance. Although we always have the option of starting that project right now, we rarely exercise it. Fatigue and distractions are the culprits that encourage procrastination, but by learning to recognize them, you can take control of your destiny. Immediate action rather than putting tasks off increases chances of success.

Starting that project today would lighten your mental load and solidify the determination to complete it, as well as other projects in the future. Set yourself up for success: Add music to the mix, or complete assignments in small bursts to make drudgery less ominous and decrease the overall fatigue.

## Get Mentally Tough

Persevering through frustration, doubt, and disappointment can help to build mental toughness over time. Weak willpower makes it more difficult to address challenges head on and easier to give up when the going gets tough. To help build the mental and emotional stamina to get through rough times, dig deep. Muster the courage to move forward even when you do not feel like it or when things have not gone the desired way.

Think of the power of the mind for a moment. It can provide the energy and focus to accomplish even a herculean task despite any feelings of mental or physical incapacity. We have all been there. It is those instances that we learn to successfully navigate the labyrinth of uncertainty, doubt, and disillusionment. Being mindful of this process keeps individuals on their toes, prepares them to face more complex challenges when they arise, as well as helps to avoid perpetual self-sabotage.

## Get Out of Your Head

Overthinking and overplanning can easily become impediments to success. Despite the fact that execution requires some degree of thinking and analysis, it should not go on forever. Unlike procrastination, this problem manifests itself by being stuck in the initial phases of a strategy for too long. We have seen it: Someone wants to start a new business, but for one reason or another cannot move past the four corners of the business plan. The editing never ends and, of course, the business never gets off the ground. Avoid this eventuality. Take an inventory of daily habits and notice how they affect performance.

Likewise, make a list of any behaviors that are causing stagnation. Work to eliminate them individually. Then, notice how much closer you are to achieving goals, based on your fluid progress. Understanding the importance of getting out of your head and knowing how to do it, should be the motivation for taking immediate action and avoiding the complications associated with becoming stuck.

## Journal Questions

1. List three previous decisions that fear clearly influenced. Do you regret having made them? Why or why not?
2. Identify two chronic excuses that interfered with your ability to achieve an important goal. Do those excuses seem justifiable now?
3. On a scale of 1 to 10, how would you rate your current level of mental toughness? Explain.
4. How did this principle help you better understand your role as a leader? How will its mastery enable you to cultivate greater effectiveness?
5. How will you use the preceding strategies to advance the commitment to eliminating self-sabotage?

## Leadership Challenge

Name three ways you have stood in your way in the past. What have you learned from these experiences that will help you avoid repeating mistakes in the future? What are the three key ways that you can get out of your way right now? Write them down and put them on your refrigerator to serve as a constant reminder.

## Note

1. Damasio, A. R. (2005). Descartes' Error: Emotion, Reason, and the Human Brain. New York: Penguin Books; Hampton, D. (2015, January 12). What's the Difference Between Feelings and Emotions. Retrieved September 12, 2016 from https://www.thebestbrainpossible.com/whats-the-difference-between-feelings-and-emotions/.
2. Debbie Hampton, What's The Difference Between Feelings And Emotions? (https://www.thebestbrainpossible.com/whats-the-difference-between-feelings-and-emotions/)
3. Damasio, A. R. (2003). Looking for Spinoza: Joy, Sorrow, and the Feeling Brain. Orlando: Harcourt.

# 4

# You Are Your Own Best Barometer

*Effective leaders develop a strong sense of self and trust the wisdom of their guts. When you are led by a strong sense of self and trust the wisdom of your gut, you avoid the trap of seeking praise and dodging blame because you are comfortable in your own skin, and stand firm as your own best barometer.*

Whereas trusted advisors are an important component of any smart leader's decision-making process, confidence in one's thinking, both in times of tranquility and great turbulence, is a linchpin of effective leadership. A self-reliant leader has an increased likelihood of being a high performer, of fully leveraging his or her potential, and of experiencing long-term leadership success.

Being your own best barometer is not about residing in your head and avoiding all constructive feedback. Such behavior would prove detrimental to the overall process. On the contrary, it is about relinquishing the persistent need for affirmation from others. The crux of this principle is learning to trust *yourself* first, which does not happen overnight. Self-reliance is built on the foundations of clear thinking and good decision making amassed over time.

Other important building blocks in this process include discovering who you are and being comfortable with it. An additional layer is knowing what you think about yourself matters more than what others do. The core beliefs you hold about who you are form your self-concept, so they must be grounded in self-love and integrity with an eye on self-actualization. Without question, positive self-esteem and self-efficacy must drive these beliefs if they are to support a healthy self-concept.

Although most leaders are comfortable providing advice to others, the most effective ones are also comfortable following their own. Using the wisdom gleaned from a lifetime of experience—both positive and negative—is essential to achieving the goal of self-reliance. It takes courage, though, and a

© The Author(s) 2018
K. Mariama-Arthur, *Poised for Excellence*, DOI 10.1007/978-3-319-64574-2_4

willingness to trust your judgment, especially when cynics weigh in. Being enamored of praise and trying to avoid blame are external challenges to becoming self-reliant. Neither inclination provides the context for inspiring it. Continuously seeking validation from others prevents the development of a healthy and autonomous sense of self because it forces you to question the value of your own thinking and behavior. By giving someone else the power to define your worth, you lose a bit more of yourself with every appeal. This behavior is antithetical to good leadership.

We are all human, therefore we err. Even still, we often forget this basic maxim to our detriment. Dwelling on past mistakes and being self-critical are internal challenges to becoming self-reliant. Attempts to avoid blame circumvent the benefits of experiential learning. Just like being enamored of praise, this behavior also is inconsistent with good leadership. There is no shame in making mistakes and no honor in pretending to be perfect. Mistakes are a necessary component of long-term learning, so why not fail enthusiastically as you move forward and make more mistakes, faster? If you can embrace your mistakes and learn from them, your decision-making skills will improve, and your ability to advise others will likewise increase.

Self-reliant leaders strive to regularly assess their strengths and weaknesses to self-actualize. Even though everyone has a balance of both, we cannot recognize them in ourselves unless we are willing to take a closer look and honestly examine them for what they are. Once we fully assess them, we can begin to improve on weaknesses and fortify strengths. There is no limit to how great a leader you can become, so never stop trying to exceed your expectations. As a rule of thumb, the most driven leaders expect more from themselves than anyone else.

Because self-confidence is linked to self-reliance, smart leaders strive to strengthen it daily. They take every opportunity to increase their self-confidence by building positive emotional momentum. To this end, they not only care about and accept themselves, but also push themselves to grow beyond their comfort zones. They do not allow the opinions of others to negatively influence their self-concept. What others think does not factor into their day-to-day decisions. It is none of their business. Smart leaders turn a deaf ear to naysayers and act as competent self-guides as they move through the world and face its challenges head on.

Behavioral alignment creates integrity of service and builds the foundation for trust in oneself. It is impossible for a leader to behave in a way that contradicts their platform and yet garner the respect and support of a committed base. Leaders who strive to become their best barometers check in regularly and ask themselves if they are living up to the principles they espouse and demonstrating the behaviors they expect from others. Clearly aligning principles with behavior is the key to accomplishing the goals that you set for yourself as a self-reliant leader, and when practiced consistently, helps you to eliminate the need for external validation as you strive to become your own best barometer.

Misty Copeland desired to become a ballerina since she was a young girl. However, her critics were not convinced that she could be successful.[1] They said that she was too short, among other things, and lacked the potential to excel in the field. Even still, she kept at it. She persevered and practiced incessantly with her head held high. Despite a lack of industry support, she eventually became her own best barometer: She was comfortable in her own skin, drowned out the naysayers, and leveraged positive self-esteem to inspire her stellar work ethic and self-reliance. She became an incredibly powerful self-advocate, shattering the very stereotypes that kept her pigeon-holed by critics.

For Misty, becoming her own best barometer was a necessary step to achieving her childhood goal and reaching her full potential as a world-class ballerina. Had she become despondent and allowed her critics' opinions to get the better of her, she likely would not have graced the cover of *Time* magazine, made its list of Top Influential People in 2015, or become the first African-American female principal dancer with the prestigious American Ballet Theatre—a novel feat for the books, previously unheard of in its then 75-year history.[2] Through her personal evolution, she developed a strong sense of self, removed the need for external validation, and became her own best barometer.

## Core Strategies

The strategies outlined in the following sections offer guidance for cultivating the skill and insight needed to become your own best barometer. They are distilled from the lessons I have learned from exceptional leaders across various industries.

### Determine the Value of Unsolicited Feedback

Although feedback is an important aspect of growth, not all feedback should be eagerly embraced. Unsolicited feedback, in particular, is not always beneficial. Constructive criticism offered by someone who is genuinely concerned with your well-being can be valuable. Conversely, if the person criticizing does not genuinely care about your best interests, it can be destructive. There always will be someone ready to share their opinion of you or your work, even when you have not asked for it.

Think about it. How many times have you already experienced this scenario? Hold acceptable feedback to a higher standard; be a better steward of what you allow into the vulnerable territory that is your mind. Moreover, when receiving any unsolicited feedback, first consider the motive of the person giving it before deciding to embrace it.

## Trust Your Gut

When making decisions, consult tangible frames of reference, but also trust your gut instincts. Just like relationships with others, the relationship with the self must be grounded in integrity and confidence so that you can escalate decisions of consequence without fear or doubt. You can be your own best barometer only if you remove the need for external validation and listen to your inner voice.

Try listening to your instincts the next time you make a decision of consequence. If you feel something is not right, follow your intuition and govern yourself accordingly. Regret may be the price for ignoring the wisdom of your gut. The best-case scenario is that you dodge a bullet. The worst-case scenario is that the misfortune actually materializes. Either way, you are best off trusting your instincts.

## Cash in on Past Performance

Past wins are an important frame of reference for dealing with the current problems, and they boost your self-confidence. It does not matter whether past and present situations mirror each other. What matters is that we draw critical inferences from yesterday's lessons and apply them to today's challenges. If, for example, you successfully confronted ethical misconduct by the CEO of a major corporation before, know that you can leverage that outcome, and the strategies you used to achieve it, in dealing with a similar workplace crisis. Even though the circumstances may be different, the way forward will be the same.

Recall that the stakes were also high then. Remember what it felt like moving through each part of the process, how you kept your cool and composure, and how you faced the adversarial process with confidence and clarity. Rest assured you can do it time and time again with the wins in every aspect of your life. There is no need to reinvent the wheel because the foundations you have built will suffice to propel your decision making and success.

## Eliminate Praise and Blame as Key Decision-Making Factors

When making a decision shrouded in fear, we tend to seek praise and avoid blame. Accordingly, remove fear from the equation and make the decision based solely on its merits. Not everyone will support it, of course, and criticism may follow. Embrace those hard truths, but focus on the decision's substance rather than on its superficial appeal. The next time you find yourself at a crossroads and must choose a distinct course of action, shun the opinions of others as you weigh your options and decide how to move forward.

Terminating an employee for unethical conduct may be the best course of action even if it is the most unpopular. The opinions of others do not matter in the final analysis, and you alone will be responsible for the choices you make and the outcomes you create. A good decision is grounded in proper motives with costs and benefits that have been thoughtfully considered. It is not the one that will garner the most plaudits from others.

## Be Kind to Yourself

Becoming your own best barometer takes time and effort. However, do not be too hard on yourself as you work through the process. Although it is true that you will make mistakes along the way, you also will make important progress. Learn from mistakes and strive to improve. Daily, practice by tuning out negative self-talk and empower yourself to become more self-reliant. Likewise, be intentional about rewarding yourself when you get it right. Acknowledge your efforts in a tangible way by giving yourself something you would enjoy that punctuates your progress. A treat from your favorite local bakery, a much-needed massage, or even a day off are all great ways to do this.

Celebrating your efforts will encourage you to be kind to yourself more often and help you build momentum. Your goal should be to insist on a little more self-reliance daily and especially each time you face a challenge. Eventually, you will realize just how far you have come and how powerful a barometer you can be.

## Journal Questions

1. In which ways have you allowed praise and blame, as well as successes and failures, to influence your self-concept and decision making in the past? Cite specific examples.
2. Do you feel good about who you are and value the contributions you make to the world?
3. Name an instance when you trusted your gut. How did it make you feel? Have you ever experienced regret after not following your instinct? Discuss further.
4. How did this principle help you better understand your role as a leader? How will its mastery enable you to cultivate greater effectiveness?
5. How will you use the preceding strategies to advance your commitment to becoming your own best barometer?

## Leadership Challenge

Identify five major life accomplishments and the obstacles you overcame to achieve them. Were there naysayers back then? If so, how did you deal with them? Now, make a list of five major goals you would like to accomplish over the next five years. List any perceived obstacles. Using positive self-talk, create a plan outlining how you will overcome challenges and accomplish goals.

## Notes

1. Copeland, M. (2014). Life In Motion: An Unlikely Ballerina. New York: Touchstone.
2. The American Ballet Theatre was created in 1940, and Misty Copeland became the first African-American female principal dancer in 2015.

# 5

# You Are Your Competition

*Leaders exceed their own expectations, and they always strive to be better than they were before.*

The world is full of trivial distractions. Some of the most common examples result from self-deception and are the biggest causes of personal and professional derailment. Getting bogged down in the muck and mire of competition is one of the most egregious. Commanding the very best of one's self each day requires turning a blind eye and a deaf ear to the distraction of illusive rivalries. It also requires a relentless desire to consistently outperform one's self. There is no doubt that illusive rivalries come and go, but they rarely merit the time and energy so generously devoted to them.

Effective leaders create expectations of themselves and set their own benchmarks. They focus on their progress and performance rather than the artificial rubrics advanced by others. They routinely challenge themselves and do not care what the Joneses or the Smiths are doing down the street. The forward movement of another has no bearing on their own mobility and, therefore, they are wise to avoid becoming obsessed with it. As the captains of their fate, they refuse to be distracted by the ruse of competition or the showy affairs of others.

Without healthy self-esteem though, it can be easy to focus outwardly and covet others' accomplishments. The mental and emotional urge to compete and gain status can be seductive, making it difficult to simply acknowledge other individuals' wins and move on without being envious of their success. To avoid battling phantom antagonists, leaders recognize that they are only ever competing against themselves. They know that it is misguided to compare themselves with others, and that it diminishes the significance of each person's contribution

© The Author(s) 2018
K. Mariama-Arthur, *Poised for Excellence*, DOI 10.1007/978-3-319-64574-2_5

to the world. When you feel yourself comparing your scorecard against that of another, correct your thinking. The grass is not greener on the other side. Focus on the landscape in your own backyard and work diligently to ensure that it flourishes independently of what is being cultivated elsewhere.

Collective contributions make the world a better place for all. The sheer depth and variety of these contributions are meant to foster goodwill and an earnest appreciation for their diversity. When we try to compete out of envy, we miss the mark. Each person's individual contributions are unique and cannot be duplicated; a point lost on so-called haters and earnest admirers alike. No one can do what you do, the way that you do it. The DNA of your experiences and perspectives colors everything you do in the most unique and magnificent way. That filter can never be leveraged as a commodity.

The fight for relevance and the fear of being a less desirable option fuels delusions of scarcity and feelings of competitiveness. Avoid this fight, as it is one that only results in an immense loss of self-esteem and a radical distortion of your self-concept. Scarcity, even if artificial, can become a self-fulfilling prophecy. If a person becomes paranoid about the magnitude of their value vis-à-vis others, what is true can easily be disregarded and what is aggrandized can surface as the alternative reality. Either way, the illusions are poignant and palpable.

Leaders who operate with dignity and self-love have precious little time to compare and contrast their worth with anyone else's. Their priorities are fundamentally different. They are like Clydesdales running audaciously in their own tracks. They have their heads held high and the expectations they hold of themselves reflect an intrepid mindset that urges them to dig deeper and consistently show up in excellence. Even when they have single-handedly produced an impressive upset, they strive to become better by tweaking the finer details of their performance. They purposely search for nuance, an edge that can help them distinguish the quality and quantity of their results.

Mediocrity lives at the intersection of complacency and inertia. While leaders who embrace this principle create a customized path to success by ignoring the distraction of competition, they get to work as well. They focus on their mission and are not afraid of heavy lifting. They do whatever it takes, even when they do not feel like it. In fact, that is when they become the most "gritty." They exercise discipline to maintain their attention and motivation for long stretches. Without the proper mindset and work ethic, good intentions fizzle. Even those competing against themselves will lose the race if unprepared for its rigor.

Floyd Mayweather Jr. is an excellent example of someone who lives this principle day in, day out.[1] An undefeated, five-division professional boxing champion who has successfully competed in every single weight class except heavyweight, Floyd Jr. has never tied preparation to an opponent's prowess. He trains for the sake of becoming better than before and to discover nuances that make him stronger, smarter, and more agile. With an impeccable work ethic that includes extraordinary discipline, he is known for training at odd hours while others are fast asleep. He pushes himself to the limit, acknowledging that his talent and uncommon success can diminish at a moment's notice.

Floyd Jr. does not fall below his own standard of excellence and he consistently challenges himself to reach beyond his comfort zone, adapt, and enlarge his skillset. What he knows for sure is that despite his incredible track record and consummate boxing aptitude, every next fight carries the possibility of a loss. That lucky punch is always available to a willing and discerning opponent. Floyd Jr., is distinguished by his remarkable ability to consistently exceed his expectations and determination to continually improve on perfection in its own right. There is no doubt that his legendary TKO, besting mixed martial artist Conor McGregor and updating his umblemished record to 50-0 on August 26, 2017, has proven beyond a shadow of a doubt that Floyd Jr. is indeed his *own* competition.

# Core Strategies

The strategies outlined in the following sections offer guidance for cultivating the skill and insight needed to see yourself as your only real competition. They are distilled from the lessons I have learned from exceptional leaders across various industries.

## Develop a Gold Standard of Excellence

Mediocrity means doing just enough to get by, and leaders are never content with shoddy efforts. They establish a gold standard of excellence that reflects high ideals that sync up personally and professionally. It does not mean that you must strive to be perfect; it does, however, mean that you should consistently put forth your best efforts and always challenge yourself to become better. Take a good look at your whole life. What do you see? Who do you want to become? What do you want to accomplish? Set your sights high.

Develop a five-year plan that is chunked backward into yearly and quarterly assessments. Push yourself to achieve the goal at each benchmark and then assess your progress and tweak any strategies as necessary. Even after all the work you have done on yourself, you will inevitably still have more to do.

That is the nature of being human and imperfect; however, as long as you are working to improve yourself, you are on the right path.

## Expect More from Yourself than Others Do

Even though leaders must be goal-oriented and aspire to high standards of performance, they also must be driven taskmasters in their own right and for their benefit. In addition, they must have higher expectations of themselves than those projected onto them by others. When you strike out to complete a task, do not reduce its completion to a mere run-of-the-mill transaction. Do it, but do it *well*. Put in the additional effort to make the end product extraordinary rather than simply average. Gussy things up. Show up and show out whenever you execute; let excellence be your signature. As you strive to embrace the idea of competition in a different way, you still must work to exceed your own expectations; after all, you always are competing with yourself to become better than you were before.

## Get Off Your Laurels

Your past successes can be great frames of reference when you start a new project. They give you the confidence to forge ahead. Nevertheless, you need more than just the confidence accumulated from past performances to shape the future; you need to create new goals that stretch you and inspire you to do more. Just because you wrote a stunning article that attracted the attention of millions last month does not mean you should sit back idly and ride the wave of your fame. Chances are you have many more valuable ideas to share and you should.

If you get too comfortable with the sum and substance of your achievements, you run the risk of becoming irrelevant. Although drawing from past achievements can help you determine new possibilities when you set your mind to the work, expanding the scope of your vision and activity are necessary to becoming your best self.

## Discover Ways to Innovate

Doing things the way you always have will not help you move beyond where you are now. Even though an established rhythm of "plugging and playing"— that is, conventional transactions where novel effort is not required—may be common in your workplace, these kinds of transactions have their limitations.

Discovering new opportunities requires leaders to sacrifice comfort and innovate. If current practices are not helping your organization to achieve the results that is required, try something new. Maybe a few things. Then push forward even if you receive pushback. Get creative.

Have the courage to articulate your vision and respond to the opposition with a fresh perspective. Your foresight can help your organization and its workforce achieve new levels of success by introducing cutting-edge thinking and unorthodox ways to boost collective performance.

## Evaluate Your Results

Being busy is not the same as being productive. This revelation, however, can be difficult to discover if you neglect to evaluate the byproducts of your efforts. Take a close look at the results of your last projects and ask yourself whether you accomplished what you set out to do. If not, revisit the steps that you took to arrive at your destination. Reexamine the goals and the strategies that you used.

What worked and what did not? Which specific elements could be improved the next time? Ask penetrating questions. You may even want to get feedback from an independent source who may offer a unique perspective. Make sure you do a thorough assessment, though, to avoid repeating previous mistakes that did not serve you and may cost you future gains.

## Journal Questions

1. Explain what motivates you to set goals. Do you feel it necessary to raise performance standards after you successfully reach certain benchmarks?
2. Describe the following aspects of your work ethic: quality and quantity of output, organization, discipline and timeliness.
3. Does other people's success influence how you set objectives for yourself? Discuss.
4. How did this principle help you better understand your role as a leader? How will its mastery enable you to cultivate greater effectiveness?
5. How will you use the preceding strategies to advance commitment to setting higher standards of excellence for yourself?

## Leadership Challenge

Push yourself to surpass your current expectations for this week. Select one of the most important goals that you are currently pursuing and set your intentions. Next, set three specific guidelines for how you will push yourself to the next level. Record your progress at the end of the week. Did you reap significant rewards by pushing yourself harder than usual?

## Note

1. Dixon, Tris. (2015). Money: The Life and Fast Times of Floyd Mayweather. Endinburgh: Birlinn Publishers.

# 6

# Integrity, Transparency, and Ethical Behavior Always Matter

*Integrity is how we behave when no one is watching. Leaders are expected to know the rules and are held to a higher standard of behavior—a standard that prescribes ethical behavior as a nonnegotiable leadership imperative.*

No matter what role you play in an organization, integrity, transparency, and ethical behavior always matter. Standards of behavior are typically well-established and do not change based on organizational dynamics or administrative hierarchies. In addition, the higher you climb up the ladder, the more you should know about those standards.

Leaders who do not embrace ethics do more harm than good, regardless of the overall value they bring to the organization. When ethics are subordinated to other priorities, floodgates open for bribes, side deals, and compromises that wreak havoc on the organization's reputation and the ability to successfully execute the business it was created to carry out. Fragile gains never merit the sacrifice when unethical behaviors set the tone for a bargained-for exchange.

Remember this: What you do in private eventually is revealed in public. There is an inherent danger in assuming that you are above reproach, that you can hide your indiscretions behind your title. You may not get caught the day you commit the violation, but rarely does that skeleton stay buried in the closet forever. If you are willing to take that chance by gambling with your integrity and the well-established standards of professional conduct, you do so at your own peril. The coercive influence of impropriety may be alluring, but ethical leaders will resist the urge to capitulate. They know that reputation and credibility are valuable assets to be safeguarded in a trust economy.

© The Author(s) 2018
K. Mariama-Arthur, *Poised for Excellence*, DOI 10.1007/978-3-319-64574-2_6

Ethical backsliding has significant drawbacks. First, it damages your self-concept. Even when you think you have escaped public scrutiny, you must still face the person in the mirror. When you lose self-respect, it is difficult to be an effective leader. It also is difficult to ask others to adhere to established standards of behavior when you have not governed yourself honorably. Second, it damages your reputation with others. Someone who double-deals is perceived as less trustworthy than a straight shooter. The negative impact on your professional reputation can be devastating, as we have seen countless times in business and government.

In some cases, legal consequences can be even more catastrophic. A leader must stop and ask whether the proscribed behavior is worth the weight of potential consequences. No matter how the alleged benefits are characterized, they will always pale in comparison to the probability of any negative ramifications.

Ethical behavior is not just about what *you* do, though. As a leader, you also are charged with holding others accountable for their behaviors. Do you turn a blind eye to ethical violations, encourage them, or work in concert to cover them up? Do you give passes to people you know well? If so, you should work to fix your moral compass. The assumption is birds of feather flock together. Not only that, you should be concerned that you have not created a laissez-faire environment where others feel they can do whatever they want without consequences or interference. Dignity and morality cannot exist when there is an absence of cultural integrity.

Understanding the role of transparency in leadership effectiveness also is critical to this discussion. Do you communicate openly and honestly or do you obscure motives using pretexts? Think about how you communicate vital messages and how you respond to messages communicated to you. Say what you mean and mean what you say. An ethical leader would refuse to operate using insincere motives or surreptitious means to achieve goals. Transparency requires stepping up to the plate with clear intentions and communicating them fearlessly and unambiguously, even when it may be inconvenient and resistance or resentment may occur.

A leader who wants to be taken seriously and earn the respect of peers and subordinates alike must govern themselves according to the widely accepted standards of ethical behavior. This mandate not only reveals the soul of a leader's ethical code, but also signals what they are willing to accept from others. If you are a good example of what you represent, others will be more inclined to self-police their behaviors. Part of the goal of effective leadership is to *be* the example so that explaining is not required. Strive to be the example of transparent and ethical leadership, especially when no one is watching.

The Enron scandal of 2001 rocked Wall Street and created uncertainty in the fidelity of big businesses in America.[1] With industry deregulation allowing companies to hedge bets on future pricing, it created a market environment where spiking share prices became the norm. The uptick in apparent profitability encouraged individual participants, as well as trading partners, to get on board. It also created a slippery slope that encouraged large-scale market manipulation. Enron decided to make the most of its position and disregarded its ethical imperatives. To make more money and hide its financial losses, it engaged in numerous financial schemes. One of the most shocking was called market-to-market accounting. In layperson's terms, it is a technique used to measure a security using its current value rather than its book value, which means it appears to be worth more than what it is.

To achieve its goal of eliminating losses from the books and protecting its bottom line, Enron created assets and claimed profits whether or not it had actually made any. Additionally, it would transfer any loss of revenue to an off-the-books corporation and that detail went unreported. When Arthur Andersen got involved to oversee Enron's books, it made matters worse. Despite its impeccable reputation for no-nonsense risk management, it turned a blind eye to the wrongdoings and cosigned the transactions. In the end, both entities were prosecuted for moral turpitude. Whatever financial gain the parties might have received from their misconduct was hardly worth the destruction of the individual companies, and the criminal and civil penalties that ensued.

# Core Strategies

The strategies outlined in the following sections offer guidance for cultivating your skill and insight as an ethical leader. They are distilled from the lessons I have learned from exceptional leaders across various industries.

## Know the Rules and Follow Them

The rules of professional responsibility are cast in stone in every industry. Thoroughly familiarize yourself with them and check with your human resources department if you are uncertain about any aspects. Not only will they guide your actions and sharpen your ethical instincts, but knowing the legal and regulatory landscape will keep you nimble as you navigate unfamiliar professional waters. Be aware of any changes or updates in laws, caveats that may color your particular circumstances, or any professional insights that can add to your understanding of substance or process.

Accord equal importance to the letter and the spirit of the law or the governing rules. Every letter has a spirit floating underneath it. Implementing the letter alone while ignoring the spirit kills the purpose. Ideas, values, and norms are all ingrained in the spirit with the letter only being a vehicle. Because the letter of the law can be interpreted in many ways, it is equally important to acknowledge the underlying spirit and govern yourself accordingly.

Additionally, be cognizant of any relevant policies that affect day-to-day decision making. These often impact the application of laws, which may also have ethical implications. Finally, resist the urge to maneuver outside the law no matter how enticing the rewards may seem. Regret, civil and criminal penalties, as well as job loss and damage to your reputation are all hefty prices to pay for malfeasance.

## Resist Groupthink

A position argued effectively and consistently can seem convincing, especially when adopted by a wide majority. Political rhetoric, when espoused prophetically, can urge the masses to accept it as true and even become outspoken advocates. The legacies of Adolph Hitler and Joseph Stalin are indelible reminders of this. No matter where the push or pull may come from, resist the urge to capitulate based on peer pressure. Examine the evidence independently. Think for yourself. Choosing to blindly accept perspectives or adopt delegated courses of action without first considering the source and having a handle on the subject matter is ill-advised and could have a chilling effect on your professional standing. Give yourself the time and space to better understand a position, develop your point of view, and even disagree if necessary. In the process, you may even come up with new ideas that lead to preferable results. Consider it your moral responsibility to make the best decision for yourself, as well as to contribute to the greater good.

## Look Before You Leap

It is always wise to thoroughly assess a situation before taking a specific course of action. Do not make assumptions or take for granted that what you have been told is correct. Do not rely on outdated information and presume nothing in the law has changed. You could very well be wrong and gambling with uncertainty might not always weigh in your favor.

Instead, ask good questions and gather facts. Review the law. Ascertain any nuances. Then, reassess. Do not rush to judgment. Rarely will you need to make a decision on the spot, and even when time is of the essence you can speed up this process to ensure that you have not missed the finer points. Take a beat before taking any action that could negatively impact your professional credibility or livelihood. Your peace of mind is worth the wait and its weight in gold.

## Confront Unethical Behavior

It may not always be you who is confronted with an ethical dilemma. Perhaps it is a colleague or someone you do not even know who is pitted against the law. It may even be a superior. It does not matter. How you handle these situations will determine whether people look to you as a gatekeeper or as a person willing to compromise integrity when convenient. You do no one any favors by sweeping offenses under the rug. Your wise counsel may even be the turning point for a much-needed intervention. Decide in advance to do what is right. Be courageous in the face of misconduct. Be the voice of reason and morality for the benefit of those who need it the most, which also may have a lasting impact and reverberate throughout the organization.

## Work with Others to Drive Compliance

Successfully managing risk and ensuring compliance is not achieved through the struggles of a single individual. It takes an entire team of committed professionals to execute effectively. Be proactive. Meet with your HR and legal teams to learn the best way to promote deterrence and enforce compliance. Work in collaboration to develop core messaging that is visible, influential, and consistent with the organizational mission. Determine which actions can be taken individually and which require the collective support of all departments. Then, delegate accordingly.

You can play a critical role in prioritizing compliance by demonstrating your enthusiasm and commitment to ethical engagement. Your behavior also may inspire others to raise their standards and self-police, thereby becoming more actively involved in the process, which is exactly the point.

## Journal Questions

1. In your opinion, how does personal integrity impact how others perceive you?
2. How familiar are you with the code of ethics, rules, and regulations in your industry and how they are applied?
3. If you observed someone violating an ethical standard, would you confront the person? If so, what would you say or do? If egregious enough, would you notify HR of the violation?
4. How did this principle help you better understand your role as a leader? How will its mastery enable you to cultivate greater effectiveness?
5. How will you use the preceding strategies to advance your commitment to be more transparent and ethical in your daily affairs?

## Leadership Challenge

Identify a critical area in which you have compromised your integrity in the past. Why did you do this? Create a five-point strategy demonstrating how you will behave in a different way if the situation presents itself again in the future. Keep the strategy close in case you need to remind yourself of your "why" and exactly how to proceed.

## Note

1. McLean, B., and Elkind, P. (2003). The Smartest Guys in the Room: The Amazing Rise and Scandalous Fall of Enron. New York: Portfolio.

# 7

# Leaders Create the Best Version of Themselves Without Apology

*Leaders strive to create the most polished, professional, and authentic versions of themselves without apology because they know that both form and substance matter.*

A compelling brand is the marrow of effective leadership. Without question, understanding a brand's key components helps leaders to build theirs successfully. No matter what industry you are in, your brand shapes the way others perceive you. It puts the world on notice, broadcasting who you are, illuminating competencies, possible synergies, and inspiring opportunities to collaborate. To be clear, branding is not an exercise in frivolity. It is an extraordinary opportunity for every professional to determine how they want to show up in the business world. Whatever choices leaders make toward this effort are calculated to produce specific and analogous results. When those choices are proactive and conscientious, the possibility of producing positive outcomes increases exponentially. On a basal level, even grooming and style choices send clear messages about how leaders perceive themselves and impact how others see and interact with them. Becoming the best version of yourself can be an ambitious and time-consuming process, but it is well worth the effort.

The building blocks of a compelling leadership brand include establishing a core identity and having clarity around the image you want to project. Identifying substantive expertise and developing "deep smarts" come next, a strategy discussed in Chap. 1. None of these matters, however, if a leader does not recognize his or her value and fails to distinguish himself or herself in the marketplace. Carving out your niche, the excellence you desire to be known for exclusively, is fundamental to this aim.

© The Author(s) 2018
K. Mariama-Arthur, *Poised for Excellence*, DOI 10.1007/978-3-319-64574-2_7

Even though every industry has a relevant standard for the basic ingredients of a successful brand, yours should be personalized, adding enough of yourself so that you do not come across as inauthentic or end up misappropriating someone else's. Doing so would be a professional, and potentially legal, faux pas. Either way, there are consequences for failing to do the necessary groundwork. Remember that your brand is your *identity* and is what the world relies on in determining whether or how to engage you. Instead of wandering aimlessly through the process, take the time to consider what aspects of your brand are non-negotiable, which project unmistakable excellence, and which help you to secure the exclusive positioning that you seek. Once you have clearly constructed your brand identity, you must then infuse its components into the fiber of your work.

Developing healthy self-esteem is critical to brand development. The comprehensive view that we have of ourselves—the internal dialogue that informs how we perceive and communicate our worth to ourselves and to others—establishes the self-concept. A conscientious leader, who is working diligently to become his or her best self, would not emerge as an apologist for having a positive self-concept. It is not conceit or arrogance to be comfortable in your own skin; it is a state of certainty that inspires effective leadership. Without it, you cannot build a compelling personal or professional brand. Own your moxie, your intelligence, your talent.

Your gifts are the reasons that you are where you are. Even when jealousy and envy get the best of others, confident leaders will not allow such behavior to rattle them or to interfere with their work. Instead, they will tune out negative voices, both external and internal, refusing to let them erode their self-confidence, jeopardize their brand, or undermine their ability to lead. They own their excellence, and their confidence is one of their best accessories.

Even after creating a stellar brand, if your messaging is inconsistent, your behavior erratic, arbitrary, or capricious, all your hard work would have been done in vein. What good is it to build a solid brand foundation and spend the time garnering respect and influence over time, if only to have it crumble after engaging in behavior inconsistent with your brand? To be clear, leaders are not expected to be one-dimensional or mundane in their approach. But the need to exercise creativity and variety should not result in a slippery slope. Leaders are expected to exercise decorum, avoid hypocrisy, and give wide berth to conduct that may raise questions of credibility and challenge the sanctity of their leadership brands.

Leaders create the best version of themselves by constantly learning and tweaking their understanding of the world, and this yearning for personal and professional improvement is the driving force behind every accomplishment. They aim high, not because the sky is not the limit, but because it is the gateway to infinite possibilities. Those possibilities cannot be realized, however, unless they embrace their flaws and eagerly seek to correct them. As such, smart leaders have zero interest in adopting the façade of so-called leadership exceptionalism. They become their best selves by acknowledging that self-improvement is an intrapersonal experience that transforms a person from the inside out, and its motivation must be sound and independent of any motive to compete with anyone else.

A clear commitment to doing the inevitable and most challenging work puts these high-octane leaders in a prime position to self-actualize. Self-actualization is at the apex of Abraham Maslow's *Hierarchy of Needs*[1] and is the crowning achievement—the most advanced of needs—for which humans strive. Yet, the best leaders know that self-actualization is ongoing. It is a lifelong process that cannot be punctuated by a culmination of events or achievements. It is this very understanding that motivates effective leaders to consistently pursue excellence in every aspect of life and to become the best version of themselves without apology.

The evolution of Chimamanda Ngozi Adichie, Nigerian novelist and world-renowned feminist, exemplifies the profound commitment of leaders to become the best version of themselves.[2] A consummate student of lifelong learning, Adichie began her academic career by studying medicine and pharmacy at the University of Nigeria. She left Nigeria for the United States at age 19, where she began studying political science and communications at Drexel University in Philadelphia. Later, she transferred to Eastern Connecticut State University and graduated *summa cum laude*. She then received a Master's degree in creative writing from Johns Hopkins University and a Master of Arts degree in African Studies from Yale University.

A Hodder Fellow at Princeton University, a Radcliffe Institute for Advanced Study Fellow at Harvard University, and a MacArthur Fellow, Adichie continued to clinch a legion of first-class academic experiences. She also wrote six critically acclaimed novels and in 2013 debuted in the single "Flawless,"[3] which was featured on the record-breaking album "Beyoncé" by Beyoncé Knowles-Carter. Her impressive academic trajectory and literary and professional successes are each a testament to her relentless ability to create a compelling leadership brand, while continuing to carve out new territory and enhance her ability to deliver greater value through socially conscious work.

An audacious and unapologetic thinker, writer, and speaker, Adichie is unbothered by the superficial opinions of others. Her concern lies with expressing the truth accurately and authentically. As a feminist, she is crystal clear on the composition of her brand identity—right down to her African roots and inclusive of her bold, beautiful style choices. Adichie shares a unique and consistent message of principled empowerment that resonates across genders and cultures. She is simply a brilliant example of purposeful leadership, the dynamism of human experience, and how to create the best version of yourself without apology.

## Core Strategies

The strategies outlined in the following sections offer guidance on cultivating your skill and insight in becoming the best version of yourself. They are distilled from the lessons I have learned from exceptional leaders across various industries.

### Assess the Status of Your Current Brand

It takes time and effort to become the best version of yourself. For most, a lifetime. So, commit to conducting a thorough self-assessment and to doing the work it will take to make solid progress. Are you happy with your personal brand right now? Take a hard, honest look. If you see room for improvement, and there is no doubt that you will, evaluate where you are effective and where you need the most work. Probe deep to understand why you are where you are now and then develop a strategic plan that can take you where you want to be.

Make sure your plan includes benchmarks with deadlines, as you will unlikely morph overnight into the ideal you aspire to become. Then, determine which resources you will need to tap into and successfully execute your plan. Moving from where you are to where you want to be will likely require additional development and the advice of experts who can competently set you on the right course.

### Get a Second Opinion

Getting another perspective on your current circumstances can help you move forward decisively. Consider the advice of a personal and professional branding expert who can evaluate the particulars with a well-honed eye. Choose someone with a well-established reputation that you can trust and who is qualified to give you the feedback that you need, as well as help you to successfully elevate your brand. Since you want to fully reap the benefits of the observations and evaluations, encourage the expert to be forthright with any insights that he or she can offer.

At the same time, do not be defensive. The purpose of feedback is not to stroke your ego. Instead, it is meant to bring to your attention the blind spots that you may be unable to perceive on your own, as well as to provide you with strategies for improvement that are intended to advance your intellect and performance. Embrace it wholeheartedly. Tunnel vision will not make you the best version of yourself, so eagerly reach for that second or third opinion and then use the recommendations to your advantage.

## Do the Trench Work

Grooming for leadership success requires a great deal of work and that is why many shy away from it. Whether it is getting additional education or working to develop thinking and behavior to more advanced levels, know that you will have to allot adequate resources to the endeavor, which may not be limited to time, money, or effort. The path to success is not paved in gold. It is often rough and unsightly: There are potholes, detours, and roadblocks. The province of a leader is to cruise through them and learn from the hard knocks.

As stated earlier, becoming an effective leader is a lifelong enterprise. It is not for those who prefer to dabble or engage in superficial learning and exploits. It means establishing a mindset that is ready and willing to confront fatigue, internal demons, inertia, and all that can potentially get in the way of your success. It also means being proactive and coaching yourself through tough times and also demanding more from yourself on a daily basis to arrive at the identified benchmarks. So, roll up your sleeves and prepare for the trench work.

## Frequently Evaluate Your Progress

No matter how much progress you are making, you will need to check in to assess which aspects are going well and which are not. Someone desirous of becoming a thought leader would not hesitate to repeatedly gauge his or her performance at necessary benchmarks. The person also should take a look at what specific thinking and behavior(s) generated the current results. One often overlooked aspect of evaluating progress is that a plan and its strategies can always be tweaked. They are not set in stone, nor should they be. Growth is a dynamic, evolutionary process.

Outside influences and other relevant variables also must be taken into consideration when making an evaluation. Understanding how these variables may affect your performance will enable you to tweak the next steps and identify perilous stumbling blocks along the way. As you calculate the sum and substance of your results, ask what you should do differently the next go-round and what makes sense to continue doing as you move forward and work to strengthen your positioning.

## Raise the Bar and Commit to Ongoing Learning

Simply because you have achieved a goal, or a few of them, is no indication that you should stop learning or making additional progress. Again, becoming the best version of yourself is a lifelong endeavor. With the momentum of past performances, raise your standards and push yourself to achieve a stretch goal. There are no rules that limit the amount of learning and improvement that you can do. So, make room for additional opportunities that can advance your brand, both short and long term.

If you took an introductory course on conflict resolution last quarter, take an intermediate course this time. If you read two books on executive presence this month, consider attending a workshop next month or getting 1:1 coaching from an industry expert. Up the ante. Never stop being eager to learn and advance your platform through high-value experiences that challenge you and force you to grow beyond your comfort zone.

# Journal Questions

1. Do you make a consistent effort to raise the bar on your personal and professional performance? Explain.
2. Which individual attributes make up the best version of you—physically, intellectually, emotionally, and professionally? Are your brand elements cohesive? Additionally, do you think it is fair to be judged by your appearance? Why or why not?
3. Do you diminish your accomplishments or abilities to make others feel more secure? Discuss.
4. How did this principle contribute to better understanding your role as a leader? How will its mastery enable you to cultivate greater effectiveness?
5. How will you use the preceding strategies to advance your commitment to being the best version of yourself?

# Leadership Challenge

Make a list of your best attributes and strongest skillsets. How can you maximize your performance by leveraging those strengths? Draft a 10-point plan that incorporates each and includes a strategy for maximizing specific aspects of your performance. Focus on one point of the plan each month and assess your progress the next month. Are you becoming the best version of yourself?

# Notes

1. Maslow, A. (1943). A Theory of Human Motivation. Psychological Review: Princeton University.
2. Tunca, D. (2016). The Chimamanda Ngozi Adichie Website. [online] L3.ulg. ac.be. Retrieved February 23, 2017 from http://www.l3.ulg.ac.be/adichie/ cnabio.html.
3. Adichie, Chimamanda Ngozi. (December 2012). "We Should All Be Feminists," [video file]. Retrieved December 20, 2013 from https://www.ted. com/talks/chimamanda_ngozi_adichie_we_should_all_be_feminists/ transcript?language=en.

# 8

# World-Class Leaders Lead by Example

*The yardstick that we use to examine others should be no less effective in examining ourselves.*

Leaders, as standard-bearers, set the tone for excellence and cooperative compliance. In doing so, they establish behavioral expectations in others. This, nonetheless, begs the question: Are leaders *themselves* expected to model their own standards of behavior? Of course, without a doubt. Leaders are not merely in the business of "guiding others"; they are likewise expected to be active participants in the overall process. This means not paying lip service to the beliefs they espouse, but rather being excellent examples of what they represent. Leading by example, they ascend to ranks of world-class leaders and foster an authentic sense of ownership in all that they do. What they know for sure is they must live by the sword if they are to thrive by it.

Because the question of credibility is always at stake and since standout leaders do not exist in isolation, self-awareness is key. As advocates of their own doctrines, they must align their behavior so that it openly reflects the criteria they have established and judge others against. For this reason, engaging in pretense does not bode well for leaders; it is not a game they can play and win. No matter how alluring, they are not free to rule from the mountaintops where their behavior cannot be observed or challenged. And, as we are severely reminded through countless public scandals, no leader is beyond reproach: A leader suffers the same consequences as anyone else who breaks away from clearly recognized behavioral standards. Essentially, what's good for the goose is good for the gander.

© The Author(s) 2018
K. Mariama-Arthur, *Poised for Excellence*, DOI 10.1007/978-3-319-64574-2_8

When congruent canons of behavior have been established, accountability is high. Leaders self-police and welcome constructive feedback. They are mindful of what their behavior communicates about them and how it impacts others. They are, for better or for worse, committed to the trenches and becoming their best, alongside everyone else. This results in higher-caliber leadership because there is an inherent checks and balances system in place, along with the recognition that even the leader must work to continually earn the respect and devotion of the group. When leaders understand that their reputation and influence are always works in progress, they are less likely to rely on past performance and more likely to focus on who they "are" as they strive to maintain credibility. This material shift makes a huge difference in the way they show up day in, day out.

In addition, there is a more inspired sense of allegiance by the leader. Leaders who embrace vulnerability and avail themselves of the scrutiny by others, do not fear reprisal. They also have more at stake and an even bigger dog in the fight when someone veers from the established standards of conduct. Instead of being removed from the process, they are entrenched in it and can point to the fact that even they have dotted the i's and crossed the t's. Those who "walk the walk," and not merely "talk the talk," also have a firmer grasp on nuance, those pesky little details that shape the rules that govern behavior. While they understand that so-called gray areas do exist, they make it their business to exercise clear thinking and bring consistency and fairness to the table. For them, it is so much easier to simply operate in integrity: Their behavior is the litmus test for their own credibility and, without a doubt, can directly influence how others choose to show up as well.

Those who look to a leader for guidance are empowered to stand taller knowing that the leader has taken the first and most important step in creating the example. They also feel greater respect, admiration, and devotion for a leader who "goes first." There is a strong sense that everyone is together in the "fight" to self-actualize. Collective effort and camaraderie guide every interaction, which also strengthens culture and fosters a genuine sense of teamwork. When reciprocal behavior reinforces acceptable conduct, people tend to "get with the program," even when it takes them out of their comfort zone. In the end, shared compliance pays huge dividends for everyone.

The bottom line is that a leader is the first line of defense. They are the "gold standard," so to speak. Honoring their role means accepting the responsibility that comes with it and behaving in a way that reflects this understanding wholeheartedly. That said, leaders do not get to cherry-pick the rules or how they are applied. When they have been emboldened to do so, it has proven to be a grave mistake, resulting in bitter consequences for all involved. When media giant CNN was accused of cherry-picking the rules of journalism in response to the alleged plagiarism of its celebrated journalist Fareed Zakaria, it raised the specter of similar scandals spilling throughout the journalism community.[1] Notwithstanding any final determination on the merits, it was clear that the fallout called into question the integrity of the journalism community at large, based on the conspicuous behavior of the "leaders" within it.

When leaders fail to establish congruent standards of behavior and govern pursuant to that misstep, they run the risk of losing respect, influence, and of course credibility. This often results in delegitimizing the role and encountering disdain from others. No one feels compelled to follow a "walking contradiction." Consequently, once such a discrepancy is discovered, leaders frequently find themselves in a losing battle to save face. Oftentimes, however, it is too late, as the damage has already been done. While it can take a lifetime to build a solid reputation anchored by credibility, one unfortunate incident can easily destroy it. Leaders can avoid this result by simply practicing what they preach.

I have an ecoconscious client in the financial services industry who not only practices the mantra "Reduce, Reuse, Recycle" by creating an environmentally friendly lifestyle both at home and at work, but also admonishes his employees for not doing the same. He refuses to purchase bottled water and filters, buys in bulk whenever possible (goods in bulk are less expensive as well as packaged and shipped more efficiently), uses solar panels at home and conserves energy by keeping electronics off when not in use, recycles nearly everything, is a vegan who brings his lunch to work, and walks or rides his bicycle to work or works from home.

I could go on, but the point is that he is not someone who simply "talks a good game." He walks the walk. His employees observe his conscientious commitment to preserving the environment and, in many ways, have adopted it because of how easy and beneficial it is to implement. Most of his employees follow the work-related guidance on being green, such as using power strips, recycling, commuting (with pretax benefits for using public transportation!), working from home, or keeping e-libraries instead of unnecessarily printing files. They also have taken the campaign to the streets and shared it with their families to make an even bigger impact. When you lead by example, as he has clearly done, you boost credibility and inspire others to follow your lead.

# Core Strategies

The strategies outlined in the following sections offer guidance on cultivating your skill and insight in leading by example and holding others to an equitable standard of review. They are distilled from the lessons I have learned from exceptional leaders across various industries.

## Lead by Example

Your behavior is a physical manifestation of the values, thinking, and principles that you hold dear. The best way to encourage others and wield influence is by being an excellent example of what you represent. Someone is always watching, whether you realize it or not. Conduct yourself accordingly. If ever in doubt, ask yourself if an objective observer would find your behavior troubling. If so, simply change it. Be conscientious of the way you speak and behave, making sure it reflects your core leadership standards. If you find yourself straying away from these precepts, course-correct. Even the best of leaders may occasionally find themselves a little off-kilter. However, the opportunity to make a good decision that aligns with your core values is always present. Choose it.

## Give Others the Benefit of the Doubt

Rather than readily assuming the worse of others, give them the benefit of the doubt first. Paint them in the light most favorable to the set of circumstances until and unless you discover new information that suggests you should handle the matter differently. Personal offense and knee-jerk reactions often lead to incorrect judgments. Tone is difficult to gauge in an email and maybe— just maybe—the CEO was engrossed in conversation and did not see you at the last company networking event. Why assume the worse?

Create distance between yourself and the independent set of circumstances; do not attempt to draw a connection where none exists. It is to your benefit to steer clear of this mistake, as you would want others to afford you the same courtesy. Having higher expectations of others inculcates a sense of pride in them, which translates into an impetus to make better choices in the future in order to align with those expectations. Giving others this benefit also creates a mindset of excellence in others. Finally, it frees you of the hasty default judgments that inspire offense and conjure up bad feelings unnecessarily.

## Get the Facts

It is important to understand the landscape before you draw conclusions about what you think you know. There is always a chance you could be wrong. The appearance of impropriety is not the same thing as the commission of misconduct. Impressions can be more than deceiving. Do your research. Compare notes. Fact-check and then, fact-check again. Be certain of the variables you are dealing with before you set out to act on them. The worst possible outcome is a rigorous campaign based on incorrect information. The best result is a campaign that never materializes because the facts deem it unnecessary. Do yourself a favor and get the facts right rather than moving forward with preconceived notions.

Choose to operate from a well-informed position of power that enables you to make informed decisions, not execute reactive strategies. Valuing facts over speculation also encourages others to take the appropriate steps to do the same when faced with similar circumstances.

## Evaluate Objectively

When considering the merits of an individual's situation, strive to examine the facts objectively. We all have idealistic views about how things should be, or how people should behave, based on our individual experiences. This filter, however, should not come into play while working to evaluate another person's unique set of circumstances. Look at each situation on its face. Observe the facts independently of any biases toward the person and apply objective criteria for reviewing each scenario.

Keep your personal philosophies and predispositions out of the equation to avoid coming to conclusions too quickly. This is far too easy to do. Instead, put yourself in the other person's shoes (because who knows when you might be in them!) and dig deep to arrive at a fair and optimal result. Remind yourself that impartiality is one of the most important tenets of effective leadership.

## Avail Yourself of Constructive Criticism

As a leader, you are not exempt from making mistakes. You may even find that you are flying high for a time, but there is always the potential to fall from grace. Do not operate under the false assumption that you know it all or are above reproach. We can always expand our horizons by learning from someone else. We can even discover important aspects about ourselves when someone offers value through her or his unique perspective. Constructive criticism from an objective source can shed light on the merits of your performance as well as areas that need attention. Welcome it.

Develop a thick skin by periodically asking for it from trusted sources. Eventually you will appreciate it like any other indulgence that you have become accustomed to. It is the leader, perhaps more than anyone else, who must be most open to constructive criticism. Leaders sit at the helm, confront high stakes, and are charged with advancing the big picture for the benefit of all. Feedback is not only necessary but also a shrewd mechanism that beckons excellence.

## Journal Questions

1. Do you behave consistently according to the standards that you have set for yourself? Why or why not?
2. Do you ordinarily give others the benefit of the doubt? Explain.
3. Have you ever been the victim of a double standard? Describe the situation and how it made you feel.
4. How did this principle help you better understand your role as a leader? How will its mastery enable you to cultivate greater effectiveness?
5. How will you use the preceding strategies to advance your commitment to leading by example and holding others to a fair standard of review?

## Leadership Challenge

List your top three values and explain why you hold them in high regard. Next, describe three ways in which you will hold yourself accountable to each value. Over the next month record your process and findings in a journal. What did you discover?

## Note

1. Bort, C. & Blappo, B. (2015, September 22). CNN Does Not Get to Cherry-Pick the Rules of Journalism. *Esquire*. Retrieved September 9, 2017 from https://www.google.com/amp/www.esquire.com/news-politics/news/amp30076/cnn-rules-of-journalism/.

# 9

# Leaders Own Their Mistakes and Embrace Constructive Criticism

*Leaders know there is no shame in making mistakes. They are valuable tools that teach one how to improve performance and, when shared with others, amplify the lessons that drive success.*

It is nearly impossible to get through life without making mistakes or experiencing some degree of disappointment, including failure, along the way. Hypothetically speaking, even if you could avoid, escape, or preempt mistakes, disappointments, and failure, it should in no way make these diversions aspirational. These experiences present evidence of our humanity, frailty, and the fact that no one is immune to erring. Besides, just beyond mistakes are opportunities for growth. Growth happens when we accept the choices we make as well as the responsibility that comes with them; this is a necessary component of leadership success.

Stepping boldly into the arena of life—being vulnerable without regard for what others think—invites important opportunities to challenge the innate status quo and promotes personal growth at various levels. Striving to become our best self, personally and professionally, is a potent example of such growth. Trial and error are a natural part of this process and we should welcome them with enthusiasm. When we endure them reluctantly, though, we fall into a vicious cycle of fear and self-deprecation that erodes our self-esteem and damages the self-concept. Similarly, shunning our mistakes only holds us hostage to a false ideal, one that traumatizes our psyche because it can never be realized.

Further, because we all are predisposed to imperfection, there is no reason to feel singled out when we make mistakes. Even still, hubris may cause some to adopt a persona that they believe "masks" fallibility. The thing is, most

© The Author(s) 2018
K. Mariama-Arthur, *Poised for Excellence*, DOI 10.1007/978-3-319-64574-2_9

people can see right through it. Pretense, as noted in the previous chapter, is an utter waste of time and energy. It is better to simply accept our flaws as the necessary evil that they are. That you may not realize your mistakes the moment they occur is inconsequential. You may not even perceive the mistakes made by others. Nevertheless, trust that everyone is making them on a fairly consistent basis. "To err is human" is the adage that holds universal truth. Despite this fact, we are, each of us, still pretty amazing human beings.

Subordinating the ego to a greater purpose is a nonnegotiable part of owning one's mistakes. Arrogance only hampers progress. Feeling that you need to portray an infallible public image to others is not only unnecessary, but also impractical and causes stress. Jettison this idea. Although welcoming mistakes is important, what you do after making them is perhaps even more important. Self-shaming and comparing yourself to others is a surefire way to damage your self-esteem and send you into a downward spiral of self-loathing. Instead of trying to escape the reality of your mistake, own it. Mistakes should be examined, and their value captured, to improve behavior and results in the future. Any constructive criticism given in response to a mistake should be welcomed. After all, what good it is in making a mistake when there is no lesson left behind to learn from?

Accepting mistakes and embracing constructive criticism are important facets of your leadership journey. Even though you do not have to tout mistakes as battle scars or be an open book, you should, at the very least, strive to own them. Sharing your process will undoubtedly help someone else shorten their learning curve, which is an important aspect of leading by example. By the same token, acknowledging worthwhile feedback only strengthens your capacity to improve and grow. Remember, it is to your benefit to concede that you are prone to error and imperfection. Striving for perfection only supports delusional thinking and behavior, neither of which sustains effective leadership. That said, leaders who refuse to acknowledge their imperfections or are wholly unaware of them often suffer from a dangerous form of cognitive bias that presents as an illusory sense of superiority. It is referred to as the Dunning-Kruger effect, and its consequences have repeatedly cost leaders their credibility, and, in some cases, their entire careers.[1]

The truth is, without mistakes, and without acknowledging meaningful criticism, the world would not be the incredible spectacle that it is today. Technological advancements, life-altering medical discoveries, and scientific innovation are all the result of trial and error, and of taking in the wisdom of another to shed light on your own potential. 3M, the "Post-it note giant," originally started as a mining company, and unbeknownst to many, was built on a legacy of fascinating mistakes. By embracing them, along with risk and smart innovation, the company became ubiquitous with resilience and resourcefulness, and grew into a multibillion-dollar empire.[2] Like 3M, the most effective leaders achieve success by owning their mistakes and eagerly turning them into something new and valuable. They appreciate the lessons that detours and missteps offer, but they are not defined by them. To the contrary, they redefine the path to success by embracing their imperfections and then, without hesitation, work toward a Hollywood ending. You can do the same.

It was a mistake for Microsoft CEO Satya Nadella to suggest that instead of asking for a raise, women should just trust the system to reward them for their efforts. Little did he know at the time. When Twitter and other media outlets responded with outrage and criticism, Microsoft posted a memo—a public apology—by Nadella to employees that attempted to soften the blow, implying that he had answered the question "completely wrong" and that he actually meant that both "men and women should get equal pay for equal work."[3] It also acknowledged that Maria Klawe's advice (who interviewed him at the Phoenix event and whose clear disagreement with his commentary drew cheers from the crowd) was correct. "If you think you deserve a raise, you should just ask," Nadella wrote, adding: "Without a doubt, I wholeheartedly support programs at Microsoft and in the industry that bring more women into technology and close the pay gap."[4] He also took to Twitter, stating he "[w]as inarticulate re how women should ask for a raise. Our industry must close the gap so a raise is not needed because of a bias #GHC14."[5]

Nadella owned his mistake and took the consequences in stride as an opportunity to rethink his own biases and how they translate in the workplace as well as how they might negatively influence and affect others. Despite this incident, Nadella has done well in managing the company's complex infrastructure and executing its overall mission, which, according to him, is "to empower every person and organization on the planet to achieve more."[6]

## Core Strategies

The strategies outlined in the following sections offer guidance for cultivating your skill and insight into owning your mistakes and embracing constructive criticism. They are distilled from the lessons I have learned from exceptional leaders across various industries.

### Be Honest

When you examine your overall performance, especially your missteps, it is critically important to be honest with yourself. A candid self-admission is not only a necessary step toward fostering your personal growth, but also helps you gain clarity around making better choices the next time. If you received a rejection letter from a potential employer advising that your elimination was based on a failure to draft an appropriately customized cover letter, seize that "ah-ha" moment.

Being dishonest only hurts you in the end, as you are held hostage by the missteps that you refuse to confront. Therefore, whenever you discover a mistake, be frank and admit it. Not only to yourself, but to others, whichever the case may be. Then, take a moment to reflect on why and how you made the mistake. Finally, determine quickly how to best apply the lesson learned so that you can use the insight in the future.

## Acknowledge Failure as a Component of Success

Although it may seem inviting to experience more wins than losses, failure is not only a great teacher, but an indispensable component of success. When you experience it, you learn more than if you only ever tasted victory. Think about the last time you experienced a failure. Would you agree that it provided more in terms of value than what you received with a success? Failure exploits gaps in your knowledge, thinking, and experience. It then creates an opportunity for you to experience newfound success through introspection and learning.

Acknowledge failure. Embrace it. Never regret it. Understand that even if you tried to avoid it, your efforts would fall flat. Failure is bound to happen, with or without your permission. It is an inescapable part of being human. No matter how quiet it is kept, it is failure that teaches us the most important of lessons about ourselves and helps us appreciate wins more graciously. So, fail forward with enthusiasm.

## Extract the Lesson

Neither mistakes nor failure exist for their own sake. There is always a lesson to be learned. Find the lesson so that it can be applied in context and placed in your toolbox for future reference. To experience anything without understanding why it occurred and what you can learn from it, both personally and professionally, is a waste. Dig deeper. Extract the lesson. Choose to be present so that you can fully explore the length and breadth of the experience.

What if you decided to spend a whole paycheck on indulgences instead of saving a portion for a rainy day? If you got a flat tire a few days later, how would you characterize the lesson? The power of learning through failure is not merely about obsessing over the poignant aspects, but also about combing through the nuance to discover what premium assets can be salvaged for the future.

## Share Lessons Learned

It is counterproductive to keep the insights amassed from previous experiences all to yourself. You can help others cut their learning curve in half if you share what you know. Welcome opportunities to mentor others by sharing your hard-wrought life lessons. Think of the advice you have received in the past and how it has helped you sidestep critical mistakes or even clean up messes that you already made. Do you feel it is important to provide similar advice to others? You should.

There are tremendous advantages to sharing your wisdom and experiences with others, especially in a candid, authentic way. It advances your leadership credibility and distinguishes you from those who merely tout wins out of context. Moreover, it allows others to frame your experiences as important sources of inspiration, which can be leveraged to further expand their horizons.

## Try to Avoid Repeating Mistakes

Even though making mistakes is an important part of the human experience, committing the same ones over and over defeats the purpose. Nevertheless, when you do, it is usually a result of failing to extract the lesson from the original experience. It also may occur when someone refuses to apply the lesson learned. In either case, the onus is on the individual to keep inventory of the mistake as well as any lessons learned and determine how to avoid a replay. To do so requires a willingness to be vulnerable and increase sensory acuity.

So, pay attention and be intentional about applying the lessons you learn. If you are able to see the signs and then pivot to avoid falling victim to the same set of circumstances, you have won half the battle. Successfully correcting past mistakes is a priority for effective leaders, and it enhances their ability to provide sage advice to others who are also working toward this important goal.

# Journal Questions

1. Do you have a difficult time owning your mistakes or embracing constructive criticism? Why or why not.
2. Reframe a past failure as a component of your current success.
3. Have you ever made a mistake twice? Identify the mistake and explain why you may have needed to repeat the mistake to learn a lesson.

4. How did this principle help you better understand your role as a leader? How will its mastery enable you to cultivate greater effectiveness?
5. How will you use the preceding strategies to advance a commitment to own up to your mistakes and learn from them?

## Leadership Challenge

Think about three critical mistakes you have made in the past. Reframe them as lessons learned. List three distinct ways to empower yourself because of the lessons learned.

## Notes

1. Mariama-Arthur, K. (2016, July 22). The Number one Reason Leaders Need Feedback: The Value of Feedback in a Professional Environment, Especially for Those in Leadership Positions. *Black Enterprise*. Retrieved September 8, 2017 from http://www.blackenterprise.com/career/career-advice/the-number-one-reason-leaders-need-feedback/.
2. 3M (n.d.). 3M US Company History. Retrieved September 2, 2017 from http://solutions.3m.com/wps/portal/3M/en_US/3M-Company/Information/Resources/History/?MDR=true.
3. Chowdry, A. (2014, October 10). Microsoft CEO Satya Nadella Apologizes for Comments on Women's Raises. *Forbes*. Retrieved February 9, 2017 from https://www.forbes.com/sites/amitchowdhry/2014/10/10/microsoft-ceo-satya-nadella-apologizes-for-comments-on-womens-pay/#113c0c646d2b
4. Chowdry, A. (2014, October 10). Microsoft CEO Satya Nadella Apologizes for Comments on Women's Raises. *Forbes*. Retrieved February 9, 2017 from https://www.forbes.com/sites/amitchowdhry/2014/10/10/microsoft-ceo-satya-nadella-apologizes-for-comments-on-womens-pay/#113c0c646d2b
5. Chowdry, A. (2014, October 10). Microsoft CEO Satya Nadella Apologizes for Comments on Women's Raises. *Forbes*. Retrieved February 9, 2017 from https://www.forbes.com/sites/amitchowdhry/2014/10/10/microsoft-ceo-satya-nadella-apologizes-for-comments-on-womens-pay/#113c0c646d2b
6. Microsoft. (n.d.). What Empowerment Means to Us. *Microsoft*. Retrieved January 20, 2017 from https://news.microsoft.com/empowerment/.

# 10

# Visionary Leaders Eliminate "the Box"

*"The box" is an artificial construct that hampers creativity and binds potential. Innovative leaders do not waste time trying to think outside it; they eliminate it altogether.*

Leaders do not replicate, they create. Innovation is essential to developing a compelling vision and strategy for moving into the future. Instead of defaulting to best practices, leaders innovate and develop creative ways to advance thinking and strengthen institutional outcomes. Effective leaders reject "the box" and all its rigidity. They break the rules, or they break themselves against the rules. Either way, the results usually are spectacular.

"The box" is an abstract representation of the mental, emotional, and behavioral shackles that bind our potential and prevent us from manifesting our visions. The box is an enduring purgatory that traps us until we can think our way out of it. It is institutional memory, groupthink, age-old practices and policies, or rhetoric that you grew up believing and that has shaped the way that one sees the world. Whatever the box looks like to you, know that it is an illusion that you must shed.

When you eliminate the box, you nullify relational reasoning and thinking in favor of uncommon conceptual frameworks. It is not about improving your current thinking about an existing concept or topic. It is about removing roadblocks to innovation and stimulating unspoiled and cutting-edge ideation. In practice, it means letting go of preconceived notions (i.e., the so-called hard and fast rules) about how the world works and what is possible inside it, whether these ideas were ingrained in you by someone else or experienced directly through trial and error. To become a visionary leader, one must be willing to surrender the ship.

© The Author(s) 2018
K. Mariama-Arthur, *Poised for Excellence*, DOI 10.1007/978-3-319-64574-2_10

Eliminating the box is a lot like starting from scratch, which is a good thing. Going back to the drawing board is a great way to get the creative juices flowing. You cannot achieve next-level greatness holding on to the same old thinking and behaviors that got you where you are today, even if you are in a good place. Break the chains that bind.

Begin by envisioning something that you have never before imagined. Look to the outer limits of your imagination rather than the artificial boundaries where most people operate. Expand your horizons. Challenge yourself and your tightly held assumptions. Hold nothing back. Reimagine the world as a better place because you are in it, where you improve the quality of life for yourself and for others through your contributions. This kind of focused introspection will inspire you to problem-solve and become a catalyst for change, both on your own behalf and in the world around you.

By eliminating the box, you increase your chances of achieving success, and open up an untapped world of possibilities. Ironically, those possibilities have always existed, but they are only theoretical ideas floating in the ether until someone snatches them up and turns them into reality. Look around you. Everything you see was invented by someone with an idea. The chair you are sitting on was probably manufactured in a factory that produced thousands of others just like it. There was a time, however, when the concept of "chair" did not even exist in the real world. Someone had to tap imagination and pull the idea out of the darkness. You would be sitting on the floor today if someone had not eliminated that "box."

The most effective leaders learn to eliminate the box in favor of creating new vistas and expanding their reach in all that they do. They refuse to be held captive by others' ideals and the artificial constructs that shape normative behavior. They are instead motivated to live out loud and discover what is possible through courage, ingenuity, and risk-taking, each of which leads them to experience greater success. In the end, leaders who eradicate the thinking and behavior associated with the "box" find that their lives, and the lives of those they serve, are richer and more satisfying for it.

Colleen Wegman is the newly appointed CEO of Wegmans, one of the most successful grocery chains in the United States. The most recent CEO and current Chairman, Danny Wegman (Colleen's father), understood the importance of innovating and of pivoting on a dime: He did not waste time thinking outside the box, he simply eliminated it. Wegman successfully carries the torch of innovation passed down from a long line of visionary business leaders. Wegmans was founded by the Wegman brothers, John and Walter, who began selling groceries from a pushcart.[1] In 1916, they opened the Rochester Fruit and Vegetable Company, known as Wegmans today.[2]

One of the most intriguing aspects of the company's success is that it began with this end in mind: To carve out an unconventional niche in the grocery marketplace. The idea was to offer a high-quality and affordable grocery experience for families, along with extras that you would not find anywhere else. That is, its own wine *department*, organic food, hot food bars with everything from scrambled eggs to Indian food, a cheese department, high-end catering and baking departments, specialty-ordered food on request, numerous ethic food aisles, several restaurants, home goods, and more.

Because the company eliminated "the box" from the store's inception, it stood head and shoulders above traditional grocery retailers, and it has never looked back. It also has remained sensitive to market fluctuation and competitive advantage. Go into any Wegmans and see it for yourself. What you will find are enterprising dynamics in nearly every department. Product selections change based on consumer demand, and departments are entirely reconfigured, even gutted, when appropriate. They are always looking for new ways to ideate and stay abreast of consumer behavior.

Hailed as the "Neiman Marcus" of grocery stores, customers proudly note that its prices are actually lower than the so-called competitors and the quality and selection of food is beyond compare. What brings new customers in the door is the intrigue of the undeniably opulent "beyond the meat and potatoes" experience, superior brand management, extraordinary customer service, and consistent attention and response to detail. As a result, they keep coming back. Now that is visionary leadership.

# Core Strategies

The strategies outlined in the following sections offer guidance for cultivating your skill and insight as an innovative leader. They are distilled from the lessons I have learned from exceptional leaders across various industries.

## Embrace Contrarian Thought

There are no real benefits to adopting the thinking and behavior of the masses. Innovative leaders are not interested in becoming fungible goods. They are not swayed by the ebb and flow of popular opinion. They do not care whether they are liked. They are interested in creating lasting change for individuals, organizations, and institutions. In addition, they are willing to stand alone and endure criticism to achieve that result. A virtual meeting format may not be popular, but what if the results could revolutionize the group's overall efficiency? It would certainly be worthwhile to embrace contrarian thought in this instance.

To make the shift from mundane to avant-garde thinking, consider opposing views of practices and procedures. Examine both ends of the spectrum to capture the big picture and find gaps in logic. If useful, evaluate the need for a disruptive paradigm shift. You might be surprised at how simply going against the grain and adopting a novel viewpoint can be advantageous to effectively solving problems. Search for ways to improve on the current state of affairs and turn traditional thought on its head.

## Evaluate Institutional Memory

What people know and how they behave largely depend on historical norms, principles, practices, and attitudes learned over a lifetime. It transcends the individuals themselves and is transferred to others over time. Pushing the envelope within an organization can be difficult, especially when there is institutional pushback from its hub. Examine your organization's institutional framework to determine whether it is sufficiently forward looking. Evaluate how current knowledge and practices have worked.

Look for gaps between what is known and what is needed to create new outcomes. See how well technological advances have been incorporated into the organizational fiber. There may be critical opportunities to learn and grow being forfeited in favor of embracing the doctrines of yesteryear. Gather credible information and make an appropriate decision about which portions of the collective dossier to keep or discard going forward.

## Be Skeptical of Best Practices

Practices that have been in place from time immemorial may be common knowledge and considered the "go to" methods for addressing well-defined problems; however, they may not necessarily be good for growth. Even if a method worked well in the past, it might not be applicable in new contexts or an altered landscape. What is safe and familiar may be comforting, but there may be consequences for adopting prevailing traditions on a whim.

It is better to evaluate core competencies against best practices and possible innovations to see how they measure up. Determine whether systems are outdated and whether new efficiencies or synergies can be leveraged to address disruptive technologies. Consider every possibility. The less conventional, the better. Your willingness to concede potentialities may well provide the relevant solution for which you have been searching.

## Develop a Fresh Perspective

The rhythm of everyday practices can wear on you, making it difficult to see things objectively. When you become used to what is commonplace, you can develop certain expectations without ever realizing it. To break this cycle, strive to develop a fresh perspective. Start by reconsidering what you know to be true. Play the devil's advocate. You can do it alone or ask colleagues to help facilitate the process, depending on what you hope to accomplish.

Raise objections to clarify issues and generate a healthy debate. Create a list of objective facts, pros and cons, and reconsider how they fit into the big picture. Search for any inconsistencies. No doubt, you will likely discover subtle paradoxes that might cause you to reexamine your beliefs. The point is to challenge yourself to see things with fresh eyes even when the facts remain unchanged.

## Be Creative and Break the Rules to Find New Inspiration

It is perfectly fine to be a maverick and swim against the tide. You are better off hedging your bets: Some practices are archaic and certain rules *should* be broken. Free yourself of the need for conforming to normative culture. Be willing to be the odd duck and stand alone. Color outside the lines. Take calculated risks and use creativity to drive excitement that may lead you in a new direction. Search for new inspiration and refuse to fall into old habits. By being clever and purposeful in your thinking and behavior, you are more likely to improve results. Tweak. Revisit. Reposition. There are other ways to get the results you want. A mountain of opportunities awaits the bold. Be willing to gear up to scale new heights. When you do, you may discover that the possibilities are not only limitless, but well within reach.

## Journal Questions

1. List three of your regular routines that have been difficult to break. Do they serve you? If not, why do you continue to engage in them?
2. Do you feel comfortable articulating contrarian views? Why or why not?
3. Name two distinct ways you can boost creativity and innovation in your personal and professional life?
4. How did this principle lead you to a better understanding of your role as a leader? How will its mastery enable you to cultivate greater effectiveness?
5. How will you use the preceding strategies to advance your commitment to innovating?

## Leadership Challenge

Identify one critical way that creativity and innovation could enhance the way you navigate your workweek. Maybe it is getting up an hour earlier, taking a different route, or bringing your lunch. Or, perhaps it is something a little more elaborate. List the processes involved and how you would integrate them into your schedule. Try it out for a week, and keep a journal on any improvements in your performance or productivity.

## Notes

1. Wegmans. (n.d.). Company Overview. Retrieved July 6, 2017 from https://www.wegmans.com/about.
2. Wegmans. (n.d.). Company Overview. Retrieved July 6, 2017 from https://www.wegmans.com/about.

# Part II

## Principles that Cultivate Leadership Excellence Through Disruptive Paradigm Shifts

# 11

# Strive for Progress, Not Perfection

*Leaders know that striving for perfection is counterproductive because it leads to constant dissatisfaction. It is better to strive for progress by moving forward with purpose.*

Success is not about absolutes. It is about using trial and error in the pursuit of a goal. Rarely do things work out exactly as planned, even with considerable forethought and above-average execution. Mishaps, imperfection, and disappointment each teach us there is always room for growth and the honing of one's crafts. Without a doubt, progress rather than perfection is a more constructive gauge for a leader's success. To that end, excellence should always be the goal.

Seldom is any feat achieved by executing a single task. Success is usually the result of several smaller, individual tasks executed with consistency that eventually add up to a big win. For example, becoming a lawyer does not simply involve passing a bar exam. Prior to this feat, there are numerous, interconnected milestones that must be achieved. Above average academic performance, competitive LSAT scores sufficient to gain admission into law school, passing a professional responsibility exam, and a positive determination of "moral character" all represent progress toward becoming a member of the legal profession.

Similarly, someone striving to become better at math must master the basics before tackling the complex order of operations. It is through the kaleidoscope of progress that one observes every isolated instance—every benchmark—that reveals growth. But for acknowledging its momentum, we would have no means of gauging forward movement. We need telltale signs that reveal the evolution of our growth, and progress provides the solution.

© The Author(s) 2018
K. Mariama-Arthur, *Poised for Excellence*, DOI 10.1007/978-3-319-64574-2_11

Hardship and battle scars are not signs of failure; they are proof of grit—the dogged determination to see a thing through, especially during tough times—and the unmistakable evidence of skin in the game. The ego might want flawless execution and perfect results in every endeavor, but that is just not realistic. Besides, if perfection could be achieved, what would its real value be? This utopian aspiration, based wholly on unrealistic expectations of performance, lends itself to a paltry and superficial distinction at best.

A delicious meal that is well-presented is worth far more than a visually flawless one made with a recipe that is followed to the letter, yet is unappetizing. Better to be driven by clarity of purpose and an earnest commitment to excellence as motivating incentives for success than to fall headlong in the race for perfection. That being said, do not beat yourself up if, despite your best efforts, you fall short of an intended goal. Progress is piecemeal, which means you are going to move forward in fits and starts. Expect a bit of turbulence every now and again, or you will be disappointed every time.

It may be helpful to reconceptualize progress by viewing it from an alternative perspective. First envision that you have hit the target dead center—you have achieved the goal. Then review the process backward, seeing each improvement as it occurred in segments. Now trace back the steps necessary to achieve each result, focusing on the completion deadlines and long-term, practical strategies required. Progress may feel more tangible and less overwhelming when viewed this way. Although you can always tweak your plan toward progress along the way, the act of committing it to paper encourages action. Besides, only results that are chronicled can be evaluated.

If a strategy is not producing the desired results, know that it can always be abandoned. Leaders should be open to various courses of action. If a plan is not serving the greater goal, examine it more closely. Evaluate it substantively and procedurally to determine why there is a gap between where you are and where you want to be. Is the plan to blame? Or, is it that the plan is not being executed properly? If the plan is the problem, consider moving on to a different one. Blind commitments to best practices yield little value. If it is a failure of execution, or improper execution, simply stop procrastinating and determine the proper steps so that you can accomplish the goal.

Leaders embrace progress holistically, which means that they accept imperfection as inevitable and that trial and error are essential. The important lessons they learn enable them to create plans that gradually move their organizations toward its target. By making note of these lessons, as well as any accomplishments along the way, leaders are best able to document progress and tweak strategies, which can lead to greater success.

Leaders also foster that expectation in everyone on the team. Impatience is common when everybody is eager to achieve a goal sooner rather than later. Yet even when time is of the essence, the goal of progress through excellence remains ever present. We cannot shun it—it always emerges prior to the final analysis of any goal. The most effective leaders work with their teams not only to understand and embrace progress through excellence as a fundamental value, but also to know what to look for when they see it and to apply it to the big picture.

Early in my legal career, one of my mentors taught me the importance of pacing myself and managing progress in chunks. I had been working with anticipation, hoping that the case I was working on would settle—a particularly complex one that had been dragging on for some time. It did not. Instead, there was an additional, unexpected discovery request—something I knew would unfortunately take a while to complete. I was fit to be tied. Not only was settlement no longer on the table, I now had a new mountain of discovery to which to respond. I was a perfectionist and wanted to get everything "right" to avoid any further delays. I remember my mentor sitting me down and saying:

> Young lady, the race does not go to the swift or strong, but to those who endure until the end. You have done great work on this case. The clients are pleased and things are moving forward nicely. I know you—you will be up all night poring over these responses and driving yourself crazy trying to draft them flawlessly. I was like that early in my career and learned the hard way. Pace yourself and each time you finish a section, celebrate it. Then get right back to work as soon as you can. For most things, success happens in chunks. You have to accept that. Not just with this case, but with everything that comes after it. So, get out of your head and go get to work.

Although I felt somewhat relieved after our conversation, I could not fully appreciate her advice until I encountered a new situation where I had to apply it. What I realized, however, was that even with a great work ethic, perfection was an elusive endeavor. I made up my mind that I was no longer going to seek it. I realized that good work meant being focused and giving it my best efforts, not flawless execution. This sentiment has helped me reach for progress, with excellence as the guiding force, in all my endeavors.

# Core Strategies

The strategies outlined in the following sections offer guidance for cultivating your skill and insight in abandoning perfectionist tendencies. They are distilled from the lessons I have learned from exceptional leaders across various industries.

## Complete Tasks with Conviction

Managing a task from start to finish can seem daunting. The problem is that we often try to consume them in fell swoops, which makes them appear larger than life. Chunking, which is the process of breaking down seemingly monumental tasks into more manageable feats, is an effective strategy for reducing stress and anxiety. Use it to isolate and complete discrete tasks with renewed focus and optimism. Be careful, though, not to create excessive minutiae. It can cause the exercise to backfire. Tackling a sea of miniscule tasks is just as foreboding as tackling a single behemoth one.

Chunk by coordinating related tasks into one group, rather than multiple ones. Remove distractions and adopt strategies that would help cope with challenges. Turn off the phone, television, or other technology and refrain from engaging in water cooler conversations while at work. Commit to the result from the beginning in spite of any setbacks. A positive mindset increases the likelihood of your success.

## Do Not Compare Yourself with Others

As you work toward your goals, chances are you inevitably will meet others who are striving toward theirs. Some will be further along than you are, while others will be at the beginning stages of their journey. In either case, do not compare yourself with them. You gain nothing but disillusionment or false pride. Recall the poem, "*Desiderata*" by Max Ehrmann. It explains this charge in no uncertain terms. When you find yourself comparing and contrasting strengths, weaknesses, accomplishments, and missteps with a rival, remember that you are doing it only to your own detriment. Resolve to stay in your lane and resist the urge to keep inventory or score. None of these behaviors can help you improve. They just will frustrate and distract from the real work at hand. Instead, focus on your goals and the progress you are making. Remember that you are competing only against yourself.

## Measure Results and Reward Your Efforts

When you are striving for progress, you should measure results to gauge how far you have come. Record where you were when you started and then measure the difference. It is one surefire way to identify any movement up or down. People are most accustomed to measuring results when determining weight loss on the scale, but weight is not the only variable that can be measured. You can measure the progress of any variable of consequence.

In doing so, however, do not forget to include projections. You also need be aware of how far you are from where you want to be. In addition, do not forget to reward yourself for your efforts. Success is not merely the act of crossing a hard finish line; there are countless important victories along the way and achieving some of them may prove more valuable than breaking the ultimate threshold. Make sure to recognize and celebrate each one.

## Fail Forward

It is natural to have good days and bad days. Sometimes your results will not reflect the time and effort that you put in. That is the nature of the beast. Learn to go with the flow, and do not beat yourself up when things do not go as planned. Often, there is a good reason that they do not go well. Fail forward and welcome the hiccups; they build intestinal fortitude. If you are having a challenging time mastering that second language, keep at it. Find ways to make the learning stick by making key distinctions and using a mix of modalities to enhance comprehension.

Even still, you may forget vocabulary or how to conjugate a verb from time to time. Keep your eye on the prize and do not give up. The most successful people are usually the ones who have failed the most, but they never let failures define them. You are much more than the sum of your failures, so resist the urge to let them define you.

## Correct the Course

When you discover that your plan of action needs some adjusting, course-correct. No need to remain committed to an arbitrary time frame or wait until you have completed a task in its entirety. Move with a sense of urgency, make the appropriate tweaks, and apply them immediately. The ability to approach the overall goal with fresh eyes and enthusiasm can boost your performance, especially knowing that you have discovered a more effective way to achieve the outcomes you seek.

For example, if you discover that a more effective way to invest in and fortify your 401(k) is to diversify your asset allocation (because you had all your eggs in one basket before), do it at your earliest convenience. You may need to adjust percentages here and there, along with balancing risks before you make final elections, but the bottom line is to make haste once you have made an informed decision. By being proactive and paying attention to nuance as you execute your goals, you enhance your leadership acumen tenfold.

## Journal Questions

1. Do you acknowledge your progress while working toward a goal, or do you only celebrate once it has been achieved? Discuss.
2. Do you punish yourself for making mistakes while working to accomplish a goal? What if you fail to achieve a goal altogether? Explain.
3. Identify an instance when you have compared your progress to someone else's, an instance when you did not feel like you measured up. How did it make you feel? Do you believe comparing yourself to others is useful? Why or why not?
4. How did this principle help you better understand your role as a leader? How will its mastery enable you to cultivate greater effectiveness?
5. How will you use the preceding strategies to advance your commitment to focusing more on progress and less on perfection?

## Leadership Challenge

Identify one major goal you want to accomplish during the next quarter. Then write down three strategies to achieve it. Chart your progress weekly over the next three months. How did it feel to track your progress, not merely acknowledge the end result?

# 12

## "True Grit" Beats Passion

*Even though passion is a powerful tool for generating excitement, it is no match for navigating long-term hardship and uncertainty. To get through challenging times, leaders need "true grit."*

Passion is an important catalyst; it jump-starts the energy and excitement needed to begin an endeavor. Nevertheless, it is insufficient to sustain these states while laboring through tough times. Leaders need a force more compelling to maintain momentum, something extra that helps them achieve their vision. That "something extra" is "true grit." It is the one thing that helps even the most talented leaders during dark days. And because dark days are sure to come and test one's mettle from time to time, every leader needs grit.

Psychologist Dr. Angela Duckworth, known for her work on grit, defines it as "passion *and* perseverance for long-term goals."[1] She notes that consistent focus over long periods is what turns talent into real-world skills. To avoid what she calls the "plateau of arrested development," where a person falls into mediocrity, one must engage in deliberate focus to move skills and goals forward.[2] Make no mistake, developing grit is hard work. It involves performing tedious tasks, especially when you do not feel like it, and demands countless hours of mind-numbing effort to get better at a specific skill or achieve a specific goal. Nonetheless, it is this regimen that distinguishes world-class leaders from average performers. As Dr. Duckworth says: "Talent counts, but effort counts twice."[3] Leaders who understand this principle not only are top performers, but also instill this mindset in others, inspiring them to raise their standards and perform at higher levels.

For leaders, grit is the secret weapon that trumps all others. While intellect and technical expertise are important, they are no match for the resolve needed

© The Author(s) 2018
K. Mariama-Arthur, *Poised for Excellence*, DOI 10.1007/978-3-319-64574-2_12

to confront the formidable challenges and harsh realities of the uncertain and sometimes volatile leadership territory. People with impressive pedigrees frequently strive to be successful, yet only those who develop true grit and have the wherewithal to tackle adversity will clinch it.

Grit equips leaders with an expansive and pragmatic skillset that is developed incrementally over time. It directs them to think differently when faced with a tough situation. Sticking with formidable tasks is no cakewalk. Doing it for the benefit of a future good takes foresight and courage. Once discovered, these elements can be used in a number of situations that require grit to face and overcome them. And because grit grows in potency over time, the more you dig your heels in and do the work, the "grittier" and more resilient you become.

Not surprisingly, passion persists only with the help of grit. These are reciprocal skills, each bearing equal parts of responsibility for success. The formula only works with both variables present and engaged. If you attempt to rely on passion alone, you soon will find that it is unable to assist in confronting unexpected adversities that emerge. If you rely solely on grit, you may wonder what all the effort is for because you are not experiencing joy, energy, or excitement. To experience true fulfillment, there must be an equitable integration of the two.

Grit prepares leaders to confront uncertainty and hardship with intestinal fortitude. It is a secret sauce that readies the heart, soul, and mind to work with purpose and courage until a task is completed. The most effective leaders learn to dig deep and focus on the prize despite daunting circumstances. They are more than capable of driving outcomes and preparing their teams to adjust to the vagaries of professional life when they persevere and leverage the power of grit.

Anything that requires immense effort over time usually evokes feelings of dread. Even though "hard work" may not always be inspiring, it is necessary to enjoy the fruits of your labor. Most people want the results, but not all are willing to do what is necessary to achieve them. Hard work demands a steely commitment, fueled by grit. And grit is not something you have the luxury of picking up every now and again. You must internalize and command it by making it part and parcel of who you are at your core.

If you are not prepared to give yourself to the work, it is unlikely that you are ready to lead. "Giving yourself to the work" means doing whatever it takes to complete it, short of hurting yourself or others. It definitely includes engaging in difficult and demanding work over long stretches, getting your hands dirty, and maybe even skipping sleep. Still, the most successful leaders are willing to make those trade-offs for long-term gratification. Despite that, it is not merely the physical aspect of the work that calls on grit to sustain it. It is also the mental and emotional aspects—those conversations that leaders have with themselves every day—that determine whether they will emerge from a conflict waving a victory flag or broken and unable to make the final trek to the shore. The bottom line is this: Without the success factor of true grit, a leader is ill-prepared to confront the harsh realities and overcome the formidable and indomitable challenges that lie ahead, any of which could jeopardize their resolve to succeed.

When I first began law school, I felt enormous passion for the entire experience. I was excited and eager to learn all that I could. My motivation was that I wanted to be the next Johnnie Cochran Jr., *in a skirt*! After the first week, however, I realized that it was not going to be the walk in the park that I had envisioned. Everything was novel and the work was grueling. I had to learn to read volumes of material thoroughly and consistently over many hours, digest complex concepts, and then spout them off intelligently the next day while in class. It was highly competitive and everyone had something to prove. Trust? Forget about it. The pressure led some classmates to drop out. Others did not make the cut after the second semester. In many ways, it felt like a protracted war of attrition.

When things got really intense, I questioned whether I would make it. I wondered if I had what it took to be successful—if I was smart enough, whether I could compete for my seat and keep it, not just in the classroom but in the real world after law school. After a few conversations with a handful of special people who loved me and refused to let me give up, I decided to dig my heels in, raise my standards, and do whatever it took to earn my law degree. After I made that decision, tough times continued, I must say, for many days, but I persevered. I knew that it would all be a distant memory once I crossed the threshold on graduation day. And, I was right. Although I started law school passion-drunk, I left with a hearty combination of passion and grit. And I have been "gritty" ever since.

## Core Strategies

The strategies outlined in the following sections offer guidance for cultivating the skill and insight needed to pursue passion alongside perseverance. They are distilled from the lessons I have learned from exceptional leaders across various industries.

### Embrace Risk

Playing it safe no doubt keeps you comfortable, but it does not challenge you to become better or position you to seize opportunity. Risk, on the other hand, does. It is a necessary component of success. It is a precursor to the growth needed to achieve the next levels of personal and professional development. Still, do not assume that you must take on wanton risk for it to count. Risk should be calculated. If you want to expand your business to increase scalability, do not randomly select a larger space and sign a lease tomorrow. Review market trends, competition, and your past performance before making any commitments.

Know that you will need to take on some degree of risk for expansion however. Also bear in mind that the thinking and effort that got you where you are today likely will be insufficient to take you where you want to go tomorrow. Therefore, be willing to make important sacrifices for success. Remove fear from the equation and focus on who you want to become, and what you can achieve in the process of embracing risk.

## Engage in Positive Self-Talk

The conversations that you have with yourself are the most important ones that you will ever have. We all "talk" to ourselves—a process that occurs without much conscious effort. By asking questions, repeating our opinions of ourselves and others, and processing information to make decisions, we are communing in our heads. So, be kind to *you.* Frequently remind yourself that you are capable of achieving your heart's desires and worthy of respect, goodness, and unbridled success. No one is better at speaking life into ourselves than we are.

Thoughts are easily embedded into your psyche, and they can quickly become a powerful frame of reference, for better or for worse. So, establish a strong foundation by building yourself up rather than tearing yourself down. When you treat yourself well through constructive conversation, you prepare yourself for the inevitable knocks and scrapes that come with being human, especially those instances where you are particularly susceptible to the judgment of others.

## When Things Get Tough, Dig Deep

It might be tempting to bow out when things get tough, but stick with it. Resolve to face challenges head on and maneuver through the pain and anguish with determination. No one is born with grit. Like most valued skill-sets, it is developed over time in a series of crucibles. Its success is hard-wrought. Instead of feeling sorry for yourself or surrendering to frustration and doubt, make a conscious decision to increase your willpower and stamina.

From a practical standpoint, enough sleep, exercise, and eating well can help you sustain your efforts with greater conviction.

These "little things" make a big difference, so do not take their usefulness for granted. Make up your mind that you will do whatever it takes to get to the other side of angst. Over time you will become stronger and more agile. And your growth can prove to be a remarkable frame of reference when you are faced with a new challenge. The boost in your morale and self-esteem alone can transform your attitude and reengineer your beliefs about what you can accomplish.

## Eat the "Frog" First

When dealing with unpleasant tasks, it is easy to feel uninspired. Of course, you would rather be doing something else. It makes matters worse when those tasks are fundamental aspects of a bigger goal. Because you should get them done, you must rethink the way you approach them. One proven way to move past the doldrums is to eat the "frog" first. That just means taking on the most undesirable task or project of the day and tackling it first.

The immediate benefit is that once you have completed the task, it will no longer be looming over your head. You will then have the needed momentum to complete any remaining tasks. If you wait until the end to eat the frog, you do yourself a grave disservice. You will end up grappling with a constant sense of uneasiness that will not dissipate until you finally get the daunting task done.

## Create a Support System

No matter how capable or successful you are, having a support system naturally enhances your ability to face challenges. Choose your team wisely: Select people whom you trust and who can offer solid, thoughtful advice or tough love when necessary. For instance, you may need a pep talk on a day when you are anxious to throw in the towel. We are not always willing or prepared to advocate for ourselves when we need to. A support system can help to mitigate that vulnerability. Additionally, do not assume the more advisors, the more effective the group. It is more important to choose people who are competent and reliable and who can provide you with critical support when you need it the most, even if they are fewer in number. In this case, quality is preferable to quantity.

## Journal Questions

1. When the going gets tough, how do you respond to the change in situational dynamics? Discuss.
2. Name three ways that you can motivate yourself to complete complex tasks that require a significant time commitment.
3. Do you engage in positive self-talk daily? If so, what specific things do you say?
4. How did this principle lead you to better understand your role as a leader? How will its mastery enable you to cultivate greater effectiveness?
5. How will you use the preceding strategies to advance your commitment to developing true grit?

## Leadership Challenge

Identify three trusted colleagues within your circle of influence. Who are they and why do you value their opinions? Make a pledge to seek their support when times get tough. Write down the skills and insights that each brings to the table, noting how they can help you move through tough times. Do you feel better knowing that you have a network of peers you can trust during dark days?

## Notes

1. Duckworth, A. (2016). Grit: The power of passion and perseverance (Unabridged). New York, NY: Audioworks, an imprint of Simon & Schuster Audio Division.
2. Duckworth, A. (2016, November 11). *Spotlight with Angela Duckworth*. INBOUND 2016, Boston, MA.
3. Duckworth, A. (2016, November 11). *Spotlight with Angela Duckworth*. INBOUND 2016, Boston, MA.

# 13

## Work Smarter, Not Harder

*Leadership is hard work, but working hard is not as useful a tool as working smart.*

Expending unnecessary time or energy to accomplish a goal is an inefficient application of resources. An effective leader must know how to successfully navigate the workday, prioritizing which projects are most important and allocating sufficient resources to accomplish them auspiciously. Even though working hard may produce quality work, the quality and quantity are likely to suffer unless you are also working "smart."

Traditional ideas of hard work include long hours and physically exhausting labor. Although an excellent work ethic is necessary for success, it is not sufficient. Linking the value of work to the time spent doing it is paradoxical now that technological innovations have so drastically changed the way we work. Tasks that used to take days or weeks can now be accomplished in hours or even minutes. Besides, it is irrational to think that the old ways of doing things were superior simply because they took more time.

To work "smart," a leader must eliminate distractions because they cause a loss of focus. A practical way to do this is to work on only one thing at a time and assign it a specific deadline each day. By beginning with the end in mind, you are less likely to wander off track, and you can measure your progress as you move forward. Putting off activities that can be addressed at another time is a smart move. You can always revisit them after you finish current tasks. This also would allow you to sharpen your focus and optimize resources.

Leaders who work smarter experience less stress, have more free time, and get more done. They do not expend energy on unimportant matters. They know that a sound strategy applied consistently yields the best results, both

© The Author(s) 2018
K. Mariama-Arthur, *Poised for Excellence*, DOI 10.1007/978-3-319-64574-2_13

qualitatively and quantitatively. They also understand that the key to success is increased productivity without expending unnecessary effort. A desire for measurable results fuels their enterprising mindsets and those results become the litmus test for their success.

Working smarter is similar in principle to scalability. Businesses that want to increase scalability aim at increasing profit while also increasing sales. They also align capacity with demand when specific resources are added to the mix. Leaders who strive to work smarter can achieve greater profitability and quality of output by focusing on the best application of resources. In each case, the goal is to improve net gains by optimizing assets. If achieved, both scenarios present an opportunity for unlimited expansion, profitability, and redistribution of precious resources.

Reclaiming the workday begins with one realization: You have the power to do it. Giving the responsibility to someone else or concluding that day-to-day activities are beyond one's control sends even the most promising leaders into a downward spiral. Instead of presuming that you are unable to exercise any control over the parameters of your daily tasks, exert some and see what happens. You will discover that even small shifts in effort yield measurable results, and you can leverage them to build momentum.

The most effective leaders embrace this principle as disruptors: They change the way they think about work and how to produce quality outcomes efficiently. They do not execute according to antiquated paradigms. What they know for sure is that the only way to improve on a process is to do something differently. What that "different thing" is depends largely on what they are trying to achieve. No matter what the goal is, however, a smart leader must strive to work smarter, rather than harder, to avoid squandering precious resources and settling for substandard results that compromise credibility, discourage collaboration, and frustrate opportunity.

"Million Dollar Listing Miami" star, Chris Leavitt, is a huge proponent of working smarter rather than harder.[1] Early in his real estate career, one of his mentors taught him the art of working smart. His mentor explained that he cut his workday down to three hours and could do the other things he enjoyed (e.g., tennis and golf), which provided him with a better quality of life and kept him fit. He discovered that balancing out a day between work and recreation made all the difference. He said that so many hours were wasted doing frivolous things, and he wanted to eliminate that characteristic from his day. He did—in favor of tightening his workday and focusing intently on the most critical and result-producing tasks.

Leavitt applied this strategy to his own workday and achieved similar results. By focusing on how to effectively manage his days, he found that he had more time to develop quality relationships outside of the office, contributing to a larger clientele and an increase in high net-worth sales. He also had more time to give back and mentor others. Among other things, this paradigm shift resulted in a long list of impressive successes for Leavitt, including representing the sale of a triplex penthouse in Miami Beach—the largest condominium sale in the history of Florida; it sold for $35 million. Now that is leveraging the power of working smarter, not harder.

## Core Strategies

The strategies outlined in the following sections offer guidance for cultivating your skill and insight into developing a smart work ethic. They are distilled from the lessons I have learned from exceptional leaders across various industries.

### Determine Overall Objectives

It is difficult to know how to work smarter unless you are clear on exactly what you need to accomplish. What are your clear-cut objectives—specifically the overarching goal—and how would working smarter advance it? Clarify your objectives first and then ask pertinent questions that frame them further. Who are the relevant stakeholders? What matters most to them and how do these factors impact your work? Do hours and location affect your ability to execute effectively? What are the industry politics and policies?

After you have a solid idea of what you are trying to achieve, examine current behaviors to see how they are helping or hindering your progress. Note where you can make improvements. For example, you may be confusing longer working hours with being more productive. Longer hours, however, do not necessarily equate to a better result. They are not one and the same. Overhauling your strategies may be to achieve quality over quantity of output.

In addition, you also may need to take a closer look at the conditions you are working under. The workplace environment may be having a negative impact on your efforts. Examine your schedule and proximity to others to identify any distractions. Each of these elements can impact your overall objectives. Understanding the lay of the land can help you decide how to best navigate the objectives and achieve your goals using the most effective strategies.

## Assess the Rigor of Work

If you only have eight hours a day to complete your work, you will use your time different from someone with a 14-hour window to burn through. Additionally, your work rhythm will vary depending on whether you are doing mental or physical labor. One may depend on inspiration and the ability to generate clear thought and high-quality arguments. The other may require physical strength and stamina.

"Rigor" may change depending on the season. Such is the case for accountants, especially during tax season. Another way rigor may change is at certain phases of a project. You may have a big push at the beginning or the end, but experience smooth sailing during the remaining work year. Knowing what is required to successfully complete the details of your work at each juncture can maximize success.

## Set Deadlines

If you want to be efficient, work needs to have enforceable deadlines. Be reasonable, but know that your deadline can be difficult to meet without consistent effort. One way to approach this is to create both soft (internal) and hard (external) deadlines. The soft deadline is usually aspirational, but it also can provide additional review time before submitting a final, timely product to a third party. The hard deadline is usually rigid and will dictate the project's trajectory.

You may even need to place the project on an extended timetable or, depending on what is at stake, speed it up and renegotiate the deliverables. In either case, it is best to sync outcomes with deadlines and break up the deliverables over time to make sure they are manageable and that the work is produced well in the first go-round. Time and effort are wasted when work must be redone because it was rushed. Remember that large or complex segments may require more time and collaboration to reasonably and competently push through in the time allotted.

## Manage the Workflow

After you have set your deadlines, you need to chunk the work into segments. Most projects cannot be completed in one sitting. They need to be broken up into smaller, more manageable pieces or even delegated to other team members. Part of this process necessarily involves understanding your workforce, pinpointing the experts, and knowing how much time each needs to churn out their portion if pieces must be delegated. If you are solely responsible, make sure you give yourself ample time to thoroughly work through each piece of a project. Take the time to review your commitments against project demands. Examine best- and worst-case scenarios to create a plan B just in case things do not turn out the way you thought they would. Determine the best way to proceed, and then move forward strategically.

## Execute

Once you have created a game plan, it is time to execute it. First, visualize the goal and then review the strategies that you have developed to see how each piece fits together. If the project requires the collective effort of a team, gather the group and brief them on the next steps. If a solo effort, you can review the plan and the steps calculated to produce the desired results. Next, create a monitoring and reporting mechanism. You will want to test these features to make sure everything will work fine when it is time to move forward.

Now would be the most opportune time to discover any hiccups and address them before they impact the final work product. Once you success- fully execute portions of the initial phase, you can build momentum for the more complex ones. Be sure to measure outcomes and use what you learn to apply to future scenarios.

## Journal Questions

1. Describe your work ethic.
2. Does the nature of your work require constant deadlines and deliverables? Explain.
3. What methods do you use to manage work flow?
4. How did this principle help you better understand your role as a leader? How would its mastery enable you to cultivate greater effectiveness?
5. How will you use the preceding strategies to advance your commitment to upgrading your work ethic?

## Leadership Challenge

Evaluate your work ethic by identifying both blind and bright spots. For bright spots, note how you became good at each. For blind spots, determine three specific ways that you can improve them, and then implement those strategies promptly. After a week, note whether you have noticed any improvement in the quantity and quality of your work, as well as your overall results.

# Note

1. Mariama-Arthur, K. (2014, December 2). The Star of 'Million Dollar Listing Miami' on Working Smarter, Not Harder. *Success*. Retrieved February 27, 2017 from http://www.success.com/article/the-star-of-million-dollar-listing-miami-the-star-of-million-dollar-listing-miami-

# 14

## Prepare for War in Times of Peace

*Prudent leaders prepare for change tomorrow by crafting their blueprint to address it today.*

"*Si vis pacem, para bellum*"—that is a 2000-year-old Latin adage that means "If you want peace, prepare for war."[1] Leaders understand the need for preparedness. Prudent leaders plan for uncertainty and constantly reevaluate the landscape because the mission is always at stake. They try to develop a contingency plan for every conceivable crisis and that manifest intentionality helps them to weather the storms of uncertainty.

Preparing for war in times of peace is like having a solid endgame strategy in a game of chess. Leaders do not rely on ad hoc tactics; they employ high-level strategic thinking to further their vision. Rather than react to change after the fact, leaders develop strategies well in advance of the turmoil to decrease adversity's blow—that is the unmitigated purpose behind being proactive.[2] An innovative approach to handling change breaks through the organizational roadblocks that traditionally stymie progress. Because leaders spend their time working offensively rather than defensively, they minimize damage caused by disruptive ideas or events.

Resisting change rarely stops it. Leaders are flexible and adaptable, and they can turn on a dime when necessary. Because they are responsible for so many people throughout an organization, and in many cases throughout the world, they cannot afford to let their minds stagnate. Leaders think differently; their vision is expansive. They do not blindly accept the old ways of doing things because they realize that the comfort of the familiar is short-lived and the risk of complacency great. Leaders act despite fear.

© The Author(s) 2018
K. Mariama-Arthur, *Poised for Excellence*, DOI 10.1007/978-3-319-64574-2_14

The ability to prepare and adapt to change requires that leaders keep their eyes and ears open. Eagle-eyed leaders are intimately plugged in to their immediate environment and keep close tabs on the periphery as well. They remain abreast of current affairs and determine how these events may directly or indirectly impact them, their organization, and/or their industry. When they observe certain trends, they respond proactively and adapt. They gather facts and test strategies based on the data they have before them.

Sometimes, however, there is insufficient information to identify an imminent trend. This does not hinder "smart" leaders because they are never asleep the wheel. They think ahead. They brainstorm to discover probabilities, flukes, and worst-case scenarios. They fill their coffers with supplies, and they assemble teams who are well prepared to execute a carefully-considered plan if the right set of circumstances arise. Rather than be caught off guard, they are inclined to test the waters by dipping a toe in and gaining clarity about what could be at stake.

The truth is that leaders face many potential risks that could transpire at any time. Even with the best preparation not all possible risks can be eliminated. They can, however, at least be identified, assessed, mitigated, and managed with proper oversight. These steps are critical for any leader who seeks to direct the future and long-term success of the organization or the institution that he or she serves.

Still, even the most prepared leaders are occasionally caught off guard by a sudden turn of events. They are human, after all. Here is a catch though. Because they have primed the pump prior to the crisis, they are able to adapt faster than those who are completely taken by surprise when a change in circumstances occurs. The process of preparing for war in times of peace is a golden opportunity that also demonstrates the raw capacity of effective leadership.

The United States Marine Corps is an elite fighting force.[3] Ask any Marine and they will tell you that their training was the most grueling, physically and mentally, of all the uniformed services. It is intense, highly competitive, and the attrition rate is extremely low. Attrition is low because they weed out "lukewarm" recruits in the vetting process, because recycling them can be expensive, given limited resources. Marines characteristically do not wait for a disaster to strike to respond. Their training gives them the required tools of the trade: The unmatched perceptive and adaptive ability to engage in conventional as well as unconventional warfare and to evolve and adapt to change seamlessly.[4] They are the only branch that possesses the full capabilities of all other branches of the military.

Through this extraordinary training, they can preconceive the worst-case scenarios and respond strategically. Their defenses are never down, so to speak. Because their mission is always at stake, they must be sharp, agile, and ready to respond at a moment's notice. This training also prepares them for a sudden turn of events. It is entirely possible for a Marine to encounter a novel scenario, but they successfully get through it because they draw on a familiar pool of knowledge and tactical resources. Their extraordinary capacity is the benefit of preparing for war in times of peace.

# Core Strategies

The strategies outlined in the following sections offer guidance for cultivating your skill and insight as a strategic leader who can prepare for war in times of peace. They are distilled from the lessons I have learned from exceptional leaders across various industries.

## Acknowledge the "What If"

Even though it makes sense to hope for the best, a smart leader creates a contingency plan and prepares for the worst. Accept that things may not go as planned and, accordingly, examine possible alternatives. Ask yourself which factors may contribute to potential disruptions? Are they unavoidable? Or are they only probable if you make certain mistakes? How can you reduce the blow if the worst occurs? These are all penetrating questions that must be asked and answered in advance to ensure that you are well-prepared.

Your responses will help create a solid plan and navigate uncertainty if and when a crisis arises. Experts in emergency preparedness focus heavily on the "what if" scenario and help individuals and organizations determine how to best deal with unlikely scenarios that emerge without warning. Recall the role of the various emergency preparedness and response teams that converged on New Orleans after the levies broke in 2005. Always consider the "what if" and govern yourself accordingly.

## Gather Appropriate Resources

Having the most relevant resources at your disposal is essential when you are planning for the future. Determine in advance what you may need. Is it people? Financial instruments? Supplies or other tangible items? Is it necessary to have these resources on hand, or can you request them when needed? Research and find out. Then begin to build an inventory that includes a variety of items, both tangible and intangible, that can be accessed and leveraged when you need them. Do not assume that there will always be time to create your storehouse. Disaster may happen tomorrow. This begs the question of whether you are ready today.

Do yourself a favor by beginning sooner rather than later. This will not only provide an important sense of accomplishment, but also give you extraordinary peace of mind and the confidence to set your sights on other pressing matters.

## Seek Advice

Although you may have a trove of expertise, it is always wise to consult with experts in areas where you may not be as well-versed. Seek out qualified advisors to get second opinions. They can help you get up to speed on the lay of the land and advise you going forward. Compile a cross section of experts who can identify key issues from various industry perspectives. Allow them to take the lead where you have limited knowledge and understanding. Ask tough questions, and put your ego aside to capture the benefit of their experience and advice. You should do a bit of research yourself, too, before consulting with experts. This will ensure that you are exposed to key industry terms, understand the critical issues that impact the landscape, and can ask relevant questions that likely will affect your specific organization and the goals you seek to accomplish.

## Develop a Contingency Plan

After you have perfected Plan A, get to work on Plan B. Strategy is the key. Develop a 5-point plan that includes details from soup to nuts. Create a shortened version in case you need to execute quickly. Either way, do not leave out any critical components. Make sure that each plan includes at least three different options for each point and a mechanism for abandoning it if necessary. The plan should include both conservative and aggressive approaches that can be used in a variety of circumstances. This way you can always have a direct route to steer through crises. The point is not to be left out in the cold when turbulent times arrive. You want to be able to assess, pivot, and adapt to change, regardless of the circumstances. Rest assured that every successful leader takes to heart and mind the value of an exceptional contingency plan and leaves nothing to chance.

## Prepare and Execute

Once you have a strategy in place, you must execute it. No need to reconsider, hesitate, or make excuses at this stage. These behaviors will only keep you trapped in a web of indecision. Instead, take decisive steps so that you can push forward. With the appropriate resources at your disposal, take the bull by the horns and move ahead with confidence. Connect the dots. Remain alert and continue to tweak strategies whenever necessary.

Take refuge in knowing that confidence and decisiveness are your allies and sometimes you must simply leap, rather remain captive by ambivalence. Imagine having to deplane during an aircraft emergency. Even though you have been advised on what to do, you may still be fearful. Still, inaction usually leads to a worse result. So, decide in advance to take the necessary action when the time comes.

## Journal Questions

1. Do you usually develop a contingency plan, after developing a primary one? Why or why not?
2. Describe an instance when you were fully prepared for an outcome. Distinguish it from a time when you were wholly unprepared.
3. List five ways to get ahead of a specific problem, with an eye toward avoiding it altogether.
4. How did this principle assist you to better understand your role as a leader? How will its mastery enable you to cultivate greater effectiveness?
5. How will you use the preceding strategies to advance your commitment to being a more prepared leader?

## Leadership Challenge

Do you have a contingency plan in place in the event that things go awry in any area of your life? Identify an area of your life where a contingency plan would be beneficial. Write out the plan and explain how it would work. Do you feel more comfortable knowing that you now have a plan in place?

## Notes

1. Jack, D. (2014, March 8). Address: If You Want Peace, Prepare for War—U.S. Military Pre-Eminence and Why it Matters. Hudson Institute. Retrieved January 25th, 2017 from https://www.hudson.org/research/10155-address-if-you-want-peace-prepare-for-war-u-s-military-pre-eminence-and-why-it-matters.
2. Bandura, A. & Adams, N.E. (1977 December). Analysis of Self-efficacy Theory of Behavioral Change. Cognitive Therapy and Research 1 (4): 287. Retrieved January 16, 2017 from https://doi.org/10.1007/BF01663995.

3. Simmons, E. (1998). The Marines. Triangle: The Marine Corps Heritage Foundation.
4. Smith, L. (2007). The Few and the Proud: Marine Corps Drill Instructors in Their Own Words. New York: W. W. North & Company.

# 15

## Turn "Shoulds" into "Musts"

*Leaders know that only "musts" get done, so they turn "shoulds" into urgent commitments.*

Saying that you *should* lose weight is very different from saying that you *must* lose it. "Shoulds" are suggestions; "musts" are imperatives. Leaders know that only musts get done. The most effective leaders are keen on that difference and strive to embrace urgent commitments as a clear mechanism for producing results.

Musts require great focus and discipline. They also need prioritizing, reorganizing, and reorienting. It takes determination and perseverance to stay on-task over long stretches. Excellence is hard work, and too often people are unwilling to put in the time and effort needed to achieve it. An exceptional leader sees the value in escalating priorities and works diligently to accomplish them successfully. They do not pay lip service to excellence; they put skin in the game.

When leaders turn *shoulds* into *musts*, they not only achieve their own goals, but help the organization achieve its as well. Leaders who adopt this mindset have a different way of experiencing the world. They get results because they demand results of themselves, and they do whatever is necessary to achieve them. They do not view success as optional. Instead, they see it as a nonnegotiable leadership imperative. It is the moxie behind such thinking that drives their results.

Leaders who take a passive approach to success fail to take the bull by the horns; they do not move with urgency, exigency, or purpose to get things done. They rely on whim and then hope things will go their way. They bet on the stars aligning and hope that circumstances will fall into place to "create" opportunities for them. Yet hope is not a strategy. In taking this stance, they diminish their role in manifesting their results. Leaders who refuse to act as

© The Author(s) 2018
K. Mariama-Arthur, *Poised for Excellence*, DOI 10.1007/978-3-319-64574-2_15

interested stakeholders in cultivating their own results lose the zeal to create them, and end up *should*ing" all over themselves.

Free will is the freedom to choose whatever you want, but this freedom also requires accepting the consequences of your decisions. Because there is no arbiter at the gates directing or influencing your path, you are free to go left or right. The best leaders know that freedom is not merely about making just *any* choice, but about making a good one. Leaders must examine what must be done against lesser "take it or leave it" options. It is all about prioritizing and acting to escalate priorities. For example, a leader serious about developing emotional quotient (EQ) skills would consider an opportunity to learn them as a basic requirement, rather than as a viable alternative.

From a leadership perspective, there is always more to do. Opportunities to improve a process, system, or an individual's performance are always available. The issue is not whether there are sufficient ways to generate activity, but what kinds of activities merit a leader's full attention, such that her or his vision and mission cannot do without them. When leaders choose to set clear priorities, they can succeed at what is most relevant. Additionally, what matters the most will never be at the mercy of what matters the least.

The most effective leaders are adamant about turning *should*s into *must*s. They decide what they really want and why they want it. They clearly define their goals and motivations. They do not let distractions and whims get in the way of completing important tasks. They eat the "frog" first and, whenever necessary, sacrifice everyday comforts in favor of strengthening their resolve to succeed. They know that no matter what, nothing looks, feels, or tastes as good as a job well done and executed to completion. When getting results are a real priority, "smart" leaders turn shoulds into musts.

Businessman, best-selling author, and philanthropist Tony Robbins is well known for his remarkable ability to turn "shoulds" into "musts" in his own life, as well as to help others do the same through his prolific work in personal development. Even though he did not attend college, he is well-read and a lifelong learner who developed compelling insights into neurolinguistic programming, psychology, and leadership topics that have helped people all over the world achieve incredible breakthroughs.

From United States presidents to world-renowned athletes and billion-dollar businessmen, Robbins knows how to get people to tap into the mindset of achievement by helping them focus on what matters the most: What they want and why they want it. He gets people to focus on what their lives would be like if they achieved their goals and, alternatively, what they would look like they did not.

In particular, he teaches people how to make deep emotional connections to each possibility. This stimulates them to create and to leverage the necessary motivation to turn their shoulds into musts. His incredible personal transformation is the best evidence of practicing what he preaches to others. If you are committed to success, your *musts* always get prioritized; they are the catalysts enabling you to experience extraordinary results in every aspect of your life. And when they are treated with the respect and engagement that they deserve, they become force multipliers.

## Core Strategies

The strategies outlined in the following sections offer guidance for cultivating the skill and insight to turn shoulds into musts. They are distilled from the lessons I have learned from exceptional leaders across various industries.

### Do Not Procrastinate

If you want to turn your shoulds into musts, start by executing your compelling desires. Simply talking or writing about them will not do, although either activity might be useful in getting you focused initially. Why is procrastination such a big problem? It prevents you from achieving your goals by lessening your aspiration and weakening your will. To repel procrastination, find out what kinds of tasks are most likely to promote it. It may creep up every time you have to write a speech or prepare a financial report. If a task feels foreboding to you, you are prone to wait until the last minute to do it, which usually results in increased stress and a subpar product.

Instead of succumbing to procrastination, be proactive and take decisive action, even if you do not feel inspired. In such cases, begin writing the speech outline or preparing the report, and schedule time to work on it daily. By acting (in most cases immediate action), you build momentum with each completed task. No matter how you feel, do not be derailed by pessimistic emotions, fatigue, or superficial distractions. Start moving forward expeditiously.

### Stop Making Excuses

It is one thing to procrastinate, but quite another to make an excuse. Excuses are ways to explain away an unfavorable result. There is always some reason, good, bad, or indifferent, why something has occurred. Whatever the case may be, you must understand and accept it. If your report is late, resist the urge to blame it on your heavy workload. You knew the report was due and you had time to do it, but for one reason or another, you *chose* not to prioritize it.

By the same token, do not blame your circumstances on others. Take responsibility for your whole life, including your results. Instead of making excuses, plan to succeed. If your plan fails, accept responsibility. Determine what went wrong, then develop a contingency plan. If you are serious about prioritizing "musts," you cannot make excuses for missteps along the way. You have to own the good and the bad.

## Freely Make Mistakes

You do not have to be perfect to achieve results. Actually, you *cannot* be perfect. It is not humanly possible. Choose to jump into your life and fail forward with wild abandon. Act and learn from everything that happens, even if the outcome is undesirable. Then, do it over again and again. The more mistakes you make, the more lessons you learn. Take pride in your mistakes. Use them to sharpen your thinking and performance. The people who have been the most successful are the ones who have made the most mistakes. Why? Because mistakes are full of great teachings. Even though it is true that musts feel risky because they require acting—action that could potentially lead to failure—they also yield greater rewards than the elusive nature of shoulds.

## Take Bold Action

To make musts bear fruit, you have to take bold action, or it is unlikely you will achieve results. Do your homework to avoid being reckless, but then be courageous and work diligently, without reservation. Baby steps have their place, but they are not calculated to yield the results you need when striving to achieve musts. Bold action can seem aggressive and even sensational, but that is the very nature of its purpose in driving larger-than-life outcomes.

So, instead of simply looking through the "Help Wanted" ads to find your dream job, go out and meet people who might be able to connect you with a decision maker. Attend industry events where high-touch interactions are possible. Be enthusiastic. Let people know that you are looking for your dream job and see if anyone bites. Taking bold action helps you draw universal pull into your orbit and attract the kind of support that yields results.

## Forget About What Other People Think

The more you worry about what other people think, the further away you will end up from your goals. If you are hell-bent on earning six figures within a two-year time frame, go for it. Who are your supervisors, colleagues, or naysayers to conclude that you cannot achieve it? Your goals are yours alone. If you allow others to redefine your musts, you may well end up achieving none or worse, living out someone else's dreams. Instead, focus on yourself, your purpose, and your needs.

Others' opinions are distractions, and if you allow them to influence you, your mental and emotional health will suffer. Understand that even people with good intentions can distract you from your greater purpose. By the same token, not everyone who offers advice has your best interest at heart. Rise above the negativity and block out the self-serving rhetoric espoused by naysayers.

## Journal Questions

1. What kinds of tasks make you procrastinate the most?
2. Name three signs of procrastination that you have directly observed.
3. Do you usually overanalyze before attempting to take action? Why or why not?
4. How did this principle help you better understand your role as a leader? How will its mastery enable you to cultivate greater effectiveness?
5. How will you use the preceding strategies to advance your commitment to turning "shoulds" into "musts"?

## Leadership Challenge

Identify a goal that procrastination has put out of reach. Use the strategies described in this chapter to create a plan to achieve it finally. How does it feel to push past procrastination?

# 16

# Lead with Influence, Not Authority

*Real power is derived from influence through authentic leadership, rather than the perception of authority.*

Lofty titles and the credentials attached to leaders create the perception of authority. If leadership is about influence—*and it is*—then these alone only get leaders so far. The most effective leaders bring something more tangible to the table—for example, high-caliber skillsets that inspire trust, respect, devotion, and remarkable performance in others. When these skillsets are thoroughly developed, they shape and move collective visions forward.

Focusing too much attention on your authority as a leader hardly ever results in long-term success. Even though it may signal stature and define the scope of duties, authority does little to inspire others to think differently or to take decisive action, which should be clear priorities for every leader. Treating authority as the "nexus of power" creates a rebuttable presumption that every leader must confront when perception proves to be ineffective in garnering the desired commitment and support from others.

How does one lead with influence rather than authority?

Leading with influence requires a clear purpose and the ability to develop authentic connection with others. When you lead based on a genuine desire to serve, and your decisions are shaped by your core values and true respect for others, it is easy to develop authentic relationships. When relationships are grounded in mutual respect, they thrive. And when relationships thrive, so do the organizations that they serve. This mutual synergy fosters greater organizational cohesiveness and more prolific collaborations, and helps leaders to establish more robust platforms steeped in influence.

© The Author(s) 2018
K. Mariama-Arthur, *Poised for Excellence*, DOI 10.1007/978-3-319-64574-2_16

When integrity and reputation set the tone, people are drawn to you almost effortlessly. Developing bona fide connections is what makes leading with influence so incredibly effective. Think for a moment about your own behavior. Would you feel inspired to follow your lead if you were in the shoes of your constituents? If the answer is "Yes," then good for you. If the answer is "No," step back to evaluate why, then reconsider your purpose, values, and behavior. Recalibrate them until you feel confident that you are a good example of what you represent beyond the boundaries of your authority.

To be clear, an impressive title is not a precursor to success in a leadership role. Consider the relevant examples in nearly every industry. Incompetence and moral and ethical failings have all been charges levied against well-known leaders with lofty titles. Therefore, the conscience of leadership requires more than merely showing up in name only. It also requires taking up the full and complete armor of the role, which out of necessity includes the consummate ability to leverage influence to mobilize and persuade others.

Conversely, sometimes individuals with less impressive credentials demonstrate extraordinary promise and have uncommon leadership abilities that urge recognition. Consider the front desk clerk who has not yet completed college, but brings unmatched energy and enthusiasm to her work. She arrives early, performs the duties competently, and is effective in getting the staff to take personal responsibility for shaping and maintaining the company's enterprising culture. Clearly, titles do not always rouse others to action, but influence does. Without question, interpersonal dynamics help a leader's influence to grow, which is why soft-skill mastery is vital to effective leadership. It is also why the best leaders do not define themselves with externalities such as titles; they rely on core principles and influence to guide their decisions and move their ambitious platforms forward.

The most effective leaders are keenly aware of how they present themselves to others. They know that if done well, high-touch interactions can add only a positive facet to their overall influence. Therefore, they make sure that their professional brand is a true extension of their core values, that there is consistency and substance behind the name. Each action they take represents another building block in their brand's architecture, so they are mindful of what they do. Leaders who embrace influence rather than authority find it easier to establish an impeccable standard of excellence, to deliver on the results promised, to value people and nurture relationships, to promote strategic cooperation, to resolve conflict quickly, and to develop and support others effectively and freely.

A profound sense of personal responsibility and, in turn, accountability guide leaders who know that titles alone are insufficient to accomplish their primary objectives and that having a legitimate stake in the game ensures greater overall success. To that end, when a leader strives to leverage influence rather than authority, he or she is in the best position to change the dynamics of every single relationship, transform the workplace culture, and boost individual and organizational outcomes. Besides, when the foundation of an individual's leadership is built on sustaining principles, the leader experiences greater fulfillment and inspires others to achieve greater purpose and results.

I had the pleasure of coaching a mid-level manager who found it convenient to regularly tout his "apparent authority" in an effort to generate fear and get his subordinates to fall in line. The problem with his thinking was that although his title provided him with a valid means of distinguishing himself from the employees that he managed, he had not earned their respect or behaved in a way that inspired them. The manager was unpleasant and often disrespectful. He would purposely sabotage employees and micromanage, making them feel powerless. The result was disastrous.

When a scandal broke out and he needed the support of his staff to get through it, no one stepped up to help. His reputation had been marred and there was little he could do to recoup it. The poor treatment of his staff, colleagues, and the administration left him without the support of a committed base. When someone forgets the importance of leading with influence over authority, there is always a hefty price to pay, no matter where they are positioned within the echelons of an organization. And measure for measure, karma always seeks what is due.

# Core Strategies

The strategies outlined in the following sections offer guidance for cultivating skill and insight as an authentic leader. They are distilled from the lessons I have learned from exceptional leaders across various industries.

## Set the Behavioral Bar High

Your behavior is a direct reflection of your core values. People observe leaders' behavior as evidence of who they are and what they believe. Their words are meaningless if incongruent with their behavior. And when curated intentionally, a leader's behavior is also an indication of what he or she expects from others and what others should aspire to become. Set the behavioral bar high and align your core values with it. Without an affirmative baseline for conduct based on a leader's own behavior, people find it difficult to gauge what is acceptable. As such, the onus is on all leaders to first establish those fundamental principles that guide their behavior, and then govern themselves accordingly. Do not try to be perfect; just strive to conduct yourself in a way that reflects your ideals authentically. It is when someone demonstrates a grave departure from these ideals that credibility issues arise.

## Garner Influence

Always remember that your behavior determines how others perceive and interact with you. Rather than leveraging authority to bolster allegiance, choose to wield influence. If you attempt to rely solely on your title, you may be disappointed. Titles, by themselves, do not prove useful in prompting others to long-term action. Rapport and authentic relationships offer more compelling sources of intrinsic motivation. Use yours to make short shrift of the more challenging aspects of the role, especially where support is critical to your success. Unlike authority, which often creates artificial allegiances that wax and wane or seem to matter only publicly, influence usually stands the test of time, even behind closed doors. As a leader, you need to know that your team supports you because you have set a good example and that your reputation precedes you in a way that complements the office you hold. So, strike out and begin to influence others by being the best example of the tenets you espouse.

## Treat People the Way You Want to Be Treated

You can never go wrong when you treat others the way that you want to be treated. It is an old maxim, but it bears repeating, especially in this context. Respect and consideration go a long way toward inspiring others to return the favor. Reciprocity is an age-old practice with a proven track record for building alliances. If people trust that you have their back, they will reciprocate and come to your aid in times of need. The reality is that you cannot expect more from others than you are willing to give of yourself.

Wielding the sword makes you susceptible to being sliced by it. If you have the propensity for being "the heavy," reconsider how your demeanor affects your ability to command influence. If you do not understand and master the principle of reciprocity, you will be hard-pressed to capture endorsements and buy-ins when you need them the most.

## Respect the Limitations of Your Title

Titles convey stature and distinguish the leaders from the masses, but they do little more than that. It is the behavior of the leader behind the title that generates the influence. Do not, therefore, assume that your title alone will help you garner approval or become a more effective leader. Instead, you must work to draw others in and to create synergies that inspire allegiance. A title is just one aspect of a leader's persona. The values they hold, how they convey them, how they treat others, and their ability to competently execute their role are all unrelated to the title itself, but are decisive attributes of the person behind it. A title is merely a symbol of rank and authority, whereas the leader behind it is expected to be a flesh-and-blood champion of change. Think about the stark differences in these concepts. Know where the lines of demarcation are drawn to avoid well-meaning but wrong-headed assumptions. Above all, remember that status, without more, is merely incidental to effectuating the true aims of effective leadership.

## Do Not Pledge Blind Allegiance to Others' Titles

If it is misguided to ask others to buy into your vision simply because you have a title, it also is misguided to buy into someone else's for the same reason. Smart leaders practice what they preach, so before you pledge allegiance to another's vision, allow her or him to demonstrate through behavior that the person is deserving of your devotion. Support people who lead with fundamental values rather than with superficial titles. Observe a person's actions first; actions speak louder than words. Give leaders an opportunity to demonstrate that their behavior aligns with their core values and the overall mission. Then, and only then, should you feel obliged to follow.

# Journal Questions

1. Describe an instance when someone with greater status treated you unfairly because of this differential. How did it make you feel?
2. Name three distinct power-seeking behaviors that you have observed in the past. In your opinion, why were those behaviors problematic?
3. How does your current behavior inspire others to follow your lead?
4. How did this principle help you better understand your role as a leader? How will its mastery enable you to cultivate greater effectiveness?
5. How will you use the preceding strategies to advance your commitment to achieving greater influence without authority?

# Leadership Challenge

Identify five ways that you can immediately increase your influence without leveraging authority. Focus on a new strategy each week for five consecutive weeks. At the end of the five weeks, write a one-page summary about how these strategies have influenced the dynamic between you, your peers, and your subordinates.

# 17

# Reboot and Relax

*Work without play is a recipe for burnout.*

We typically praise the person who is the last to leave the office and who works during weekends and holidays. Often, however, that person is the first to fall in the war of workplace attrition. Leadership demands long hours and great effort, but rest and relaxation are just as essential as hard work.

Go-getters often feel that every minute of every day must be filled with work, but that is just not a healthy way to live. Because more does not always mean better, a leader must learn to draw a hard line in the sand when asked to take on boundless responsibilities. Learning to say "no" is a matter of self-preservation. Leaders must take time for themselves, and they should not apologize or feel guilty for doing so. We are sons, daughters, mothers, and fathers before we are professionals, and it is important not to neglect the parts of our lives that make us the most human.

The failure to embrace "white space" can result in an acute decrease in productivity as well as the quality of the work produced. Stress causes mental blocks that hamper creativity. It also increases the likelihood of careless mistakes. From misspellings to missed details in a contract, errors caused by a lack of focus are usually avoidable. When the brain is not free from undue strain and is not functioning at its maximum potential, confusion and distress muck up the work and even the most mundane tasks become difficult.

Stress also can cause physical ailments. Headaches and high blood pressure are common in the professional world. Overeating, which is a response to stress, is another strain on the body caused by overworking. Because the mind and the body are so intertwined, when one suffers, the other does as well.

© The Author(s) 2018
K. Mariama-Arthur, *Poised for Excellence*, DOI 10.1007/978-3-319-64574-2_17

Metaphysics teaches that what the mind harbors, the body manifests, and therefore it is imperative that every leader prioritize mental and physical health as part of a daily routine.

To neutralize the stress of work, sometimes you need to forget about it and compartmentalize. Disconnect the brain and exercise the body. Physical exertion increases the body's serotonin levels, which improve mood and memory and decrease hunger and depression. When your body and brain feel well, you perform well. Your productivity, effectiveness, and attitude are each measurably better when you take care of yourself.

Your interpersonal relationships also improve when you are not stressed. When you can get to your "happy place" more frequently, you are less likely to get unnecessarily agitated. Besides, when the people around you do not have to worry about setting you off with a careless word or a thoughtless act, your workplace and your home life become more tranquil. Because of this increased positivity, your overall demeanor and performance will likewise improve. This funnel of beneficial outcomes is magnified by incorporating R&R into the rigor of the workday.

A leader who prioritizes downtime, relaxation, and self-care discovers an increase in overall well-being and in multiple dimensions of performance. Even though we know that work-life balance is a myth, work-life integration and prioritizing need the most time and attention. Agile leaders treat these principles with the same regard as the technical components of their work. Knowing that they do not have to choose between a harried professional life, family, or self-care to be successful, leaders create a life they hold dear that reflects their greatest priorities. By learning to relax and reboot, the most effective leaders ensure their lives do not resemble the bleakness of zero-sum games.

I knew a partner at a top law firm who worked extremely hard as a young associate, which paved the way for a successful and rewarding career. Work was clearly a priority for him. He would get there early and on most nights, stay late. He frequently would take work home and work on weekends, too. Not only that, he would also take on big projects outside of work that were unrelated to his primary specialization. Additionally, he sat on numerous corporate and nonprofit boards. One day, I noticed that he looked a little sluggish and asked him if he was okay.

The law partner said that despite all the work he had put in over the past 40 years, all the value that he provided to others, all the personal and professional success that he collared, he had not taken the time to really enjoy his life. Even the occasional golf games and weekend getaways did not feel like rest, he said, adding that his mental, emotional, and physical health suffered because he chose not to incorporate regular rest and relaxation into his daily routine.

To my surprise, he mentioned wanting to make an immediate and significant shift in his work-life priorities. He wanted a better quality of life. It never occurred to me that someone so accomplished could feel anything other than joy and enormous pride. However, he taught me that no one, not even the most successful leaders, can be effective without integrating rest and relaxation into their lives.

## Core Strategies

The strategies outlined in the following sections offer guidance for cultivating your skill and insight in embracing rest and relaxation. They are distilled from the lessons I have learned from exceptional leaders across industries.

### Draw a Hard Line in the Sand

Do not allow work to take over your life. You cannot have sufficient energy and focus unless you build rest and relaxation into it. Decide exactly when you need to step away from work, and make the time to do it. Turn off your cell phone, close your laptop, and shut off your brain. Create bumpers for projects during the day. "Bumpers" are discrete windows of time allowing you to focus on specific tasks, but then to move on to new ones after an identified time period.

For example, you might work on drafting a meeting agenda from 11 a.m. to noon, then take a break for lunch. You might start the next sequence of work at 1:30 p.m. and finish at 3:30 p.m. You might take a walk outside from 3:30 p.m. to 3:45 p.m. The point is to draw a hard line in the sand to create clear parameters around work and periods of rest and play. The goal is to find your natural work rhythms and give yourself much-needed breaks in between, without allowing anyone or anything to interfere with them.

### Create List of Favorite Pastimes

If you have forgotten how to have fun, you might need to come up with a list of things that you loved doing before your life became so hectic. Jot down activities that make you feel relaxed. It may be listening to your favorite music or taking a walk around the block. Look at your list when you are so exhausted that you forget what makes you happy. Put the list up somewhere in the office and at home where you can easily see it. No matter where you are you should be able to pinpoint a preferred method to relax and unwind. Also having an electronic copy on hand is wise for when you are away from the brick-and-mortar locations you frequent regularly.

## Set Aside Time to Engage with Others

Although it may be sublime, you do not always have to relax in solitude. Turning inward is important, but so is turning outward. Make it a priority to spend quality time with friends and family. Feed off their love. Welcome family and friends to be part of your tranquil time. It could be drinks at a bar, a physical activity, or a movie night at the close of the week. Or, maybe you would prefer regular dinners where you catch up and simply enjoy great food. Perhaps, even finding a way to play the way you did when you were a child could be beneficial to this aim. Whatever activity you choose, make sure you prioritize and schedule it so that it becomes a legitimate part of your schedule.

## Schedule Relaxation

Relaxation does not schedule itself; you have to make it happen, the same way you make meetings happen. Look at your calendar a month in advance. Identify any major projects and determine how much time you need each day to move them forward. Now figure out two specific times during the work-week when you can unplug. Decide what you will do and when you will do it. Put it on the calendar, and do not talk yourself into scheduling that "one extra meeting" in the space you have set aside for relaxation.

Because you have planned for downtime, take it no matter what you have going on. This holds true whether you are in a busy or a slow work season. You will feel rejuvenated and ready to return to the rigor of work when you build in time to step away from it.

## Live in the Moment

When you are relaxing, relax. Be there, and nowhere else. It is far too easy to be swayed by distractions. Resist them and choose to live in the moment. Do not think about the tasks that you have not yet accomplished and do not think of relaxation as an interruption of your work. That walk around the block is just as important as preparing that spreadsheet for accounting. When you give yourself the gift of relaxation, fully appreciate it. Smell the roses, enjoy the sunlight gleaming on your face, feel the weight of the concrete under your feet, the swift wind at your back.

Enjoy your time with yourself and/or with your loved ones. Rest just as purposefully and as mindfully as you work; you will find that you experience greater joy and focus as you strive to integrate the most important aspects of your life into one wholesome, glorious experience.

## Journal Questions

1. When do you make time to unplug during the week?
2. Create a list of 10 favorite activities that generate excitement and enhance your ability to unplug and relax.
3. Describe your work rhythm. Do you know when to stop, reevaluate, and recharge?
4. How did this principle help you better understand your role as a leader? How will its mastery enable you to cultivate greater effectiveness?
5. How will you use the preceding strategies to advance your commitment to unplugging and relaxing?

## Leadership Challenge

Create a workweek calendar that includes time for you to relax and unwind. When do you schedule "me time"? What do you plan on doing? Plug in blocks of time for play that complement the blocks of time for work. Now see how this new rhythm feels. After a week, assess your physical and mental state. Did it feel good to have time for self-indulgence?

# 18

## Always Look for the Silver Lining

*Leaders inspire others to perform at their best by finding the bright side of every situation, even when others only see darkness.*

A Chinese proverb holds that every crisis is an opportunity riding the dangerous wind. This should be the mantra of every leader. It is all about perspective; it is all about the ability to find the positive in the negative. Problems are inevitable, but suffering is a choice. Leaders who understand the power of perspective do not fear hardship; they can see beyond it and shift their mindsets, and thus, their realities, in response to adversity.

If you merely focus on what went wrong in a situation, you will be miserable. If, however, you also focus on what went right, you will be on your way to becoming an effective leader. When a company goes bankrupt, most people wring their hands and fret over the future. A leader, however, sees an opportunity to go back to the drawing board and start anew. A leader looks at what went wrong and learns from those missteps. No matter how bad circumstances may seem, thoughtful leaders discover the lessons, and those lessons provide context for future decisions.

Finding the "silver lining" means thinking of creative ways to reframe situations. It does not mean burying your head in the sand or denying the cold, hard reality. It means studying the facts of the failure so thoroughly that their insights become a part of you. When you know precisely why you failed yesterday, you are less likely to fail again tomorrow. You are also in the best position to help someone else avoid the same mishap.

Without taking corrective action, finding the silver lining is an exercise in futility. After dissecting a failure and brainstorming with advisors to uncover

© The Author(s) 2018
K. Mariama-Arthur, *Poised for Excellence*, DOI 10.1007/978-3-319-64574-2_18

possible strategies for addressing it, leaders makes the necessary adjustments and tries again. Sometimes they fail again, but they do not let failure overtake them. They view it as another opportunity to learn, and then they try yet again. Leaders welcome failure as a necessary component of every success.

If Albert Einstein, history's greatest physicist, had failed to look for the silver lining as he developed his life's work, especially when he was dealing with trial and error, he may have never developed his ground-breaking general theory of relativity, nor had such an incredible impact on the philosophy of science. He always looked for a takeaway, a simple nuance, and a new way to approach his work to perceive of a new result. Einstein mastered this principle early on, and the world has reaped the benefits of the silver lining embedded in his awe-inspiring perspectives.

When a situation initially unfolds, the facts are not always as clear as they become after being fully digested. Smoke and mirrors can hide the true meaning behind a seemingly negative outcome. Being fired from a job, receiving a devastating medical diagnosis, or an unexpected fall from grace are all familiar examples. Being too close to a situation also can create confusion and further distort the facts. If you react, you cheat yourself out of an opportunity to learn more and delve deeper to discover what may be lying just below the surface. Like diamonds and gold, the silver lining also must be mined for.

Analytical leaders choose to suspend judgment and knee-jerk reactions in favor of searching for the hidden truth, an important lesson and a best-case scenario for how all the details matter in the grand scheme. They avail themselves of critical information and gain a greater understanding of the situation, which provides important context for navigating the lucid as well as ambiguous frontiers of leadership. By resolving to see the virtue in every storyline, the most effective leaders create value where there was none.

My grandma Lily Mae always looked for the bright side in every situation. Her life was full of wonderful experiences, but it also had its fair share of bitter hardships. Nonetheless, she never succumbed to any of them. She was soft-spoken and good-natured. She lived her life much like an open book and was always ready to help others, even if it meant giving away her last dollar. When it came to me, she was always eager to make adolescence bearable. Grandma said: "Baby don't worry about this and that. Everything will be alright. There is a good reason—better than you can imagine—why everything happens the way that it does. Even if you don't understand it right now, I promise you there'll be a rainbow on the other side of this crazy storm."

Then, she would share a relevant example from her experience. She knew very well what to say at the right moment. She helped me learn at a young age that things are sometimes not what they appear to be and that most of the time you can find a silver lining. You just should look for it.

# Core Strategies

The strategies outlined in the following sections offer guidance for cultivating your skill and insight mining for the silver lining and embracing a positive outlook. They are distilled from the lessons I have learned from exceptional leaders across various industries.

## Maintain a Positive Perspective

When things do not go as planned, it can be difficult to move forward. Disappointment and uncertainty can take a toll on you. Try not to focus on the crisis, but the opportunity. Look for the bright side. Sift through the failure and find the lesson. There is always one hidden deep down. When you can anchor your perspective in positivity, circumstances emerge as having some inherent benefit, rather than misfortune and disadvantage. Instead of seeing a layoff as a setback, consider that there may be a bigger opportunity in the works. Perhaps one that may not have materialized had you been tethered to your previous job. Instead of defaulting to pessimism, let faith and optimism guide your thinking.

## Tune Out Negative Influences

Negativity can be a powerful influence, but you can refuse to let it get the better of you. The choice is always yours. Choose to tune out people and things that cause you to feel challenged by negativity. They may be family members, close friends, or office associates. It makes no difference—a negative influence is a negative influence. People who wallow in the dark are people who cannot inspire you to act. Their negative influence may even make you change your perspective for the worse. If you find yourself slipping down that slope based on others' adverse influences, change the conversation, the environment, or the nature of the association, which may mean cutting it off altogether.

## Find Your "Happy Place"

If you struggle with negativity, practice positivity. Give yourself three ways to feel good and practice them on a daily basis. It may be meditating, listening to your favorite music, or chatting with a good friend on your way to work. It may even be dashing out for that mid-morning cup of Starbucks' coffee.

The point is to have a few useful activities at the ready that can help you find your happy place. These can be your go-to exercises when you need a quick fix, or simply be used to start the day off on the right foot.

I have a friend whose aunt wrote her an inspirational poem when she was a child. She would read it every day at the same time, without fail. She said that it boosted her self-esteem and helped her to feel gratitude on a regular basis. She knew how to find her happy place. Your job is to find yours.

## Make a Visceral Connection

How can you create an immediate and visceral connection to positivity? You have to feel it, deep down in your gut. Even though doing exercises can help, they fall flat if not tied to purpose and emotion. How you do the exercises is equally important as what you do. Choose one that works for you. Practice by connecting it to a specific emotion that evokes positivity. For example, instead of just listening to your favorite song and enjoying the tune, go a few steps further. Think about the words and the energy.

Does the song galvanize you to be your very best? If so, envision yourself becoming better every time you listen to it. Think about the things you will do to advance an important goal. Feel the emotions surge as you see yourself accomplishing it. The stronger the connection to positivity, the easier it is for you to feel, believe, and act on it.

## Evaluate

Evaluation is essential to developing and maintaining a positive outlook. Ask yourself whether your exercises have worked. Have your moods changed? What about your perspectives? If not, add some new activities to your list and abandon the ineffective ones. If the afternoon walk encourages you to grab a chocolate ice-cream cone and you usually feel guilty afterward, walk another way or take that route before the shop opens. An overall assessment is necessary to make sure you are on the right track and not being drawn back into a negative mindset.

Become aware of your thoughts, feelings, behaviors, and interactions on a daily basis. Self-awareness, which promotes consistent self-evaluation, is the key to developing a positive perspective over time. Do not be afraid to take a hard look at yourself and how you show up. Then, make the required shifts to ensure your success.

## Journal Questions

1. Do you see the glass as half empty, half full, or refillable? Explain.
2. When others exude negativity, does it influence your mood? Discuss.
3. Have you ever manipulated your feelings to change your emotional state? Explain.
4. How did this principle help you better understand your role as a leader? How will its mastery enable you to cultivate greater effectiveness?
5. How will you use the preceding strategies to advance your commitment to positivity?

## Leadership Challenge

Identify an outcome that you did not feel good about. What went wrong and why were you unhappy with the results? Now, flip the script by reframing the value of the outcome. Describe how it taught you a lesson or gave you some other intangible benefit. Do you see how this exercise can help you push past disappointment and leverage adverse experiences into positive ones in the future?

# 19

## See the Forest *and* the Trees

*To execute their visions, leaders must see the entirety of the landscape clearly—the big picture and the nuances.*

Juggling mounds of information can be taxing, but an effective leader will learn to do it competently. Leaders are responsible for handling the small print to ensure that key details have not been overlooked. At the same time, they also must monitor the big picture, scrutinizing all those pesky details that fit together to form the mosaic. It is the integration of the two that make leaders so valuable and the work they do so important to the organizations and institutions they serve.

Great leaders seem to have eyes in the back of their heads. They seem to see everything and hear even more. They are constantly searching for new information and analyzing it to determine how it can benefit their organization. Leaders know that they cannot take anything for granted. They try to avoid assumptions. They make every effort to acquire fresh perspectives and then try to translate them into practical strategies and policies.

Details can be easy to overlook. They are often overshadowed by whatever is urgent. A good leader remembers that when details are missed, competitive advantage is lost, relationships fail, and economies collapse. On the flip side, being mindful those details can seal deals, clarify otherwise cloudy processes, and even trigger ground-breaking innovation. As that cliché goes, "The devil is in the details," but there are plenty of angels in there, too. A similar line of reasoning emerges when examining the big picture. A blue unicorn will be invisible to the naked eye when one's vision is blurred by a rainbow of minutiae. Without a doubt, leaders need remarkable agility to skillfully navigate the contours of this paradoxical domain.

© The Author(s) 2018
K. Mariama-Arthur, *Poised for Excellence*, DOI 10.1007/978-3-319-64574-2_19

When analyzing critical issues, the pressure to perform can frustrate even the most competent of leaders, making shortcuts easier to indulge, and resulting in only a portion of the terrain being explored. Deadlines and high expectations can create an artificial sense of urgency. When this occurs, steps are missed and valuable assessments are left undone. Leaders who habitually come to the table ill-prepared and unable to engage stakeholders to address the sum and substance of the issues at hand are seen as casualties, rather than assets, and often encounter irreparable harm to their reputations and professional relationships as a result.

Make no mistake that both the forest and the trees each merit an independent, meticulous review. When leaders fail to see the big picture and are focused exclusively on the brass tacks, they miss situational anatomy. Without the structure, it is difficult to see how all the pieces fit together. It is like trying to determine the final picture of a jigsaw puzzle with, say, 5000 pieces spread randomly across the floor. Even for the best of geniuses, it would be challenging to make sense of it all. Having context for the finer details is necessary.

Imagine trying to interpret financial data on a spreadsheet and all you see are numbers, pluses, minuses, and totals. Later, you discover it is a profit-and-loss statement. If you knew that it was a P&L statement to begin with, you could have easily applied the data to the appropriate algorithm. Yet, without having this big picture perspective, all the random data amounts to little more than gobbledygook.

On the flip side, when a leader only sees the big picture and misses the important details, the results are similar. Imagine that your best friend is getting married in June at a resort in the Caribbean. Yet, knowing nothing else, you are expected to attend. How can you make plans to attend without having the most important details available: The date, island, province, and resort? Too many details have been left out and though the wedding appears to be a "go," you will not likely be in attendance without first getting those pertinent details squared away. Details add texture and context, and therefore must be treated as a critical component of any competent business analysis.

Big picture perspectives are just as important as the technical details. Being able to bring all those into focus requires great vision. Without it, you end up getting lost in the minutiae. By synthesizing micro issues with macro ones, the most effective leaders develop a comprehensive perspective that allows them to diagnose and act on complex organizational challenges with greater insight and confidence. Being mindful, curious, and committed to a holistic investigation of the issues, problems, and/or challenges that come their way also ensures the collective success of all interested stakeholders. Leaders who master this principle find they experience greater success than those who merely focus only on one aspect or the other. Being wholly tuned into the nuances of the leadership landscape allows for a greater understanding of what is at stake and, of course, more astute counsel. These outcomes can be measured and leveraged to meet short-term and long-term organizational objectives.

General Colin Powell is an extraordinary leader known for his remarkable ability to see the forest *and* the trees while executing his duties as a statesman and a dedicated public servant.[1] As National Security Advisor under the Reagan Administration and Chairman of the Joint Chiefs of Staff under George H. W. Bush, he successfully advised on matters of the United States security, intelligence, military conflicts, diplomacy, policy, strategy, and more. His integrity and history of pragmatic decision making, especially in high-stake scenarios, fueled his career and made him one of the single most sought-after political advisors in U.S. history.

Notable public figures, who have consulted him and sought his ongoing advice, include former Defense Secretaries Casper Weinberger and Frank Carlucci. Make no mistake that it was Powell's exceptional ability to perceive nuance and distinguish the "devil in the details" minutiae, as well as synthesize it to construct a big-picture panorama, that made his advice so invaluable and influential in the contexts of both national affairs and international relations. From operations like Desert Storm and Desert Shield, to the Iran controversy and zealously advocating for better treatment of the Guantanamo Bay detainees, Powell will forever be respected for his incredible insight, exercise of good judgment, and the ability to see the forest and the trees with peerless vision.

# Core Strategies

The strategies outlined in the following sections offer guidance for cultivating your skill and insight as a perceptive leader who can skillfully manage the complexities of the leadership landscape. They are distilled from the lessons I have learned from exceptional leaders across various industries.

## Home in on Details

When trying to understand a problem or a challenge, you need the ability to see nuances. Small things can make a big difference. A missing detail could mean that a contract fails for want of specificity or that a consumer suffers a fatal crash because of a brake malfunction that went undetected during the R&D process. Details are everywhere. The problem is that we do not always pursue them. The next time you scan a Sunday newspaper sales circular, look for the inconspicuous details, such as exclusionary clauses. No doubt there will be a few hidden amid the compelling bargain language. Take an enthusiastic approach and be relentless in the hunt for overlooked particulars. It is only to your advantage, after all.

By being proactive and taking the time to comb through the chapter and verse, you avoid the pain of regret and the bitter consequences that eventually follow. Find what others could not and then analyze those details ad nauseam for context. Challenge yourself to find the needle in the haystack. Discover points of differentiation, which you can always use to your advantage as they can be leveraged when other aspects appear fungible. Even if you find the process intense, know that your diligence will be well rewarded.

## Observe the "Big Picture" Landscape

The big picture is what people normally extract from a situation. The big picture is the key takeaway; it is the bullet-point summary. It is relevant to the overall analysis because details alone do not help you formulate a comprehensive understanding of the issues, problems, or challenges. You need to absorb them in context to understand how and why they matter.

When the City of Flint switched its water supplier from the Detroit Water and Sewage Department to the Flint River in 2014, numerous fine-line issues surfaced. Nonetheless, the big picture involved determining how best to address the public health crisis stemming from contaminated drinking water, which was directly linked to its decision to cut costs. When you analyze a situation, do you see the big picture? Or, do you get bogged down in nuances and fail to apply the details to the whole? Step back. Try to see all of the details coming together like a puzzle. Ignore distractions. Remove bias. Look at the forest and not the trees so that the landscape materializes and allows you to make sense of it all.

## Review for Holes and Inconsistencies

After you have a good understanding of the big and the small pictures, it is time to review for any holes and/or inconsistencies. What did you miss? What thoughts or ideas were left incomplete? What could have received further treatment? Did you make any critical mistakes or were there any lapses in logic? You almost always miss something on a first pass, so pull out your microscope and hunt for the flaws in your thinking, planning, or vision.

Consider executing this review only after you have had a good sleep or a sufficient break and can apply fresh eyes and thinking to your examination. Time away will make an appreciable difference and often improves overall clarity and resoluteness. After all, what is the use of conducting a review if you are unable to conduct it prudently?

## Cultivate an Informed Opinion

After you have reviewed for any holes and inconsistencies, it is time to make a well-informed decision and walk away. Going back and forth is counterproductive and should be abandoned in favor of gaining clarity and taking a firm stance on the issue. How do you get from murkiness to complete clarity? By laying out the evidence before you and taking a second look with fresh eyes and an unambiguous understanding.

Carefully examine the key elements and seek to understand the "whys" just as plainly as the evidence itself. Cover your bases by consulting a few relevant sources and see how well they line up. Once you have done that, you should have sufficient information to cultivate an informed opinion. Draw your conclusion and trust your judgment.

## Ask for an Independent Analysis

Even after cultivating your own opinion, sometimes you can be too close to a situation to see things clearly. To avoid missing the mark, seek a second or even a third opinion from someone you trust, someone who understands the landscape in which you are currently operating and who can home in on the details to discover nuances. For example, if you are a trial attorney litigating a pharmaceutical case, you might call in an industry expert to pore over the technical issues and ensure that you have not misunderstood any of the functional distinctions within the case.

Of course, searching beyond your immediate professional circle may be necessary to eliminate any potential bias. You want an honest, straightforward analysis of what is at stake. No matter how much effort you put into a project or how celebrated an expert you may be in the area, it may still be difficult for you to see either the forest or the trees; so, find someone who can help open your eyes to one or the other. You will be glad you did.

## Journal Questions

1. Do you consider the big picture when making decisions? What specific factors do you include in a big-picture analysis?
2. How do you self-police for bias when analyzing information? Discuss. If not, what are the three key ways that you can eliminate bias during this process?
3. Do you look for nuances, the tiniest details that could significantly influence decision making? Why or why not?
4. How did this principle help you better understand your role as a leader? How will its mastery enable you to cultivate greater effectiveness?
5. How will you use the preceding strategies to advance your commitment to shrewdly managing your perspective?

## Leadership Challenge

Select a controversial issue about which you have a strong opinion. If there has been legislation or public policy discourse on the topic, make note of it. Analyze both sides of the issue, making a list of the top five arguments for each. Make a second list outlining the big picture and detailing any nuances. Do you now feel you have gained a more informed perspective on this issue?

## Note

1. Powell, C. L. & Kotlz, T. (2012). It Worked for Me: In Life and Leadership: 1st HarperLuxe ed. New York: HarperLuxe.

# 20

# Think of Fear as an Ally

*Do not be intimidated by fear. Courageous leaders know that embracing fear is an opportunity to transform it into an ally.*

Fearful leaders are a danger to themselves and a liability to the organization. "Fear" kills creativity, communication, and drive. It can also compel a person to take two steps back for every two steps forward. When a leader exhibits it, others lose courage and fall back on old, convenient habits. Fear breeds stagnation, negativity, and conflict, and it often marks the beginning of a downward spiral that can quickly decimate an organization.

There are countless fears—fear of success, of failure, of the unknown, of rejection, of what others think, of making mistakes, of losing face, of change, of being misjudged. We all endure one or more of them on occasion, but just because we are afraid does not mean we should act with cowardice. We can choose to act boldly in spite of fear. Even though some choose to pretend that fear does not exist, it is far more prudent and constructive to simply acknowledge it.

Moreover, consider that its presence might be useful. For instance, fear may be urging you to take swift action to protect something of value. That value may be tangible or intangible. The person who is never afraid may fail to see the significance of fear as an equitable barometer. There is such a thing as being too risk-friendly and that brazenness can make you highly susceptible to inconspicuous threats.

Leaders regularly make decisions of consequence. They juggle perception, volatile resources, and bottom lines. When there is so much at stake, it can be easy to feel angst when uncertainty is imminent. Even still, people depend on a leader to move through uncertainty. In striving to balance their considerable responsibilities, leaders do not want egg on their faces for making bad decisions

© The Author(s) 2018
K. Mariama-Arthur, *Poised for Excellence*, DOI 10.1007/978-3-319-64574-2_20

or causing others to suffer the consequences of them. The uneasiness that comes with great contemplation is more than a notion. Yet, this is the reality for every leader, regardless of industry or expertise.

Remember, though, that fear is not all bad. Fear can provide extraordinary benefits to those willing to embrace contrarian thought and turn it on its head. Take a moment to consider the benefits of developing greater sensory acuity by embracing fear. That is, you become more aware of your surroundings, including the people and physical spaces. Fear feeds one information. It is a delivery system that alerts you to nuances that you might not otherwise detect and provides you with a valuable opportunity to examine them. It makes you more curious and that heightened awareness is like having a sixth sense.

Beyond enhancing a person's sensory awareness, fear also provides motivation for shrewd preparation. When someone's back is up against the wall, fear steps in to remind them that failure is not an option. If preparation is not adequate, failure and disappointment are imminent. To avoid these results, fear urges us to step up to the plate and engage in specific behaviors to achieve our goals. In its most basic sense, it helps us avoid being complacent. By merely taking requisite action, it also increases feelings of well-being and overall confidence. Think about an annual report that is due and, to complete it, you need an expert willing to contribute his analytical wisdom and insights. The fear of missing the deadline, or else submitting a subpar report, will spur you into action: No doubt you will locate the needed expert and avoid the worst result.

Fear also prompts us to think on our feet when time is short and we are in the midst of a crisis. It jolts us to action rather than allowing us to succumb to inaction. Threats are everywhere, and they can strike at a moment's notice. The dark ally. The impending deadline. The missed detail. Fear swoops in to give us the intestinal fortitude to "grit" through a hairy situation, rise to the occasion, and do whatever is required to get to the other side. When viewed in the light most favorable to it, fear emerges as a remarkably powerful indicator. Indeed, one that should neither be discounted nor be ignored.

Leaders who embrace fear rather than run away from it know the great sense of accomplishment that comes with facing what we fear. They also know that facing fears helps others face theirs. Remember that someone is always watching, sometimes even judging, how you conduct yourself. If that "someone" can take a page from your playbook, you have helped her or him overcome one of nature's most formidable forces. When you make fear an ally, it is no longer the big, bad adversary you once dreaded because you have transformed it into a useful force for good.

One of the most common issues I deal with in my work is fear. Clients find it difficult to confront and often allow it to sabotage their success. If, for example, they are afraid to ask for a raise, they would much rather forego it than simply request it. If they are being bullied by a coworker, they would rather work from home than deal with the incessant and demoralizing tactics they are subjected to on a regular basis. Fear is real and can be an immobilizing force for even the most accomplished professionals. Instead of allowing my clients to capitulate, I challenge them to step out of their comfort zones.

I tell them to confront their fears and examine them more closely. Then, I ask them to explain the role of fear in that scenario. I push them to be creative, especially when they are struggling with seeing the benefit of fear in their lives. I explain that acknowledging fear is not a weakness, but an act of tremendous courage. I also make clear that while everyone experiences it, not all will confront or embrace it. Hence, I urge them to be one of the extraordinary few who do. Experience teaches that once fear is embraced courageously, it is no longer seen as a foreboding force, and it can be dealt with swiftly and enthusiastically.

# Core Strategies

The strategies outlined in the following sections offer guidance for cultivating your skill and insight into ways to embrace fear. They are distilled from the lessons I have learned from exceptional leaders across various industries.

## Acknowledge Fear

To overcome fear, you must first acknowledge it. There are no benefits to pretending it does not exist. That thinking only keeps you beholden to it. If you are afraid of heights, simply admit it to yourself. No need to grab a bullhorn and profess it to the world. Acknowledging fear is to your advantage, preparing you to eventually take the steps necessary to eradicate it. In addition, while not required, in some instances, it might be useful to talk about your fear with someone you trust. The person may be able to probe more deeply to help you unpack it.

To begin the process, examine your fear more closely. Become clear on exactly what you are feeling and why you are feeling it. Then mentally prepare to confront it. Do not let it immobilize you. Take baby steps if necessary, but make sure those steps bring you closer to it, not away from it. Dodging fear only will amplify your anxiety and move your further away from resolution.

## Determine Where Your Fear Is Coming from

To effectively address fear, you must determine where it is coming from. Does it stem from a previous experience? Is it a random dialogue that keeps replaying in your head? Is it caused by something that someone else said or did? A reluctance to develop substantial bonds, whether platonic or sexual, could be related to a deep-seated fear of abandonment established early in life. Those memories may have been repressed in an effort to protect your psyche. Dig deep to get to the root of your fear.

Once you connect the dots and identify its source, ask yourself whether it is justified. Is this a legitimate fear that must be worked through? Or, is it something else. If justified, determine what triggers conjure it up so that you can recognize the tell-tale signs and address them accordingly.

## Recognize the Benefits of Fear

Accept that fear has tangible benefits that are difficult to recognize when in the clutches of the emotion. To perceive fear differently, you must first understand that it actually can help you. You must literally turn it on its head. Adopting a disruptive approach will expose you to the guiding principles that an unconventional perspective brings. It also will help you to redefine fear, because, after all, "meaning" is truly a subjective concept. And we assign meaning based on whatever we choose to believe. Do you genuinely fear that your presentation to the board of directors will be ridiculed and dismissed because it lacks merit? Or, would simply doing a bit more research and preparation transform your fear and enhance your ability to deliver a presentation that could "wow?" Chances are your fear is sending you a strong message, that with adequate preparation, you can avoid a worse result.

Interpretation is always up to you; therefore; choose to curate meaning that is beneficial. Once you reassign meaning to your fearful experiences, you will be well on your way to recognizing its benefits. The goal is to identify and apply them to your unique set of circumstances. Look deeper to peel back the layers to appreciate how fear can serve you.

## Resolve to Act despite Fear

The most potent and straightforward way to move past fear is to simply move toward it. By gradually inching forward mentally, emotionally, and in many cases physically, you can ease the fear a little at a time. Although what you do in each instance may vary, acting is all that counts. Your steps may involve making a simple phone call, sending an email, or having a tough conversation. Whatever those steps may be, however, know that they each pave the way for greater confidence and enhanced well-being. What may have initially felt like an insurmountable climb may now feel like a small feat when you take it in small steps. Remember, when you make the true decision to confront your fear, take steady, definitive steps forward. Delay and hesitation thwart your best efforts and leave you full of regret and, yes, fear.

## Evaluate Your Progress

Like with most other strategies, the best way to gauge progress is to take a hard look at your results and evaluate them. Refuse to water down your assessment. Be honest and thoroughly examine the steps you took to confront your fear. Were you able to turn it on its head? If so, how did you change your perspective and assign it new meaning? If you decide to at least "wade" in the shallow end of the pool, and before you would not even dip a toe in it, you have made progress. If you reframe the narrative surrounding your aquaphobia, citing that learning to swim could save your life, you have done well.

The whole point is to take a serious look at your outcomes to determine whether you are closer or farther away from overcoming your fear. Did you begin to feel overwhelmed or helpless recently because of fear, despite taking action? Or, did you stand up to it and take action anyway? Weigh in on what you did and decide what the next course of action should be.

# Journal Questions

1. Are you often challenged by fear? Discuss.
2. Name three key ways that fear has interfered with your personal or professional progress.
3. How can you motivate yourself to act despite fear?
4. How did this principle help you better understand your role as a leader? How will its mastery enable you to cultivate greater effectiveness?
5. How will you use the preceding strategies to advance your commitment to embracing fear?

## Leadership Challenge

Write down three of your biggest fears. Acknowledge and embrace them as challenges that you must face. Now choose one, and write down three ways that can help you move past it within the next 30 days. Implement the strategies daily. At the end of 30 days, assess your progress. Were you able to successfully push past this fear?

# Part III

## Principles that Nurture Leadership Excellence Through Benevolence, Collaboration, and Value-Based Service to Others

# 21

# Honor Human Relationships

*Quality interpersonal relationships are a testament to the phenomenal power of human connection, trust, and interdependence. They also help leaders generate influence and support.*

Making a genuine connection with another human being is a sublime experience. It instantly makes one feel more alive and radiates warmth and esprit de corps. Even though it would be ideal to experience these feelings with everyone we meet, it is also unrealistic. Sometimes, we simply fail to connect with others. This can be frustrating, and even painful. In these instances, it is useful to remember that not all interactions will result in developing deeper bonds and that is no one's fault. Learning to navigate interpersonal interactions and develop meaningful relationships, however, can make a huge difference in the quality of our lives.

Humans are hardwired to socialize. We generally enjoy interacting with others because it brings us pleasure. We also want to give the same pleasure to others. We seek to build relationships because we want to connect with, be accepted by, and appreciated by others on an ongoing basis. Emotional refueling and reciprocity feel good. By the same token, we know that rejection makes us feel miserable. This disapproval, however, usually has more to do with the other person than with us, so it is to our advantage to let go of the need to control perceptions extraneous to ourselves. Just like beauty is in the eye of the beholder, so, too, are feelings of connectedness.

Although learning how to manage relationships is important, understanding their value may be even more vital. Human interaction, especially in business and professional settings, is often structured superficially. Our roles and

© The Author(s) 2018
K. Mariama-Arthur, *Poised for Excellence*, DOI 10.1007/978-3-319-64574-2_21

the nature of quid pro quo transactions usually dictate how we interact. Because of this, people are usually focused on what they are getting out of an interaction rather what they are contributing to it. They disregard the human element, the importance of getting to know, understand, and honor the people involved. This misplaced focus and the inorganic framework of these exchanges make genuine connection difficult in highly structured environments.

Despite these realities, leaders must still learn to develop genuine connections, and successfully manage them over time. Navigating the labyrinth of human interaction requires courage and the willingness to meet people where they are. It also means being vulnerable. A hard exterior discourages more intimate exchanges and sends a signal that a leader does not want to let others in. Demeanor matters. When a leader is open to developing deeper connections, however, to be effective those exchanges must be organic and dynamic, not superficial or merely procedural.

People will only buy into a leader's vision when they feel connected to it. Typically, that does not happen without first developing an affinity for the leaders themselves. Knowing that a leader has the best interests of all at heart, however, usually will seal the deal. Surely, the art and science of making authentic connections has been the secret sauce of effective leadership since the beginning of time. Charismatic leaders like retired business executive and former chairman and CEO of General Electric John Francis "Jack" Welch Jr. know this all too well.

It is no secret that people everywhere want to be treated well. To that end, everyone usually seeks the best results from their relationships—that is, connection, trust, respect, integrity, reciprocity, love, and support. Coincidentally, people treat others the way we treat them. When you intentionally curate what you put out in the Universe, you do not have to fear bad karma circling back your way. In addition, because we teach people how to treat us based on our own behavior, we must take responsibility for the critical role we play in framing interpersonal interactions and how the dynamics of our relationships play out.

Humans are pretty intuitive. We know when someone has put us on the backburner or has chosen to interact with us when it is merely convenient or beneficial to them. No one enjoys feeling mistreated or unappreciated. To avoid making people feel insignificant, a thoughtful leader will be a good listener and regularly look out for others' well-being. They freely will admit when they are wrong and put forth their best efforts not to commit the same offense twice. They have high expectations of others because they are led by a strong, internal belief system that guides their behavior: They expect no more from others than they expect from themselves.

By honoring human relationships, we elevate every interaction to a wholesome place that transcends superficiality, self-interest, and pretense. When leaders take their responsibilities seriously, they create strong and lasting connections that result from purposeful service. What they know for sure is that every single life is valuable and worthy of respect, kindness, and decency. They also know that whatever they put out into the Universe eventually will come back to them, so they choose wisely. The most effective leaders are compassionate, recognize the sanctity of our common humanity, and honor the dignity of human relationships.

I met an extraordinary communications professional at an international conference at the European Union a few years ago who really made a great impression. She had great energy and really seemed to develop rapport with almost everyone she spoke to. I was impressed by her generosity of spirit as well as her open demeanor and quiet confidence. Her kindness and sincere love for people was more than obvious. She was curious about others and wanted to learn more about their unique gifts. She was honest in her approach. Her warmth felt intuitive. At the same time, however, her motives did not reflect impropriety. This made her even more intriguing.

When this professional invited me to have breakfast with her on the last day before my final talk and offered to help me with the final details of my presentation, I got to know her a bit better. She was deeply interested not just in my work, but who I was and *how* I was. She asked lots of initial as well as follow-up questions. She maintained great eye contact and her smile generated extreme warmth. During our discussion, I learned that part of her work involved ensuring the well-being of her clients on mental and socioemotional levels. This explained her compassionate demeanor. Not surprisingly, she was also a thought leader in her field. While we talked, I learned more about her and also watched how she interacted with others. She shared her philosophy about friendship and the importance of honoring human relationships. She seemed to instantly fill the room with more joy and everyone there appeared compelled to speak to her. The whole thing got me thinking about how humans connect.

This woman honored the art and science of communication and of relationships. She cared how she came across and seemed to bring out the best in others. She focused on maximizing every single interaction, making each individual that she spoke to feel like he or she was the only person in the room. Since then, we have developed a great friendship and a flourishing business relationship that each reflect the generosity of the human experience and why honoring human relationships is such an important aspect of effective leadership.

# Core Strategies

The strategies outlined in the following sections offer guidance for cultivating your skill and insight in developing and maintaining quality relationships. They are distilled from the lessons I have learned from exceptional leaders across various industries.

## Learn to Make Meaningful Connections and to Build Healthy Relationships

Making meaningful connections and building healthy relationships are vital to effective leadership. No man is an island and, therefore, requires the support of others to sail through the world, even in the simplest of endeavors. Every relationship begins with a solid connection. The easiest and most effective way to connect with others is to be curious and develop rapport. Give good eye contact. Smile. Demonstrate genuine interest and ask good questions that require further follow-up. The other person will feel your focused energy and often reciprocate. Self-absorbed leaders rarely make meaningful connections because they make everything about themselves.

Remember, the best way to create healthy relationships is by building a firm foundation. The initial phases determine how the subsequent phases turn out. So, begin by being honest, by acting with integrity, and by building trust. The best relationships evolve organically. Forced relationships quickly crumble. Spend time getting to know someone beyond superficial niceties before entering into any substantive business transaction. You will discover, sooner rather than later, it is well worth the investment. Also, no matter what, do not sacrifice relationships for personal gain.

## Offer Value

Relationships are about give and take, and you should always try to give more than you take. If you find yourself taking too much, pull back, even if the other person is happy to give more. Turn your attention outward. Find out what the other person needs and give it generously. Then ask how you can give more without seeking anything in return. You always should come to the table ready and willing to provide bona fide value.

Know your worth and be prepared to share it with others at the outset of an interaction or, whenever most appropriate. Do not wait to be asked. If you have great ideas that could, for instance, improve your colleagues' accounting practices, share them. Why allow them to languish by wasting precious time and money on what they are currently doing? Go first and offer value of your own volition.

## Exercise Reciprocity

No one should walk away from any interaction feeling exploited. One-sided transactions do not benefit the team. Exhibit gratitude and appreciation for acts of kindness. Even though you do not give to get, reciprocity engenders goodwill and inspires further kindness. But it should never be requested. Allow the other person to reciprocate of her own volition. Do not ask that the person to "even the score." If you must urge someone to reciprocate, that is a clear indication of the inequities within the relationship and how value is being perceived.

Both parties should be offering value freely, openly, consistently, and of their free will. Consider whether the relationships you have established contain these vital elements when assessing their overall value. One-sided relationships tend to topple over. Take a closer look and examine whether you, too, are exercising reciprocity. If not, determine how you can do a better job doing this in the future.

## Communicate Effectively

Good communication is vital to healthy relationships. Although there are many avenues of communication, the goal should always be the same: To forge a deeper bond and to develop a greater understanding. Effective communication requires effort and follow-up. To show your commitment to this aim, return calls, emails, and texts as soon as possible. By the same token, do not send reactive emails or return a call when your emotions are raging. Saying what you mean and meaning what you say are difficult when emotions dictate. And once you have pressed "send" or said the unthinkable, it is often too late to take it back. Press pause on knee-jerk reactions with all forms of communication. On the flip side, be proactive about initiating communication where necessary to address misunderstandings and resolve conflict. Do not let bad feelings fester. Confront them and encourage others to do the same, even when resolution requires a difficult conversation.

Likewise, strive to be consistent when you communicate. People will know if you really care based on what you do, not what you say. If your friend truly has been on your mind, reach out by calling or sending a nice note. Telling him that you have been thinking about him a week later is just not enough.

## Expand Your Relationships' Circle

Strive to expand your circle of influence exponentially so that it includes people outside of your industry and, where relevant, your region. Attend conferences and other professional development events that require travel locally, regionally, nationally, and internationally. Break out from the comfort of current, familiar relationships. Even though they may have served you in the past, they will not help you to expand your reach. The whole purpose behind expanding your circle is to make valuable new connections and to encourage growth. A key way to leverage your newly expanded circle is to explore ways to use mutual synergies to collaborate and improve the work that you do.

Additionally, network with a singular focus on meeting new people with differing interests. Opposites attract and can provide new, exciting ways to experience the world, personally and professionally. Together you may even discover new hobbies or ways to challenge each other to step outside your comfort zones. As an added bonus, you will no doubt continue to improve your interpersonal communication as you engage with new actors during the process.

## Journal Questions

1. Are your closest relationships grounded in trust, respect, and reciprocity? Explain.
2. When the integrity of a relationship is challenged, what do you do?
3. Do you actively network or otherwise engage with others on a regular basis? Why or why not?
4. How did this principle help you better understand your role as a leader? How will its mastery enable you to cultivate greater effectiveness?
5. How will you use the preceding strategies to advance your commitment to creating and maintaining quality relationships?

## Leadership Challenge

Research three networking events scheduled for next month. Make sure to only select events with professionals from outside your current industry. Get to know at least two interesting people at each event and follow-up with them afterward. Did you establish any meaningful connections? How did it feel to move outside of your comfort zone?

# 22

# Use "Honey" to Catch Flies, Not Vinegar

*Methods of interpersonal engagement matter. By using "honey" rather than vinegar to their advantage, smart leaders earn the social cache they need to influence others and move their visions forward.*

A hostile disposition undermines effective governance. It frustrates a leader's ability to inspire trust, spark chemistry, and rouse influence. Yet, far too many leaders believe that being callous and detached works to their advantage. They see it as a way to command respect and create "required distance" between them and everyone else. Even though establishing boundaries is an important aspect of leadership, creating them artificially is counterproductive. Congeniality is not a bar to being held in high regard. You can have a pleasant disposition and still be a well-respected leader among peers and other members of an organization.

A good rule of thumb is to ask yourself how you would respond if the leader you admired the most acted out. Would this change your opinion of him or? Would it cause you to shift any of your thoughts about their leadership style? Behavior matters a great deal and influences how a leader is perceived as well as how others respond to him or her. Think about how you want to be seen. Consider your leadership brand. If you have ever read Niccolò Machiavelli's *The Prince,* you already may have some great perspective on this. If not, read it and come back to this question more informed on creating a leadership identity, and what it means to genuinely connect with others.

Regarding boundaries, leaders still must create them. Yes, they must. Sure, leaders may play nice, but again, their behavior also sets the stage for how others interact with them. So, leaders must draw hard lines in the sand, but

© The Author(s) 2018
K. Mariama-Arthur, *Poised for Excellence*, DOI 10.1007/978-3-319-64574-2_22

without having to be cruel to earn respect. You have, of course, seen those who time and again have played this primitive card. Nonetheless, the result is not usually a good one. Tyrants are just one example of those who find themselves on the rough edges of the civility spectrum. Smart leaders are careful to avoid behavior that can transform their otherwise noble administrations into oppressive regimes for others.

How do you know where to find your "happy medium"? It may seem like trial and error at first, but there is always a better litmus test. First realize that neither throwing your weight around nor pandering for affection will achieve a positive result. Instead, strive to be respected and treat others with respect; these precepts are consistent with effective leadership. Remember, respect can be earned without being callous. So closely examine your behavior and notice how it influences the perception that others have of you. Are you closer to or farther away from your goal of influencing others with honey rather than vinegar? If you are in the ballpark, tweak it slightly. If you are way off, whatever you are doing clearly is not working. So, determine which factors are contributing to this result and then try to find your happy medium once again.

A leader who mistakenly assumes that clout and goodwill magically come with the territory must tread lightly. Leaders get as good as they give. Behavior is an objective variable easily evaluated by anyone. If a leader exudes pretense and negativity, offending others should come as no surprise. Leaders who lack the gravitas required by the role soon find that "honey" is the better choice. No leader is exempt from this truism. Unfortunately, President Donald Trump, who is well known for his petulant demeanor, has made this point painfully clear. His interactions with the general public, as well as prominent heads of state, such as Angela Merkel, Chancellor of Germany, have been particularly illustrative of how this principle can play out—not only at home, but also on the world stage.

Blurred lines and hidden agendas make using honey ineffective. A leader who forsakes the tenets of the role and gains alliances through cowardice muddies the waters of leadership. Respect rather than adoration must instead be the goal. Whether they are "liked" by the masses should be immaterial. Pandering for social cache always leaves a gross deficit and a hefty price to pay. At best it produces marginal gains that are short lived and result in resentment, betrayal, and disappointment. Because pandering begins and ends with some level of gross deception, it thwarts the process and overall goals of authentic leadership. Above all, leaders should never sacrifice their integrity to sweeten the pot, so to speak.

Leaders who learn to use honey rather than vinegar to their advantage not only do earn respect, but also take great comfort in knowing that pretense is an unnecessary artifice. Inaccessibility and prickly demeanor will not transform you into a glorified protagonist. Rest assured: Vinegar is sour and is hard to get down. Honey is a far better alternative and proves useful not only in establishing rapport initially, but also in developing long-term relationships of substance. Smart leaders choose to be authentic and exercise integrity. They use honey to create nuanced interpersonal relationships, invite widespread opportunities to influence others, and earn the social cache they need to succeed in their overall endeavors.

I had the honor of working for an internationally known attorney early in my career. He was renowned for his brilliant legal mind, but also for the way he treated others and the way he made them feel. He was charismatic and lit up a room when he entered. He was well-dressed and had a bright smile and so much "swagger" that it just seemed to spill out everywhere. He treated staff and fellow attorneys with great respect. Even though he had high expectations, he had no aspiration to wield power with an iron fist. It was unnecessary.

The attorney would ask nicely and say "please" and "thank you." He would always smile. A lot. He shook hands and gave hugs. He was eager to acknowledge a remarkable work ethic, or praise someone for accomplishing an extraordinary feat. He did not create an artificial distance between himself and others based on his title or larger-than-life fame within the legal community.

As a case study, it was interesting to see how his demeanor did not negatively affect his professional standing: He was not considered a pushover and no one ever stepped beyond the bounds allotted by his cordial behavior. Although it could have been just as easy for him to pound his fists or walk around brandishing an angry and off-putting scowl, he chose not to. What he knew for sure was that he could catch more flies with honey than with vinegar, and he did catch his fair share of flies.

## Core Strategies

The strategies outlined in the following sections offer guidance for cultivating your skill and insight in leveraging with honey to your advantage. They are distilled from the lessons I have learned from exceptional leaders across various industries.

## Smile

A smile—especially a big, bright, and earnest one—is a wonderful way to greet and engage others in a professional setting. A "Top of the morning" greeting to welcome colleagues fuels them throughout the day and sends them out on a high note as they depart. Pretense is useless. Putting on a superficial frown and puffing up makes you look ridiculous. For sure, projecting an acrimonious demeanor does more harm than good. Instead of achieving the desired result and getting people to see you as an authority and to respect you, it often accomplishes the exact opposite. People see a person who puts on airs as cold and disengaged. With employee disengagement already at record lows, this kind of behavior only makes it worse. So, smile big and welcome the world in. Remember that smiling usually encourages others to do the same.

## Authentically and Enthusiastically Engage with Others

Although smiling is a positive mechanism that can invite deeper and more meaningful interaction, it only goes so far. To effectively leverage your "honey," you must take the initiative to engage others with authenticity and enthusiasm. Infinite opportunities for interpersonal interaction are always present. You not only must recognize but also create them. So do not be passive and wait for others to come to you; engage them first when possible.

When you are having a conversation, convey your enthusiasm by being present and using active listening techniques. Also, present the real "you." If you would normally laugh at a funny joke and it is office-appropriate, go ahead and laugh! There is no need to pretend to be someone you are not, which creates awkwardness and unnecessary distance, making the entire interaction counterproductive.

## Show up and Participate

Purposeful interaction takes this principle a few steps further. Although it is great to meet others in the hallways and at the water cooler, how many times have you planned to attend a work-related event and be an active participant? Consider bringing a dish to the next potluck and sticking around to eat and talk to others during the meal. If your office has a summer picnic, the same thinking applies. The point is to intentionally put yourself in environments that compel meaningful interactions and provide an opportunity for you to leverage your "honey." When you are away from the office or in low-key scenarios within it, you should focus on authentic and enthusiastic engagement rather than the rigors of the work.

## Nevertheless, Create Boundaries

Sure, we are talking about all things "nicety" and how to escalate the warm fuzzy feelings within a professional environment; however, do not mistake these strategies as an open invitation for others to overstep their boundaries. To the contrary. Leaders who engage their workforce with open arms do not have to finish last; they do not have to get walked on. Freely establish boundaries at the outset of every new relationship using whatever mechanisms you have at your disposal.

Setting boundaries and leveraging your honey are not mutually exclusive. It is both art and science. If you fail to set boundaries in favor of what you perceive as "being nice," you will be deeply disappointed by how others respond to you. If you give an inch and a mile is taken, you only have yourself to blame if you do not address the infringement.

## Get 360-Degree Feedback

You may not be completely off-track, but you may never know unless you ask. So ask. This will allow you to perform a self-evaluation, as well as get honest feedback from your peers, supervisors, and subordinates. Getting 360-degree feedback is executed anonymously so that participants can feel free to provide open and honest remarks. You can request feedback on any number of areas, depending on what you are trying to gauge.

When you receive your assessments back, do not be defensive. Instead, take some time to sit with the commentary. Think about what was said and also, perhaps, why. Be honest as you strive to align your understanding with the feedback. Retain what is helpful and disregard what is not. After all, the exercise is only useful if you can extract value and apply what you learn to leverage against any inappropriate behavior in the future.

## Journal Questions

1. Do you prefer to use honey or vinegar to set the tone of your professional relationships? Explain.
2. Have you worked with a leader who insisted on being "contrary" to create distance and gain respect? If so, how did it make you feel?

3. In what ways can you leverage a positive disposition to successfully establish professional boundaries?
4. How did this principle help you better understand your role as a leader? How will its mastery enable you to cultivate greater effectiveness?
5. How will you use the preceding strategies to advance your commitment to using honey rather than vinegar to your advantage?

## Leadership Challenge

For the next 30 days, actively prioritize the needs of others. Force yourself to commit by subordinating your personal wants and wishes. Next, identify three key ways to effectively execute this exercise. How do you think you have added value to others having done this?

# 23

## Give Credit Where It Is Due

*Because leaders are confident in their abilities, they praise the brilliance of others eagerly and often. They know that celebrating the "light" in others will not diminish it in themselves.*

There is plenty of genius and ability in the world. Anywhere you go, you will find an abundance of wonderfully talented and accomplished people. The Creator has endowed us all with unique gifts, so we should all stand tall. In addition, knowing that we have each been equipped with such remarkable faculties should be reason enough to celebrate it in others. When there is no fear in giving credit where it is due, leaders can stand confident in their abilities while, at the same time, celebrating the beauty and faculty in others.

If we were all exactly alike, without any distinguishing characteristics, it would be impossible to tell one person from the other. Not only would life be boring if we were all identical, but it would be difficult to have special feelings for anyone. There would be no excitement or anticipation and no impetus for discovering anything novel when meeting new people. Living in a world populated with carbon copies would be dreadful. Thank goodness for the imperfections; nuances; and the sundry of physical, emotional, intellectual, and personality differences that make us each stand out individually. Each of these attributes makes us unique and generates magnetic appeal in a sea of sameness. We should each be extremely grateful for such impeccable distinctions.

Our differences, coupled with free will and drive, make for a collective existence of fascinating individuals with tremendous potential. Each person has value, and that value ought to be acknowledged. Our species has learned to harness the energy of the atom and has sent probes to the farthest reaches

© The Author(s) 2018
K. Mariama-Arthur, *Poised for Excellence*, DOI 10.1007/978-3-319-64574-2_23

of the Solar System. We have accomplished these feats of collaboration only because we have been able to see beyond our superficial differences and set aside petty jealousies. Besides, if we are to continue accomplishing wondrous exploits—if we are to indeed continue as a species—we must continue to acknowledge and celebrate the beauty and novelty in others. If we fail to acknowledge this simple truth, we are doomed to stagnation and probably much worse, in the long run.

It takes nothing away from us when we give praise to another person. The goodwill that it inspires often starts a powerful cycle that promotes further goodwill. A small act of kindness can make a big difference and show up in places that you might not expect. Kindness, just like animus, leaves a discernable footprint. Like the butterfly effect, compassion and generosity can ripple throughout a community and then spill over into larger ones or even the next generation. Embrace benevolence. It is cause-worthy of the efforts needed to keep it migrating in perpetual motion. We all benefit from good karma when widespread humanitarianism is at work.

If you find it difficult to repress an incessant craving for attention, or if you are often overwhelmed by feelings of jealousy and contempt, look into your heart to figure out what is missing. If your self-esteem is not as high as you would like it to be, your perception of others will be colored by your insecurity; you will be unable to see the good in others and inspire them to achieve greater feats. Closely examine your thoughts, actions, and motives. Consider consulting someone who might be able to help you work through any insecurities. You will be in a much better position to lead others if you are comfortable in your own skin. Liberate yourself from the insecurities that feed the green-eyed monster within.

Giving credit where due means you have removed the shackles of jealousy and freed yourself to respect the divine in others. You are drawn to their "light," which is magnified by acknowledging its unmistakable existence. That acknowledgment gives the receiver the power to own their excellence, then take it to the next level. And, more often than not, they do. The most effective leaders do not hold praise back, and the people they lead respect their graciousness and emotional generosity. It eventually becomes a barometer for their own behavior, and they pay it forward. Smart leaders know that appreciating the skills, talents, and accomplishments of others only gives the Universe more reason to circle back with additional favor for them.

Oprah Winfrey is a great example of someone who gives credit where it is due. She has enjoyed an amazing career chock-full of varied successes. She has earned her stripes and is comfortable in her own skin. A prominent and well-respected public figure and a highly successful businesswoman, she could very well have turned inward and basked in her own glory. Instead, she has devoted her career to turning the illustrious spotlight onto others.

Winfrey gives credit where due and holds nothing back because she knows that uplifting others is a win–win scenario. Her light still shines brightly no matter how resounding her praise is for others. Whether it is leveraging her platform to bring attention to an important cause, sharing the compelling personal stories of ordinary Americans, or collaborating with other public figures to advance a message that matters, Winfrey is a conduit for celebrating the greatness in others at a high level.

What she knows for sure is that we were all placed on this Earth for a reason and once our purpose is ignited and put into action, the universe will give it wings: Those remarkable individuals and their incredible successes deserve to be recognized and celebrated. Oprah's wholehearted commitment to this principle is evidenced in all that she does to elevate others, as well as the gift of her own continued success—an obvious reward from the universal powers that be.

# Core Strategies

The strategies outlined in the following sections offer guidance for cultivating your skill and insight into giving credit where it is due. They are distilled from the lessons I have learned from exceptional leaders across various industries.

## Recognize the Inherent Value in Others

Every person you meet is a reservoir of untapped value. Look for it. Your light will not be dimmed by celebrating the accomplishments of others. Acknowledge the value that other people add to your life, your organization, and encourage them to continue being excellent. Do not think twice about giving praise to anyone deserving of it. Consider the colleague who always give 100% but never receives any recognition. Let him or her know how much the person's efforts are appreciated and add value to the collective good.

Set aside your ego and your fear and open your eyes to the talent around you. Opportunities to seek it out and praise it arise almost every day. Do not take them for granted. Consider it your duty as a leader to rise to the occasion and recognize the value in others.

## Do Not Hog the Spotlight

If you have an opportunity to participate in a joint venture, take it. But, resist the urge to soak up all the accolades. You do not need all the glory; there is plenty to go around. Sharing the spotlight only adds to your glow. Consider basking in that idea. The next time there is an opportunity for you to take all the credit for a shared accomplishment, *do not*. Let someone else take it. Graciously remove yourself from the center of attention. Remove your name from the program as a "major sponsor." Ask not to be announced at the gala. Do the work and enjoy the rewards of quiet contribution. Humility is an important part of the praise equation. Master it by creating healthy self-esteem and a healthy self-concept that is grounded in self-love and balanced by altruism.

## Praise Genuinely and Enthusiastically

When offering praise, give it generously and with enthusiasm. Make sure it does not sound "canned." Tell the person exactly what she or he has done well and explain why it deserves to be acknowledged. Remember it is not just what you say that matters; it also is how you say it. People can hear earnestness in your voice and see it in your body language. They also can see, hear, and feel the opposite.

Look individuals directly in their eyes when talking to them and mind your body language, too. Smile and look the valet attendant in the eyes when telling him how well-fitted his suit is and how professional he looks. If you are not genuine and specific when you offer your praise, it will come across as insincere. Pay close attention to how you communicate and notice how others receive praise.

## Practice Altruism with Conviction

You should not expect a reward for everything you do. Do them simply because they are the right things to do. If you practice altruism on a regular basis, eventually it will become second nature. Periodically, give of yourself in a way that stretches you and your resources. Spend more time at the shelter volunteering instead of playing golf.

Perhaps you could give the same portion of a month's earnings that normally goes into your 401(k) account to the homeless shelter or to a family in need. Expect and accept nothing in return. To practice altruism more regularly, commit to carrying out three random acts of kindness each week and create a journal entry for each experience, noting how you can have more of an impact the following week.

## Encourage Others to Embrace Altruism as a Core Value

In a culture that places so much value on individual success, it can be difficult to think about others. A good leader does exactly that, though, nonetheless. Support the people around you and encourage them to support others. Be the voice of reason and compassion for those who might not yet have learned the value of selflessness. If you notice opportunities for others to provide praise and practice altruism, encourage them to do so as well.

For example, you might ask someone to help a coworker, who is stressed about an impending deadline, complete a complicated report. No doubt that extra help would lighten the person's load and brighten up the week. As an added challenge, look for opportunities to discuss altruism with someone new at least once a week. Explain its benefits by giving examples from your own leadership experiences.

## Journal Questions

1. Do you find it easier to criticize others or to offer praise? Discuss.
2. Are you sensitive to actual or perceived competition? Explain.
3. Do you enjoy being the center of attention? Discuss.
4. How did this principle help you better understand your role as a leader? How will its mastery enable you to cultivate greater effectiveness?
5. How will you use the preceding strategies to advance your commitment to giving credit where it is due?

## Leadership Challenge

Every day next week, find three new people to compliment on different aspects of their performance or character. Offer your remarks genuinely and enthusiastically. Notice each person's reaction. At the end of each day, reflect on how it felt to uplift those individuals. Are you feeling more motivated to do this regularly?

# 24

# Promote Fairness and Consistency

*Leaders strive to be fair to all members of the workforce.*

Everyone holds some form of intrinsic bias, but a fair-minded leader learns to recognize it and removes it from the decision-making process. Equity must guide every interaction, and behaving consistently with everyone should always be the goal. Not to mention fairness and consistency translate across all leadership styles. When leaders are fair and objective, there is no room for ambiguity, and their behavior requires no interpretation.

Leaders can nurture fairness by first establishing objective performance standards and providing equal opportunities for all to be heard. Refusing to play favorites, even when there are long-time allies positioned throughout the ranks is a must. When people feel that they are being treated equally, they are less apt to fight against rules and regulations. In addition, when people know that they have an opportunity to make their cases, they have greater respect for the leaders and the system. They also will be less likely to assume there was any double-dealing if things do not go their way.

In addition, a leader must try to conduct an objective examination of the facts whenever they require review. They must put themselves in the other person's shoes and dismiss preconceived notions, emotional reactions, and fickleness. Each inclination interferes with the ability to listen without judgment and to make competent, even-handed decisions. When someone considers how they would want to be treated if in the same situation, it helps the person to reach for a more neutral standard and give others the benefit of the doubt. That said, a leader usually will reach a more just conclusion when fairness is used to distill their interpretation.

© The Author(s) 2018
K. Mariama-Arthur, *Poised for Excellence*, DOI 10.1007/978-3-319-64574-2_24

Fairness, however, also has several layers of inherent complexity within it. To execute it dutifully, sound judgment must, at times, also come into play, and it may not always appear black and white. Although objective standards and equal opportunities set the stage, there are instances when circumstances merit a judgment call requiring a different, yet otherwise fair administration of the facts. Leaders must be ready to exercise good judgment in these instances. An annual review that reveals above-average professional performance and results in a sizable bonus is just one relevant example.

However, nurturing consistency may seem to be a more straightforward concept than nurturing its counterpart, fairness. Whatever rules, policies, and procedures have been decided on should invariably be carried out consistently. People will develop expectations based on the standards that have been set. Those expectations act as a compass for how they navigate the work world. If priorities are constantly shifting and substance and procedure are in chronic flux, employees lose confidence in the overall machine. Unfortunately, leaders cannot afford to absorb the fallout from this kind of grave departure. Better to simply execute the rules, policies, and procedures with consistency.

Leaders who are perceived as being biased do not earn respect or commitment from their teams. Subordinates equate the lack of consistency to insincerity and untrustworthiness. Besides, if a leader is deemed untrustworthy, she or he quickly loses all credibility. Once credibility is lost, it is extremely difficult, if not impossible, to get it back. Because there is such an inherent risk of loss when being perceived as partial, it simply makes good sense to do whatever it takes to avoid even the slightest notion of it.

The overarching goal for every leader is to capture hearts and minds by demonstrating good faith and the aspiration to serve honorably. There is nothing more valuable than trust and commitment when well earned. It powers everything that leaders do and serves as a compelling filter for how the rest of the world interacts with them. When leaders operate from a locus of fairness, it fosters unity and brings the collective together under an umbrella of cohesiveness. Of course, leaders' own thinking and behavior drive this effort. When leaders self-police and promote fairness and consistency as fundamental values throughout an organization, it sets the tone for the building blocks of an equitable culture. When everyone inside of it adopts the same principles and, in turn, holds each other accountable, the organization thrives.

I have a colleague in higher education who is very outspoken. She speaks her mind and offers honest feedback to all. One of her guiding principles is that practicing fairness and consistency are the best ways to build the foundation for effective leadership. She speaks from a place of conviction and finds teachable moments wherever she can. If she sees injustice rear its ugly head, whether from an administrator, colleague, or a subordinate, she confronts it.

She demands that all be accountable. She also prides herself on behaving in a way that promotes these values. She is tolerant of others who hold differing perspectives and who stand tall in their uniqueness.

This higher education colleague also believes in consistently practicing what she preaches to create this expectation in others so that they know what to expect when dealing with her. What she taught me was that no matter how high up you are on the chain of command, you can never be too big to be accountable for your behavior. Likewise, she notes that every leader is called on to speak truth boldly and unapologetically. If you want to lead from the front, she says, "You must promote fairness, tolerance, and consistency in all that you do." She is certainly right about that.

## Core Strategies

The strategies outlined in the following sections offer guidance for cultivating the skill and insight needed to promote fairness and consistency. They are distilled from the lessons I have learned from exceptional leaders across industries.

### Think Objectively

It is easy for a bias to creep in if you do not work diligently to protect your mind from it. Before we can address them, we must first become aware of biases in our thinking and behavior. How many times have you judged someone unfairly based on ethnographic biases? Have you made assumptions about someone's intelligence or capabilities based on an unfair bias that you held? What about because of their religious or sexual preference? We must shift the paradigm to remove bias in favor of more objective thinking. To do this, clear your mind of all influences. Imagine a completely clean slate and then try to reassess the situation in context, without the distraction of bias creeping into the equation. Whenever you feel the bias resurfacing and influencing your thinking, begin again.

### Put Yourself in Another Person's Shoes

To fully understand where a person is coming from, you need to put yourself in his or her shoes and embrace a different train of thought. This means putting ego and bias aside and welcoming the opportunity to learn something new. That drug store clerk did not have it out for you when she insisted on the receipt for processing the return. Little did you know, she almost lost her job when she failed to do it the last time. Try not to be so easily offended and take things so personally.

Often what you see unfolding has nothing to do with you. Appreciate other people's experiences with fresh eyes and try to see where they are coming from based on the way they think and how they understand the world. You may notice that doing this consistently will increase the level of compassion you feel for others over time, which is a good thing.

## Try to Be More Self-Aware

Being self-aware is the first step to fairness and open-mindedness. Go inward and tap into the power of mindfulness. Daily meditation can help you accomplish this. Set aside a few minutes to do it each morning. It may even help you notice when you are letting bias creep in. It can also help you start the day off right, in peace and free from the negative influences that converge on the work day. Often, they pop up without us ever really thinking about them.

You can preempt them by being present and leading with positive frames of reference. Examine your thoughts to gain clarity and understanding. You cannot fix a problem unless you are aware that it exists. Usually that involves going beyond the surface and unearthing issues at their source. Avail yourself of the opportunity to learn more about yourself and examine your own thinking on a deeper level.

## Actively Promote Fairness and Consistency

The only way to truly lead from the front is to simply do it. Take the steps necessary to facilitate these principles in practice; open your mind and your heart to actively promote them. Examine the current rules, policies, and procedures. Do they pass muster for the equitable culture you are trying to create and maintain? If not, some revisions may be in order. Challenge yourself to see the injustices in the workplace and to confront them courageously. Situational awareness is key, as infractions can happen at moment's notice. Being nimble will help you respond to them thoughtfully.

Likewise, instead of waiting for a triggering event, you can always challenge yourself to behave more consistently with the values you espouse. This can be practiced daily. Do not just talk about it. Get out there and do the work. When others see your obvious commitment to these principles, it not doubt will inspire their own.

## Take Stock of the Results you Have Produced

After all is said and done, take a close look at your results. Have you been successful in your attempts to promote fairness and consistency? You cannot move forward if you fail to assess where you have just been. If you did not achieve the exact results that you intended, there is no need to beat yourself up about the past. Accept it and move on. You can grow by examining your missteps and learning how to pivot. You can always do better the next time.

You may have thought that the weekly roundtables were a great chance for the employees to voice their concerns among their peers in an open and supportive forum. Turns out that no one wants to participate and it just wastes time. Perhaps meeting with employees individually would be a more conducive strategy. Reviewing outcomes matters. So, take the time to pull back the curtain, examine the thinking and behavior that produced your current results and tweak things where necessary.

# Journal Questions

1. In which ways do you actively promote fairness and consistency?
2. What do you do when someone is intentionally trying to influence your decision-making process for their benefit or someone else's?
3. Do you course-correct if your perspective becomes colored by negativity? If so, how do you do it?
4. How did this principle help you better understand your role as a leader? How will its mastery enable you to cultivate greater effectiveness?
5. How will you use the preceding strategies to advance your commitment to being more open-minded and objective?

# Leadership Challenge

Identify a topic about which you have been biased in the past. Shift your perspective by listing six new ways to view the situation. How difficult was it to reframe your perspective on this issue?

# 25

## Confront Workplace Bullies

*When the bully moves from the playground to the corner office, it is a leader's job to stand up to that person.*

Think back to the third grade. Remember the playground? The bigger kid pushed the smaller kid and took her lunch money. You probably thought that was over when you graduated. Then you landed your first job as a professional (or maybe your first leadership role) and realized that there were bullies in the work world, too. Some adults still like to throw their weight around and to exercise control over others to feel more powerful. It is sad that some people never grow up.

Bullying in the workplace is a systematic campaign that includes "repeated, health-harming mistreatment of one or more persons (targets) by one or more perpetrators. It is abusive conduct that is: Threatening, humiliating, or intimidating; work interference—sabotage—which prevents work from getting done, or verbal abuse."[1] When someone is bullied at work, the person may experience physical illness at home or in the office, an uptick in medical problems related to stress, avoidance of work, obsession with work outside of the office, shame, or an inability to enjoy their favorite activities.

Workplace bullying is a silent, pervasive illness. It is a disgusting and vicious abuse of power that gives perpetrators an artificial sense of superiority while making their victims feel defenseless. Research indicates that workplace bullying is on the rise, which is unfortunate and unacceptable. In its 2017 U.S. Workplace Bullying Survey, the Workplace Bullying Institute found that 60 million Americans are affected by it, 19% of Americans are bullied, another 19% witness it, and 61% of Americans are aware of abusive conduct

© The Author(s) 2018
K. Mariama-Arthur, *Poised for Excellence*, DOI 10.1007/978-3-319-64574-2_25

in the workplace.[2] Still there is no legislation on the books, which is why there is a great need for workplace advocates who know what to look for and how to support victims, as well as policies that punish harassment at work. This is especially important because most of the time this behavior goes unreported, and its victims suffer in silence.

Many people do not believe that workplace bullying exists or that it *could* exist. To a larger extent, it is a behavior that, in theory, has been relegated to the confines of elementary school. To complicate matters further, it is difficult to know what to look for or how to recognize it when it occurs. However, even though workplace bullying is widely considered a silent illness, the signs of abuse are not wholly obscure. This begs the question of which factors contribute to these incidences and how they continue to go on for so long without intervention. Considering the increasing number of people affected, and how dramatically it affects their ability to work, it is stunning that little if anything has been done to stamp it out.

The sad fact is that not many people take it on themselves to stop adult bullying, which is why it is so important for leaders to take charge and stand up to offenders when others will not or cannot. When leaders refuse to give a safe haven to bullies, they empower others to stand up for themselves and to create a healthier, more supportive workplace environment. Leaders who protect their people are the leaders who the people will come to trust and also protect, should the need ever arise. Because leaders are generally so visible and oftentimes perceived as equally powerful, they are expected to do the "right thing" and nip workplace bullying in the bud once discovered.

Bullies are often discreet predators, not vocal, making it fairly challenging for a leader to identify them in the workplace. Bullies realize that they would be moved against if caught, thus their discreetness. Even still, bullies usually fall into one of two categories. Flagrant bullies are easy to identify and deal with because they are highly visible. Inconspicuous bullies can only be felt and, therefore, are much harder to detect. Leaders need to keep looking around not only to see bullying but, more importantly, feel it. In this scenario, they must use their faculties more than usual. Also, the fight against bullying in this context has two facets. One, to contain the bully tactfully and, two, to help the victim survive. Even though there can be multiple effective ways to deal with bullying, a tested method is to visibly side with the victim, sending a message across to the bully that the behavior is unacceptable. This entire exercise requires tact, patience, determination, and, above all, vigilance.

No matter the circumstances, the most effective leaders always confront workplace bullying. They appreciate the gravity of what is at stake, and know that because they can successfully leverage their positions to deal with the offender, they most often can end the behavior and facilitate the appropriate punishment. They also can help the victim overcome the fear and uncertainty that come with the territory through various support mechanisms. By being both a confidant and an advocate, leaders can helping victims deal with the complex issues related to workplace bullying and improve the overall quality of their lives. In some cases, however, such support can even help save lives.

If there is ever a question of whether an incident or a series of events amounts to workplace bullying, it makes sense to assume that it does. Take seriously whatever has happened. Waiting around and hoping that things are not what they seem is counterproductive and may only embolden the offender. When a bully's behavior amounts to covert, yet a systematic campaign against the victim, time is always of the essence. Smart leaders know that it is always better to play it safe than end up sorry. They make informed decisions about workplace bullying and strive to resolve it sooner versus later. They know that most times the difference between a bully being caught and the victim being made whole is the ability to prudently confront the offending behaviors without hesitation and to address anomalies in due course.

When I was in high school, I worked for a fast-food restaurant. One of the managers was a workplace bully. He would make unreasonable demands on the crew and threatened their jobs if they did not comply. Some took exception to his demands and left of their own volition. Others who really needed the job were less vocal and instead chose to simply do what he asked, even if they suffered because of it. The litany of his demands included working burdensome, additional shifts, coming in during days scheduled off, cleaning up horrible messes in the bathroom, doing other "special cleaning duties" that should have been farmed out to a third party. And, as if those "directives" were not enough, he also made staff perform "repeat after me" exercises to spotlight their mistakes and publicly humiliate them. It was demoralizing for everyone involved.

One day it was my turn. While I was shocked at his undignified request to perform excessive shifts, it was the unexpected sexual harassment that troubled me the most. Instead of succumbing to his outlandish behavior, I, like many before me, decided to quit. Not before I sent a "special" note to HR, though. I explained to the department exactly what had been going on and what he asked of me. At the time I was proud of myself for standing up and confronting the bully. In hindsight, however, I realized that this behavior amounted to a great deal more than workplace bullying and the legal consequences were severe. Nevertheless, I learned two very important lessons from the experience. One, I would never treat anyone the way he treated us and, two, I would never let anyone bully me or anyone else at a workplace.

# Core Strategies

The strategies outlined in the following sections offer guidance for cultivating your skill and insight in confronting bullies. They are distilled from the lessons I have learned from exceptional leaders across various industries.

## Know What to Look for

There are specific signs of bullying at the workplace that should be recognized. Not surprisingly, they resemble the bullying we all saw on the playground in elementary school. In professional settings, you may notice that bullies often are outspoken and insecure and push other people around at every opportunity. Although it may seem counterintuitive, be sure to scrutinize the behaviors of the bully and the bullied, separately, as you may not see the interaction directly.

For example, notice whether a coworker who never wants to eat in the lunchroom or interact in a group setting. Or, you might take notice of another coworker who is consistently cracking crude and excessive jokes about the mailroom clerk. By the same token, look for any behavior that appears questionable. If it appears suspect, it probably is. Also note the significant toll that bullying takes on its victims. They can have physical, mental, or emotional problems that persist long after the workday ends. Whenever you notice a sharp decline in work product, increased socio-emotional distress, or anything else that seems awry, investigate it. Do not leave any unfortunate possibilities to chance.

## Confront the Bully's Behavior

Once you discover a bully, be unapologetic and call them out on the bad behavior. The truth is that bullies do not want to be discovered or held accountable for their dirty work. A bully's entire goal is to keep the campaign going and to escape any intervention. Your job is to make sure that the person is exposed. Be vocal. Say something, even if it means confronting the bully in a public setting. If the situation requires it, do not hesitate. Ending the bad behavior is the first step in helping the victim to find relief. If you do not feel comfortable doing it, enlist another colleague to be your witness and provide moral support. There are probably plenty of people you could call on and who would step up to the plate.

Remember, there often is power in numbers. In addition, no matter how you decide to approach the situation (alone or with a colleague), make sure you are specific in your admonition. The bully should know that you directly observed or are otherwise aware of the bad behavior. Do not give the bully any wiggle room.

## Take It up the Hierarchy

Just calling out a bully is sometimes not enough to stop the behavior or to right the wrong committed against the victim. In some instances, you may need to get the HR and the legal departments involved. If you must escalate an intervention, prepare a detailed account of the behavior in advance; it should include your observations as well as firsthand accounts by the victim. Present a timeline to both departments, along with any other evidence that might help with the investigation.

If you need, for example, an affidavit to support your claim, make sure you have one prepared and notarized ahead of time. If there are witnesses, make sure that they have put their statements in writing and that those statements are included in the collective submission as well. Also make sure that you have several copies, including an electronic version.

## Follow-up with the "Powers that Be"

It is important not to leave departments to their own devices. Even well-meaning individuals can forget or get distracted with other competing responsibilities. After initiating the appropriate administrative procedures, follow-up. Find out what each department discovered. Ask for copies of any reports or responses that they have filed. Determine whether they have sufficient evidence to move forward, and if so, what they plan to do next. Ask whether anything else is needed on your end and, if so, offer to provide it as soon as possible.

Also, it would be a good idea to know what the policy is in your office. Are these matters dealt with internally, or do they get handed over to third parties at some point? Whatever the case, find out the preliminary conclusions and next steps toward the final resolution. Make no assumptions and leave nothing to chance.

## Support the Victims

It can be easy to forget, while the investigation is taking place, that the victim needs your support. Do your best to facilitate this process. Paid time off might be in order, or the victim might want to work from home for a time. She or he may feel uncomfortable being in the presence of their peers while everything is so raw, which is to be expected. The bullied individuals should be given sufficient latitude on this point, and afforded scheduling flexibility as needed, especially until they feel comfortable enough to return to work.

In addition, counseling could be necessary. Make sure that their benefits are in order to easily facilitate this possibility. Those affected may need to work through numerous issues related to the bullying and mulling it over alone may be insufficient. Even though it obviously is important to deal with the perpetrator, do not lose focus of the victim. The person needs the support to move past the injustice.

# Journal Questions

1. Are you familiar with workplace bullying? Discuss.
2. What are some possible ways to combat it?
3. In what ways can you support the victims of workplace bullying?
4. How did this principle help you better understand your role as a leader? How will its mastery enable you to cultivate greater effectiveness?
5. How will you use the preceding strategies to advance your commitment to confronting bullies, no matter where they are?

# Leadership Challenge

Develop an action plan to combat workplace bullying within your organization. Enlist the help of your human resources and legal departments. Once you have formalized a policy, post it so that all employees are aware of it. Then host a formal training so that employees know the signs of bullying and have the resources needed to confront it. This should also serve as a deterrent for potential bullies. How do you feel having implemented this policy?

# Notes

1. Namie, G. (2014). The WBI Definition of Workplace Bullying. *The Workplace Bullying Institute*. Retrieved September 12, 2014 from http://www.workplace-bullying.org/individuals/problem/definition.
2. Namie, G. (2017). 2017 Workplace Bullying Institute U.S. Workplace Bullying Survey. San Francisco: Workplace Bullying Institute.

# 26

# Collaborate with Experts to Maximize Results

*Leaders understand the extraordinary power of collaborating with experts. They know how to pool synergies to drive results.*

Self-reliance is a decisive measure of effective leadership. Indeed, the person who is self-sufficient can usually accomplish a great deal without seeking much assistance. Nevertheless, no man is an island and no leader achieves great success in isolation. The support of a competent team of expert advisors—a dream team—who can help turn dreams into reality is an invaluable component of a smart leader's superlative tactical strategy. Smart leaders—no matter how bright, talented, or experienced they are—eagerly welcome the wise counsel of capable and resourceful minds.

Discerning leaders know that no matter how well they operate in their respective arenas, they will always have chasms—blind spots and knowledge gaps—that must be addressed. At the same time, they know that merely acknowledging them is not enough. To move visions forward, leaders must pool high-caliber knowledge resources that provide new perspectives and uncommon direction to produce extraordinary results. Amassing relevant insights from credible advisors effectively achieves this ambitious goal.

This, however, does not mean that leaders can sit back idly while others do all the work. While leveraging a talented team of advisors is certainly necessary for success, such efforts will fall flat without the strategic involvement of leaders throughout the process. Laziness has never landed a person in a corner office. Leaders must come to the table hungry and ready to expend their best efforts, too. When they have reached scorched earth, however, they proactively seek the surety of the brain trust. A leader must strike a balance between self-reliance and reliance on others. Teams only win when everyone contributes.

© The Author(s) 2018
K. Mariama-Arthur, *Poised for Excellence*, DOI 10.1007/978-3-319-64574-2_26

The best teams are comprised of best-of-breed members. The team's interactions are high-touch and its members are high-caliber. They include experts who are often "thought leaders" and whose brilliant ideas and wise counsel transform their respective industries. In organizing such a team, certain matters must be thoughtfully considered. To make the impossible plausible, the person at the helm, the leader, must be a team player. He or she must be clear on the purpose of the collaboration, impervious to undue influence.

The advisors must be narrowly focused on delivering value and be free from hidden agendas. All players must perform at optimal levels to maximize the goals of the collaboration. When each team member sets aside extraneous desires and focuses on the mission, phenomenal things happen.

Experts can be incorporated in any number of ways. They can be entrenched within the organization itself, especially when there is an ongoing need for their involvement in day-to-day operations or comprehensive decision making. Or, they also can be hired as consultants, offering advice and focused oversight on a project-by-project basis. The goals of the mission and the organization will determine the nature and frequency of an expert's involvement. Nevertheless, whatever arrangement is selected must reflect the most effective use of resources so that the insights can be fully maximized and implemented successfully. There is nothing worse than wasted time and talent, so it is critical to engage experts in a way that captures their full potential.

Make no mistake: When experts are not engaged, organizations suffer. Trying to maneuver in the absence of critical knowledge reservoirs forces an organization to spin its wheels, thus wasting time and other valuable resources in the process. There is no question that specialized knowledge is needed more and more in today's growing global economy. As workforces collaborate across industries and, in many cases, continents, the likelihood of requiring access to an expert's unique skillset is great. Because of this new workforce dynamic, it is in a leader's best interest to manage this facet proactively. Oftentimes that means having core teams already assembled, which can prove particularly advantageous under the right set of circumstances.

The most effective leaders identify their strengths and leverage them to maximize their success, but they also recognize their weaknesses and know when expert collaborations are necessary to propel their visions forward. Trial lawyers working on white-collar crime cases often will round up forensic accountants to analyze the alleged financial misconduct by the parties. What they uncover can make or break those cases: Their deep smarts provide stakeholders with a practical understanding of complex issues and a window into key distinctions. Assembling a team of experts to help navigate uncertainty and problem-solve should be an option that is always on the table. It can also make the difference between success and failure. Smart leaders choose success and, therefore, begin with the end in mind by welcoming insights from expert advisors to maximize their results.

Part of the work that I do involves consulting leaders on the creation of expert advisories. Although I firmly believe that a leader should own his or her expertise, achieving more complex outcomes often requires collaborating with others who know more than you, both within and outside of your industry. When an organization is at a crossroads and needs to solve a problem beyond the scope of its expertise, I advise members of the C-Suite on how to assemble knowledge experts and how to best leverage their contributions.

Whether a single or a multifaceted engagement, the team is always interested in learning how to vet, engage, and collaborate with experts. Sometimes my work involves navigating the waters myself and at other times, simply offering straightforward advice on how to integrate expert insights and develop a work plan that produces results at a high level. In either case, the results have been remarkable, as the clients' positions have always improved. What I know for sure is that collaborating with experts, regardless of industry or expertise, is critical to achieving above-average results. And when leaders embrace this principle, they set themselves up for extraordinary success. There is no doubt that building and leveraging a team of experts help a leader to be more effective and deliver on the promise of results with greater clarity and confidence.

## Core Strategies

The strategies outlined in the following sections offer guidance for cultivating your skill and insight into connecting and collaborating with experts to maximize results. They are distilled from the lessons I have learned from exceptional leaders across various industries.

### Determine the Need

Do you really *need* an expert? Or, should you simply engage in some good old-fashioned research? Well, if you come across an area of which you are fundamentally unfamiliar and the level at which you require enlightenment or engagement is beyond superficial, it is very likely you will need to consult with an expert to navigate the terrain. To avoid wasting your time, or the time of the expert, make sure you are clear on the project requirements and how the expert would add value. Engaging an expert may not be free, so consider the overall budget in assessing the need.

Likewise, realize that in a situation where the expert input will make or break the project, you probably *need* it. So, do not skimp on costs when the input is imperative to the goals of the overall mission. In making the final determination, consider what the results of the project could possibly be without the expert's involvement.

## Find the Best and Most Relevant Experts

Not all experts are created equal. If you are going to engage one or assemble an entire team, you want only the best. So, check their credentials, results, and references. To make sure their insights will be relevant, make certain that you select the right subject matter expert for the job. There is a big difference between a renowned pediatrician and a renowned neurodevelopmental pediatrician. Whomever you choose should have the requisite education, skills, and experience to help you bring the project to fruition successfully.

Going a step further, once you have narrowed your choices down to a few, you may want to interview them and see whether you have good rapport. It would be a shame to select the best-credentialed and well-known actuary only to discover that they have a bad attitude or difficulty adapting to the organizational culture, especially if it is to be a long and high-touch engagement.

## Develop a Strategic Plan

Once you have selected the most appropriate experts to work with, you also must develop a plan that will help you be successful in the time allotted. Make sure you are maximizing the expert's capacity and assigning tasks that allow the person to perform fully. If the expert can perform cutting-edge research and conduct the analysis, she or he should. Making appropriate assignments at the outset will help the entire team make the most of the contributions. In addition, outline expectations and explain any ambiguities before you begin.

There is nothing worse than having someone come back to you once a project has started to complain about its scope. Get that right initially and build your deadline and benchmarks around the project's scope. Additionally, examine where there might be some crossover and how the individual team members will work together until completion.

## Execute the Collaboration

Schedule a kick-off meeting so that everyone can meet in advance of the frenzy and be formally introduced, regardless of whether you are bringing on one expert or an entire team. It is much easier to begin working together once you have broken the ice. If you are bringing on a team of experts, make sure that there is ample time for networking and relaxing before and after the work details have been sorted out. This meeting should energize the group, not stress them out and make the project foreboding. Schedule a lunch on the first day of the collaboration to get people talking and connecting offline to build additional rapport.

An introductory team-building exercise also might be a nice touch. Because the group is in a nascent stage, you want to select an exercise that is light-hearted and fun and provides an opportunity for everyone to simply get to know one another better. Also, make sure that everyone's contact information is shared so they can be in touch afterward. Follow your strategic plan to execute the nuts and bolts of the collaboration so that nothing important is overlooked.

## Assess the Value of Collaboration

Determining the success of an engagement should be a straightforward process and must be done to establish whether it was a good fit and whether the team should collaborate again in the future. Start with the technical results you hoped to accomplish. Were they the results that you expected? Are they subpar or better than expected? Was the project completed on time? Also consider the facilitation, supervision, and execution. Were the expectations clear from the very beginning? Was communication regular and well-disseminated? Did the expert work well with the team? What feedback did you receive from the team?

Again, even a highly sought-after expert may not be asked back if they lack interpersonal skills. Think about each area where you wanted to excel and whether the expert's involvement helped or hurt those desired outcomes. Whatever you learn from your assessment should be used to create more effective collaborations in the future.

## Journal Questions

1. Describe three key benefits of collaborating with an expert.
2. In what ways can you leverage your own expertise to make projects more successful?
3. Do you consider yourself a team player? Why or why not?
4. How did this principle help you better understand your role as a leader? How will its mastery enable you to cultivate greater effectiveness?
5. How will you use the preceding strategies to advance your commitment to connecting and collaborating with experts more strategically?

## Leadership Challenge

Challenge yourself to collaborate with an expert outside of your industry to bring your next project to fruition. Your skills should be complementary, but you should each be in different industries. After completing the project, assess how you feel about the work you have done together. What skills did you learn? How can you do a better job of collaborating with an expert in the future?

# 27

# Challenge the Status Quo

*Leaders should not be besotted with the comfort of best practices. Instead, they must welcome change and boldly challenge the status quo.*

Institutional memory seldom provides the best context for confronting current challenges. While it must be examined in the grand scheme of things, a common mistake is to arbitrarily apply the thinking and decision-making from time immemorial to present-day challenges—especially as a perfunctory measure. Change is a constant variable, even though people and processes do not always move with it. Yet, understanding how people and processes have evolved to create a culture is important when considering why changes may be appropriate.

First, understand that change is never instituted for its own sake. Certain conditions must hold to justify it. When people are suffering, an organization is struggling, or the business or political landscape has shifted, change is probably necessary. Even when these conditions beckon change, it still can be met with significant resistance. Change can be scary. It can be a lot of work. Nevertheless, it also can be illuminating and transformative. In addition, no matter what criticisms abound or what opposition may exist, it is a leader's job to evaluate the need for change and, where appropriate, challenge the status quo.

The problem is that the status quo often lulls people into complacency. It makes them overly comfortable with the ways things are and provides little motivation for learning something new or doing things differently. This rings true even when current policies are detrimental to the overall mission and neither individual nor organizational interests are not being well-served. Time-honored policies and procedures can give people a false sense of security, making them believe that the established decision-making processes are good

© The Author(s) 2018
K. Mariama-Arthur, *Poised for Excellence*, DOI 10.1007/978-3-319-64574-2_27

as is. If no one takes the initiative though, problems will never get solved, an organization will become even more entrenched in its ways, and people continue to suffer.

How do leaders confront the status quo? They begin by observing the current landscape and decision-making mechanisms to discover where improvements can be made. They are honest with themselves and others. They confront individuals or situations causing dissension within the ranks, and/or preventing the evolution of ideas and growth for the benefit of the organization. They have conversations about revamping policies, procedures, missions, manuals, and more to move the organization in a new direction with a renewed sense of purpose. Then, they decide whether an incremental or global change would better serve the overall strategy. Whatever they decide, however, they make sure that there is significant momentum moving the organization forward and that people's feet are being held to the fire.

Collaborating and delegating are essential when considering how to best execute change. Assigning projects to teams is key to promoting efficiency and increasing the quality of output during transition. In some cases, such as mergers and acquisitions or transitioning to a new presidential administration, a formalized "transition team" should be created. In fact, it is an essential component of the due diligence process. It ensures that the transition occurs in an organized fashion, that people are well informed, and that communication flows freely throughout the organization. Although the individual team members may vary, commonly representatives come from IT, finance, HR, and the C-Suite. When the team is cohesive and change is well integrated, there is less anxiety and the organization can move forward with determination.

Notwithstanding the instances where change is appropriate, leaders still must understand the practical implications of how the past affects the present and what changing old procedures could entail for everyone involved. They also must determine whether any aspects of the old guard's platform remain relevant and, if so, the rationale behind it. In performing their analysis, leaders are proactive and do not wait for others to determine when the time is right to consider change. They do their homework to avoid missteps and then take the bull by the horns to marshal the organization in a new direction and take it to next levels of success. Steve Jobs understood this well and, for this reason, was incredibly instrumental in introducing innovation and influencing Apple Inc.'s tremendous success.

The best leaders know that being wed to best practices and the comfort of the status quo does more harm than good. They look for opportunities to innovate and disrupt archaic regimes in favor of improving them. Even if they experience pushback, which is often the case, they remain committed to the greater good of the institutions and organizations they serve. It is this mindset that separates the most effective leaders from those who simply go along to get along and fail to serve their constituents' best interests. But then again, fear of making waves has never been the guiding principle for standout leaders. They move against the tide enthusiastically knowing that the greatest reward is on the other side of it. If there ever were a truer definition of a maverick, it would certainly be a leader who is emboldened to challenge the status quo.

I have been a member of various organizations since college. Some of them have been worth the effort of membership, others not so much. One of them stands out in my mind because of its standards and tremendous leadership legacy. In particular, it is interested in attracting active members who uphold its values and are committed to serving the greater community. Although its institutional memory is strong, the organization remains dynamic and agile. It is not opposed to examining where it can improve and serve its members and the community even better. In fact, it conducts regular performance assessments and welcomes feedback from the membership.

The organization finds every opportunity to challenge the status quo and reinvent itself for the greater good. Whether it is the organization's website, marketing, or educational materials, it always is making tweaks to benefit the brand and to bring it into clear alignment with its mission. The members do not fear change, whether they are leading it, or simply helping to facilitate it. Each individual member is empowered to lead change for the benefit of the whole and is fully supported by the entire organization. It is one of the main reasons that I am most excited to renew my annual membership and participate in its regular activities throughout the year.

## Core Strategies

The strategies outlined in the following sections provide guidance for cultivating your skill and insight in challenging the status quo. They are distilled from the lessons I have learned from exceptional leaders across various industries.

### Assess the Status Quo

Take a good look at the status quo before you decide to disrupt it. Getting a sense of the big picture is necessary before resolving to alter what may not require any modifications at all. Take time to learn and understand how the institutional memory was established and what is currently keeping it alive. Does it serve the individuals within the organization and the organization itself? Is, for example, promoting from within a help or hindrance to building a robust leadership pipeline?

Ask the right questions of the right people and do a bit of independent research. Look at historical data, organization charts, and changes in law and policy. Find out what preceded the status quo and examine any possible rationale for changing it. If none exists, focus energies elsewhere until and unless an appropriate opportunity presents itself.

## Apply Disruptive Thought

Now that you understand the existing system, and determined that there is a need for change, ask yourself how you can turn the current thinking on its head. Start from scratch and build from the ground up, rather than executing prophylactic measures and applying band aids to the situation. Note that there are aggressive as well as conservative ways to effect change. Determine whether one approach is better than the other, or whether a hybrid approach would best serve the organization. Explore ideas and strategies that might seem counterintuitive. An overnight shift for the administrative staff? Just a thought—a thought that might be cost-effective and result in greater productivity across the board.

Again, you want your thinking to disrupt patterns and challenge assumptions. Do not be tempted to fall back into older, more engrained ways of thinking and behaving. Even if they have worked well historically, you must persist in forward-thinking and focus on current realities to drive innovation and advance organizational goals.

## Step Outside Your Comfort Zone and Embrace "Why"

When you are committed to challenging the status quo, there is obviously something at stake for you as well as the organization. Whatever is driving you, use it to fuel your energy and sustain your attention. Then, force yourself to work outside your comfort zone because growth does not happen inside it. Remember that change for the organization also means change for you. This may initially conjure up some feeling of discomfort. But remember that you, too must evolve to facilitate this epic turnaround.

Notice where you are comfortable and commit to breaking the chains that bind your thinking and performance. Then determine the distance between where you are and where you want to be. Finally, determine exactly what you need to do differently to get to where you want to go. Your previous level of thinking and performance will not help you negotiate success under the new regime.

## Develop a Fresh Perspective

After compiling your research and creating various angles from which to proceed, take two steps back and try to develop a fresh perspective. What do you truly envision as you think about effectuating change at this level? What are the goals you hope to achieve? Are there any challenges that you failed to consider that might circumvent your efforts? Are there relevant stakeholders that could benefit, but were previously unidentified?

Lay your biases aside so you can look at the situation objectively and with fresh eyes. A fresh point of view will help you navigate the newly developing landscape as you strive to gain needed clarity. It will also ensure the best results as you challenge yourself to step away from the status quo into the brand-new arena. Therefore, urge yourself to confront archaic thinking every chance you get: Throw down the gauntlet and pursue unconventional ideas with wild abandon.

## Take Bold Action

Now that you have developed a plan of action, execute it competently. Remember that a plan is only as good as its execution. Determine what the first steps should be, how they should be organized, and when they should be carried out. Has your transition team been assembled? Do you need expert advisors to make this transition? Are the necessary financial components in order? Determine what you need to do and what needs to be delegated. Then move boldly, without hesitation. If the plan scares you, know that you are moving in the right direction. Regardless of any challenges you encounter during this phase, do not become anxious or retreat.

Challenge yourself to execute more boldly each time you tackle a new task and you will become more confident with every new experience. Think big. If scheduling a meeting with the CEO would help jumpstart progress, then by all means, pick up the phone and give her a call. The point is to take bold action to move change forward, even if it makes you feel uncomfortable.

## Journal Questions

1. Do you usually feel more comfortable going with the flow, or will you make waves when necessary? Discuss.
2. Do you find it difficult to develop a fresh perspective when you have become accustomed to the status quo? Explain.
3. Do you care what other people think of your decisions, especially if they are personally affected by them? Why or why not?
4. How did this principle help you better understand your role as a leader? How will its mastery enable you to cultivate greater effectiveness?
5. How will you use the preceding strategies to advance your commitment to challenging the status quo?

## Leadership Challenge

Identify one key area in your life—personally or professionally—that has been hindered by the status quo. How can you mix things up? Make a list of five ways you can innovate to improve this area. Implement one strategy over the next five weeks. How did you challenge the status quo?

# 28

# Leverage Leadership Ethos to Shape Culture

*Workplace culture is an amalgamation of beliefs, behaviors, and policies. Leaders must successfully mold that culture to move their visions forward.*

Leaders play a crucial role in influencing organizational culture. Buy-in requires that employees see a big picture that resonates with their core values and calls for a level of inspiration fueled by how leaders carry themselves. Because what leaders believe influences their own behavior, they must be intentional about assessing and refining their thinking. That process may involve recalibrating beliefs to bring them into alignment with their vision. Likewise, it may mean acquiring relevant professional development and substantive experience to prepare for a specific leadership role.

Culture is not aspirational. It is based on the sum and substance of what people actually do rather than what they hope for. Abstract principles that are not expressed through behavior often are dismissed as empty rhetoric or as "all talk and no action." Leaders must "walk the walk" not just "talk the talk." When both are at play, however, they must be congruent. When there is a disconnect between beliefs and behavior, it is difficult to earn the respect and support of the team. People question the integrity of a leader who fails to practice what they preach. In addition, when people start to whisper, morale drops and culture becomes strained.

We have all seen the poignant examples of celebrated leaders who fell from grace when actions spoke louder than words. A recent instance involves the retired United States Army Lieutenant General Michael Thomas Flynn, who is also the former National Security Advisor to President Donald Trump. General Flynn's alleged attempts to conceal his contacts with Russian government officials lead to his untimely resignation from the Trump Administration.

© The Author(s) 2018
K. Mariama-Arthur, *Poised for Excellence*, DOI 10.1007/978-3-319-64574-2_28

Behavior matters for its own sake, but it also influences how others think and behave. Such behavior also influences culture.

Values that are reflected in behavior and reinforced through policy are compelling influences on an organization. Leaders lean on values and behavior to drive performance and shape culture. When ethos is linked to business objectives, employees follow the path of least resistance. They try their level best to do the "right thing." This shift in thinking and behavior results in higher productivity, increased creativity, and other intangible benefits.

When employees understand the symbiotic relationship between ethos and culture and govern themselves accordingly, everyone wins. Google's culture is a great example of this. The bottom line is that when employees understand how specific behaviors advance organizational goals, they are compelled to get behind them and further support a leader with unconventional ideas—ideas that catalyze change. By all accounts, leveraging ethos simply makes good sense.

Although rules and regulations are important building blocks for compliance, they do not necessarily determine how ideas are transformed into actions. Values and policies dictate what actually happens at the workplace on a day-to-day basis. They are the rousing undercurrent that flows swiftly and entirely through it. That said, leaders must be keenly aware of what happens at both the micro- and macro-levels within the workplace environment. A level of broad-mindedness is required to successfully navigate its complexities and to purposefully shape culture. Often, those inner workings reveal how members of the collective establish boundaries, determine acceptable behaviors, and engage one another.

A mission is a complementary component that reinforces the structural anatomy and culture of every organization. Without a mission, an organization cannot establish its true north. Organizations need a compass that clarifies its purpose and is available for all to see, which encourages everyone to achieve "big-picture" goals. When ethos bolsters the organizational mission, sparks fly. More than simply giving people an objective to aim for, a mission inspired by ethos empowers employees to take personal responsibility for creating culture. It also provides clear direction and a solid rationale for how to achieve an organization's overarching strategic goals.

Leaders who understand how values, behaviors, and policies interact know that leveraging ethos is a powerful method of influencing culture. Employees expect leaders to be good examples of what they espouse, not merely good advocates. When they are, they are in the best position to lead others and transform the organizational dynamics from the inside out. Leaders rely on employees to embrace key values and behaviors that drive individual and collective performance. When they do, the individuals help to create and maintain a culture that thrives. In the process, leaders must remain well-informed and attentive to ongoing nuances: Culture has the potential to evolve and devolve organically. By leveraging leadership ethos, the most effective leaders model the change they seek and inspire others to follow suit in shaping cultures that flourish within the organizations and institutions that they serve.

I am the president of a global advisory board of an international leadership organization that serves women around the world. I was recruited by the organization's president and we are now great friends. She has a distinct leadership brand that exemplifies honesty, integrity, and a wholehearted commitment to critical issues facing women around the world. She is easygoing but has a clear-cut expectation for an excellent work ethic and performance. She has taken the time to build each component of her organization from the ground up, including handpicking her board leadership based on the idea that though values must mesh, organic rapport also must exist.

Not surprisingly, the culture of the organization of this president mirrors her deepest desires for it. It is full of amazing, enthusiastic, talented, and committed women from around the world. They each work hard and put their best foot forward, as they work diligently to effectuate the organization's mission. It is all done within the context of the beliefs, values, and policies that have been established and influence the way people interact, the way protocol is executed, and the general tone of the organizational environment. Had it not been for this president's extraordinary leadership and the ethos that she infused into the organization, its overall success, and particularly that of the board, would not have materialized.

## Core Strategies

The strategies outlined in the following sections offer guidance for cultivating your skill and insight into creating and maintaining a culture grounded in leadership ethos. They are distilled from the lessons I have learned from exceptional leaders across various industries.

### Identify the Organizational Goals and Determine How Leadership Ethos Can Support Them

Before you decide to take the bold step of using ethos to shape culture, you must first decide on the values you want to create and why. To avoid negative consequences, do not proceed haphazardly. Do not make random assumptions based on what has worked with other organizations. Customize your experience and take the time to reexamine your own values, attitudes, and behaviors. Evaluate how well they mesh with the kind of culture you seek to create. Next determine the ideal values, attitudes, and behaviors and how each can be linked to organizational objectives. Ask how these components can drive performance effectively and make employees more accountable for contributing to strategic outcomes. You want to align synergies at the outset and strengthen the rationale for each as you go along.

## Align the Vision, Mission, and Organizational Goals

The organizational mission and its goals must be in sync to use them to shape culture. It is counterproductive to attempt to form culture without a powerful vision or mission to reinforce it. First, decide the most basic way of articulating the organizational vision. The vision is aspirational—so think big. Then, do the same for the mission. Both should be straightforward and influential. Describe them each in no more than two or three sentences. Brainstorm with key decision makers to develop each one so that they resonate and embody the sentiment that you seek to convey.

As you work to finalize each, test them to make sure they fit the organization's goals. If the organization's vision and mission are already in place, you might need to do this process in reverse, which amounts to refining rather than creating the vision and mission statements and aligning them with the organizational goals.

## Educate the Entire Workforce

Employees will not adopt a vision or mission or embrace a culture that they are unfamiliar with. Host an introductory event where employees are educated on the vision, mission and the goals of the culture you seek to create. Discuss the purpose and benefits of each part of the statement, as well as the overall expectations of employees at every level. Make it interactive so that they can discuss and role-play. Invite them to ask plenty of questions. Provide handouts and reference materials so that they have resources to review after the event.

You want your workforce to be as educated as possible. Do not force them to find the information for themselves; give it to them to review. Follow up after the event to make sure that everyone is on the same page and is ready to move forward. If they are not, be sure to encourage questions and clear up any misunderstandings that may exist.

## Reinforce Ethos Through Activities and Signposts

Even after you have held an introductory event, some ideas will take time to process. So, be prepared to host regular meetings to address questions or concerns, and post information around the office for all employees to see. You should provide every opportunity for the people who make up the culture to freely access the information and to learn about how to make the most of their contributions. A fun way to reinforce this is to schedule a contest or trivia game and give out prizes to anyone who can write down or recite the information correctly.

In addition, keep everyone focused on maintaining an enterprising culture by framing some the sentiments and place around the office—in the hallways and other common areas for good measure. The more you reinforce something, the more it becomes second nature.

## Determine the Impact of Ethos

What have you learned through this process? How has your thinking, values, and behavior impacted the process? Have employees internalized ethos and drawn the necessary connection to culture? Have they used the tenets of the vision and mission to guide their purpose? Are they taking personal responsibility for their role in the process? Has it helped the organization thrive? What are the results of the shift? Assess the answers to all these to discover where you may have gone wrong and where you have made good choices.

In doing so, consider whether the process was communicated effectively and whether your follow-up was beneficial. As you continue to refine the process, you will be able to clarify your thinking and improve the strategies for leveraging ethos to shape culture and achieve the best results for your organization.

# Journal Questions

1. What is your company's mission?
2. How do the values and visions of the leadership contribute to its culture and reflect its mission?
3. How is culture nurtured within the workplace?
4. How did this principle help you better understand your role as a leader? How will its mastery enable you to cultivate greater effectiveness?
5. How will you use the preceding strategies to advance your commitment to contributing to a culture that reflects your organization's mission?

## Leadership Challenge

Host a board meeting to discuss ways to enhance workplace culture. Before you begin, make sure every member has a copy of the mission statement. Decide on the specific objectives that would improve the workplace culture and ensure that each person has a role. Create a plan that can be executed immediately and evaluated in 30-, 60-, and 90-day intervals. What did you discover about the evolution of culture at each interval?

# 29

## Practice Tolerance

*Patience, understanding, and an appreciation for differences are critical virtues for leadership.*

Thanks to new and faster ways to communicate, travel, and learn, the world has become smaller, and the people in it, more accessible. The new technologies also have helped us discover that, as a species, we are more alike than we are different. When we come together to appreciate our commonalities, we cast off fear, doubt, and arbitrary feelings of resentment. We also get a unique opportunity to explore alliances based on substantive characteristics rather than superficial distinctions. Understanding that the world has transformed into a synergy-rich global marketplace, the need to develop cultural intelligence is perhaps greater now more than ever before.[1]

A hunger for learning and an openness to change are the foundation for developing "tolerance." Deep down inside each of us is an innate desire for uncertainty. To keep life interesting and invite new opportunities to learn and grow, we must break up the monotony. But as we reach for new frontiers, we must also reach for tolerance. New experiences rarely emerge without exposing us to new people and paths less traveled. Resistance to the people and things that are different from what you currently know undermines opportunities to learn and grow. Contrast is everywhere and attempting to avoid it will only make you miserable. If you are not exposed to new people and fresh ideas, it will be difficult to become more knowledgeable, increase cultural competence, and experience all the idiosyncratic goodness that the world has to offer.

Being tolerant means accepting that everyone is not the same, that real differences in people and ideas do, in fact, exist. To a greater extent, it also may mean making the effort to get to know someone or being a good listener and

© The Author(s) 2018
K. Mariama-Arthur, *Poised for Excellence*, DOI 10.1007/978-3-319-64574-2_29

resisting the urge to react when you perceive differences. Whether that difference is an accent, a style of dress, a religious preference, and/or a socio-economic distinction, do not let the "difference" become a distraction. Tolerance means thinking before you speak. If an employee uses his or her breaktime to pray rather than eat or walk around the block, that is entirely the person's prerogative. You may be curious, but all curiosity does not merit an unwarranted and intrusive query or comment. Kindness is the precursor to patience, and patience is the key to developing interpersonal relationships that can help you grow. Consider welcoming differences with open arms rather than shunning them with narrow-mindedness and hypersensitivity.

Understanding is a linked to tolerance. It means going a step beyond merely "accepting" differences. It means making a sincere effort to learn more about people, cultures, and new ways of thinking. It is an active approach that requires taking deliberate action that can enrich your experiences and allows you to develop a more informed perspective. "Understanding" means that you try to see where a person is coming from and *why*. You may not necessarily agree with the opinions, but you cannot dismiss a person simply because he or she has a different outlook. In addition, learning about the origin of different viewpoints can be useful. You never know when the need to speak up on someone else's behalf may arise or an opportunity to enthusiastically exchange ideas may present itself.

Appreciating differences builds reciprocal synergy that we can use to make our organizations and our entire world better. When we learn more about each other, we do more than merely gather a trove of encyclopedic information. We learn how to help and heal one another, how to multiply our successes, and how to celebrate the things that matters most, together. By definition, it also increases mutual respect and helps to build stronger alliances, which benefit all. Make no mistake: We are invariably stronger together than when we cling to the fragile strands of selfhood and isolation. Exercising tolerance establishes good karma that opens door now and in the future—that is, "tolerance" is a priceless gift that keeps on giving.

When leaders are not tolerant, understanding, and open to differences, they alienate themselves from the world around them. People do not feel connected to an intolerant leader, which makes it virtually impossible to influence them. When people know that you value their differences, they also become more tolerant of yours. Yes, we *all* have differences. Perspective is merely in the eye of the beholder. So, be aware that the way you see others impacts the way others see you. Besides, what you put out in the Universe will no doubt make its way back to you—good, bad, or indifferent. Choose wisely, and consider the consequences of intolerance before acting imprudently.

The most effective leaders are tolerant and welcome the uniqueness in others. They also become more fearless about sharing their own differences with their organization and the world. Tolerant leaders filter out the bias in their thoughts and wholly embrace the humanity in others. They know that everyone can contribute to the success of an endeavor with exclusive insights that will only complement the final outcome. Homogeneity is an attribute of the most cohesive, collaborative, and successful organizations and societies anywhere in the world. Look around you and see for yourself. When open-mindedness and magnanimity regulate a leaders' moral compass, they rarely are led astray.

Dr. Martin Luther King, Jr., will forever be remembered for his whole-hearted embrace of humanity and exercise of tolerance. He believed in the sanctity of humans, not the superiority of one race over the other. His passion for equality and value-based ideology breathed life into the Civil Rights Movement. Nonviolence was a key component of the messages he disseminated. As a historic leader of the Civil Rights Movement, Dr. King challenged America to cherish the sum of its differences and to acknowledge the powerful ways that make us alike. What he taught us through altruism and humility is that tolerance is a critical aspect of effective leadership. Without tolerance, leaders cannot unify others, but only divide them further.

By creating a visceral message of unity that resonated with people across races, cultures, and socioeconomic lines, he demanded that we look inward to examine our beliefs and confront fallacies related to intolerance. Dr. King gave us a vision for the future where we could embrace each other without reservation and where our children and their children would develop substantive relationships based on the content of our character rather than the color of our skin. Indeed, tolerance is a compelling leadership imperative—one that we will never forget thanks to the noble teachings of Dr. King.

# Core Strategies

The strategies outlined in the following sections offer guidance for cultivating your skill and insight into developing tolerance. They are distilled from the lessons I have learned from exceptional leaders across various industries.

## Decelerate and Shift Your Lifestyle Priorities

You may not realize it, but tolerance is difficult to develop when everything feels harried and you are beleaguered by stress. Fast-paced days and anxiety make it difficult to appreciate anything except what is urgent and relevant to your own life. You will have little time or tolerance for anyone else when you always feel "on." Your capacity to be open-minded and considerate will wax and wane. Your tendency to blurt out whatever is within your stream of consciousness will increase exponentially. So, slow things down.

Stop with the impossible schedules and deadlines. Long hours and little sleep with no time for anything in between leads to poor performance and declining health. Take a breath to be in the moment. Cut things out of your schedule. Get up earlier and make your commute to work more leisurely and enjoyable. Produce less and spread things out to relieve unnecessary pressure and build latitude for being more relaxed and easygoing.

## Make a Concerted Effort to Learn More About Others and Embrace New Experiences

You cannot increase tolerance by simply hoping to have more. Yes, it does start with an earnest desire. But that desire must be followed up with action. Take the time to read about various people, cultures, and places. The history of nationalities can be quite telling and help you to develop a genuine understanding of their unique human experiences. The History Channel is a great place to explore this kind of knowledge (i.e., an auxiliary source of information and insight). In addition, where possible, travel and directly experience other people and cultures up close. Eat their food, navigate their environment, respect their laws, and learn to speak their languages.

Increasing tolerance, however, is not simply about the human aspect. Exposing yourself to new ideas also is part of the learning. Learning about a variety of ways of thinking and negotiating the world are also critical to developing tolerance on a grand scale. Open your mind, heart, and soul to the possibilities that it represents.

## Self-regulate Because Tolerance Requires It

You have a little voice inside that can help you maintain your composure whenever you feel the urge to speak out of turn or act out. This voice is particularly useful when you are striving to increase tolerance. You will not always agree with someone else's views or the choices they make. Nevertheless, that does not give you a license to be impolite or confront the differences in opinion. Sometimes tolerance is just about quiet contemplation. Tune in and notice when your emotions start to take you where you do not want to be. Trust that inner voice to get you out of an unpleasant or antagonistic state.

Resist the urge to judge and condemn people—they have a right to own their thinking and behavior, just as you do. "Live and let live" should be your guiding mantra.

## Practice Exercising Tolerance Daily

You can learn to harness this important trait by consciously practicing it a little each day. Start by setting yourself up for success. When you wake up, take a moment to appreciate the diversity in the world and how it enhances who we are as a people, and what we have been able to accomplish as a species. Think about your own unique attributes and outlook on life. Ask yourself how you would feel if others prejudged you and treated you unfairly based on those attributes and ways of thinking. How would it make you feel? Hurt? Rejected? Whatever you might feel is probably what others feel when they are mistreated because of their differences.

Humanizing tolerance helps to create a visceral connection to its purpose. Then, after you leave the comfort of your home, try to be kind, understanding, and respectful of others who are not the same or have different circumstances than you do. The beggar on the street. The office cleaning crew. The store clerk with the thick accent. The woman passing by wearing the hijab. When you begin with tolerance, you end up with gratitude and compassion.

## Assess the Results and Tweak Your Thinking and Behavior as Needed

What did these exercises teach you about being tolerant? Has your stress level decreased? Have you started feeling better about your daily routine? Have you begun to feel more connected to others and more appreciative of their unique differences? Have you self-regulated when you felt like reacting? If so, you know that you are on to something. If not, you may need to take a closer look at how you are negotiating your days and the experiences within them. If you are more reactive than proactive, stop and take a beat. Remind yourself of why it is important to become more tolerant and the influence it will have on your life when you do.

Think about the gift you give to others when you become more tolerant. Change the narrative that you are operating under if it does not encourage tolerance, then govern your behavior accordingly. Remember, tolerance is not just an idea that resides in the deep recesses of your mind, it is a way of being.

## Journal Questions

1. Do you usually have difficulty exercising tolerance? Explain.
2. What are some key ways to self-regulate while striving to become more tolerant?
3. Name three ways that you can increase tolerance in your daily routine.
4. How did this principle help you better understand your role as a leader? How will its mastery enable you to cultivate greater effectiveness?
5. How will you use the preceding strategies to advance your commitment to cultivating tolerance?

## Leadership Challenge

Select one area in your personal or professional life where you are having a difficult time exercising tolerance. Write out three reasons for increasing tolerance in this area, as well as three strategies for achieving it. After implementing each strategy, assess whether you have become more tolerant or need to spend more time developing this area.

## Note

1. Livermore, D. A. (2015). Leading With Cultural Intelligence: The New Secret to Success. New York: American Management Association.

# 30

# Create a Vision that Inspires

*The foundation of competent leadership is a compelling vision that inspires commitment to a higher purpose and spurs others to action.*

A well-defined vision is essential; it is the roadmap for creating a compelling future in advance. A vision, though, is not created merely for a leader's own sake; it must also be shared by the individual members of the organization. A "shared vision" is one that requires individuals within an organization to synchronize their efforts to achieve a common goal. Without such a vision, there is no reason for people to follow a leader. To get buy-in, a leader must create a "binding force" that cultivates commitment to a higher purpose and spurs others to action; that "binding force" is a vision that inspires.

The existence of a compelling vision is not the be-all and end-all, though. Leaders must also communicate their visions enthusiastically to successfully win commitment and to inspire others to act. Leaders must have passion, but they also must be able to convey the big picture in a way that resonates with others. A clear vision helps an organization to orient itself toward the future and to build momentum around a creative narrative. The narrative varies depending on the mission and the culture of the organization, but the passion behind the narrative is a feature common to all of them.

Leaders should spend a fair amount of time envisioning the future to create it, but they do not have to do it alone. By soliciting input from others who can provide context and direction, leaders can pull the best ideas together to form a coherent plan for the future. Being a good listener and having a genuine interest in the ideas of others help to fuel this effort. Leaders who fail to win the support of the people find it difficult to move their vision forward. A vision without the support of the people perishes rapidly. Inevitably key

© The Author(s) 2018
K. Mariama-Arthur, *Poised for Excellence*, DOI 10.1007/978-3-319-64574-2_30

details will fall through the cracks. Important projects may only receive mediocre efforts, or worse, none at all. This, however, is what happens when a single ship sails to sea for battle. Although a leader may be competent and energetic, he or she can never fully realize the dream without enlisting true commitment from others.

The growth and direction of any organization is rooted in its vision of success. Take Amazon's extraordinary expansion over the past decade, for example. As the world's largest online shopping retailer, it has transformed the way the world interacts with the retail marketplace. While it began only selling books in its infancy, it has expanded to selling nearly everything under the sun. Its trajectory is due, in large part, to the extraordinary vision of its CEO, Jeff Bezos. He wanted to expand the company's legacy beyond its humble beginnings and was motivated by the possibilities. He, like many other successful leaders spearheading dynamic organizations, understood early on that change is a constant variable and the future is whatever *you* want it to be. He knew that the future could be created in advance through a vision that inspires.

Not surprisingly, though, a compelling vision also helps an organization to stay on track. In the beginning, passion may be strong and a desire to achieve common goals may win the day. Then something happens. A major organization-wide scandal, layoffs, or the leader loses credibility. Then, a formerly committed base is seemingly worn down by attrition. Whatever the source of the frustration, and when all else fails, it is that all-but-forgotten vision that can bring everyone back to ground zero. Reviewing it can remind people of their "why" and provide a sense of renewed purpose. It can also lessen antagonism and speed healing when the culture has started to crumble from the inside out. It is a sweet balm in times of chaos that encourages the collective to cling to strengths and commonalities, rather than frailties and differences.

The most effective leaders create a vision that inspires as the hallmark of their standout administrations. They know that a comprehensive blueprint, followed by strategic execution, is essential to making an organization's dreams a reality. Therefore, they begin with the end in mind. In creating their vision, they consider the goals of the organization and develop a thoughtful plan of action to bring them into fruition. They use ethos to bind purpose, inspire commitment, and energize the hearts and minds of the people. What they know for sure is that without a compelling vision that inspires, there is no impetus for forward movement. Thus, they anchor themselves and the organizations they serve, to a greater purpose that is indelibly etched in the soul of their vision.

Elon Musk, CEO of SpaceX and Tesla Motors, is an innovative leader who has revolutionized entire industries with his out-of-the-box thinking and willingness to take big risks to win even bigger.[1] His vision for the future has always been inspiring, multifaceted and, to some, even a bit outrageous. Nevertheless, he has captured the attention of the masses because his vision is so compelling; it has galvanized the world to see things differently and imagine new possibilities. One obvious reason is that his ideas bear sizable fruit. When both of his companies faced bankruptcy in 2008 and Musk was forced to decide between allocating his remaining funds between them or focusing on just one. He felt compelled to support both the companies. Not surprisingly, the risk paid off.

In mid 2017, Tesla trumped both Ford and General Motors with gross profit margins well over 20 percent, while SpaceX was one of two companies chosen by NASA to develop the next generation of systems to take U.S. astronauts to the International Space Station. There is little doubt that his winning streak will continue well into the foreseeable future. Musk also believes that driverless cars will be on the scene sooner than we think and has even considered building a network of tunnels under major cities in America to address the congestion caused by heavy traffic. Even though his ideas may seem to be incredulous to some, Musk is a visionary and his leadership has inspired the new generation of out-of-the-box thinkers and doers, too. Without a doubt, Musk's success illustrates why having a vision that inspires is essential to effective leadership, regardless of industry or expertise.

# Core Strategies

The strategies outlined in the following sections offer guidance for cultivating your skill and insight in creating a compelling vision for the future. They are distilled from the lessons I have learned from exceptional leaders across various industries.

## Determine What Is at Stake

To create a compelling vision, a leader must first determine what is at stake. That means understanding the goals of the organization, who the stakeholders are, and what kinds of shifts (including benefits or harm) could result once those goals are achieved or not. To competently handle this question, start with a broad brush. Categorize goals as aspirational, feasible, and those that are low-hanging fruit. Then, distill them down to the granular level. Decide what matters the most, the finer points. Any nuance impervious to being finessed must be prioritized because it can make or break an organization. Remember that the purpose, or "why," guides this process. When the "why" is compelling, everything else usually falls into place. Make sure that you are clear on yours as you conduct your analysis.

## Crystallize Your Vision

Once you know what is at stake, you need to make your vision plain. Do not use vague language to describe what you would like to see evolve. Be specific. How does it look, taste, and smell? Who should be in charge? Are there any things that need to change? If so, should those changes be wholesale or incremental? What does the ideal culture look like? How should employee performance be rewarded? How about bad behavior? Successes? Also, what specific things about this organization make your vision particularly compelling? Make sure it is not generic. Speak exclusively to the heart of this organization. Lastly, your vision must be so clear that anyone in your organization can easily articulate it. After all, it is their compass, too.

## Develop Objectives

Once you know exactly what your vision is, you must develop objectives to carry it out. Create at least five core objectives that support your vision. Make sure that they are robust and also support your organization's mission. Put them side by side and notice any parallels. Write down the ways in which they complement each other. In addition, make sure the objectives are executed according to a specific deadline; they must be feasible. So, set up specific deadlines at 3-, 6-, and 12-month intervals (longer where necessary). Remember that the goal is to bring them into fruition. Finally, be sure to delegate. The collective must also bear responsibility for bringing the vision into focus.

## Develop a Strategic Plan

Once you have the five key objectives in place, you must develop a strategy to help you achieve them. Do not confuse objectives with strategies. Objectives are the outcomes you want to achieve; strategies are the methods used to achieve them. At this stage, you should be describing a path that includes detailed steps about how to get to an endpoint; this is not a surplus declaration of what you hope to achieve. You should have at least three strategies for every objective. Make sure that the strategies vary in form and difficulty. You want low-hanging fruit, but you also need to challenge yourself and your team to stretch in the process. Remember that your strategies must be calculated to achieve results, not be merely perfunctory measures.

## Execute

Once you have created your strategies, you need to put them into action. A plan may look great on paper, but unless it is executed, you can never be quite sure of its efficacy. Try out a few strategies and then determine which are providing the best return. Do you see your vision coming into focus based on these strategies? If so, determine why; you will want to repeat whatever worked. If not, determine why not. In any case, review what you have done and assess the preliminary results. In your review, you may discover that you were "right on the money," that you need to tweak some of your strategies, or that you must abandon some altogether. Remain flexible during this process. The fact that you are putting your plan into action is the most important point.

## Journal Questions

1. Describe your leadership vision in the context of your organizational mission.
2. List the top three outcomes you seek to accomplish as a forward-thinking leader within your organization.
3. Which strategies have you outlined that will help you to execute your vision?
4. How did this principle help you better understand your role as a leader? How will its mastery enable you to cultivate greater effectiveness?
5. How will you use the preceding strategies to advance your commitment to creating a compelling vision for the future?

## Leadership Challenge

Create a "vision board" for one of your current leadership goals. What kind of activities should it include? What is the timeline for completion? Be creative and have fun with it. Once completed, frame it and hang it on your office wall. You may find greater inspiration for achieving your goals if you can see them every day.

## Note

1. The Henry Ford. (n.d.). Elin Musk: Founder PayPal, SpaceX, Tesla Motors & Solar City. *The Henry Ford*. Retrieved February 16, 2017 from https://www.thehenryford.org/explore/stories-of-innovation/visionaries/elon-musk/.

# Part IV

**Principles that Promote Leadership Excellence Through Fundamental Calls to Action**

# 31

# Delegate!

*Although leaders may be capable of juggling a mountain of various tasks, delegating some is always a better choice. Leaders who embrace this principle are more efficient and effective at every stage of their leadership activities.*

Leaders strive for excellence by working diligently to achieve their expansive visions; however, their can-do attitude often leads them to bite off more than they can chew. Although taking the initiative is always important, one cannot go too far, or too fast, without delegating. When leaders fail to delegate, they keep their noses to the grindstone and take on the "world" and the enormity of its burdens without any support. They add unnecessary stress to their lives and risk burnout. Additionally, they rob others of the opportunity to learn, grow, and move up the professional ladder.

Delegating can be difficult because it means letting go and trusting others to do the work based on your ironclad standards, which can be difficult for a leader at times. Nonetheless, letting go is necessary to orchestrate a vision that requires the input of a myriad of actors to execute. Delegating does not mean second-guessing but giving others the autonomy they need to function and achieve the collective goal. It also means knowing what should be delegated and what should not. Making the wrong decision about which tasks should be delegated can result in disaster.

When tasks are assigned inappropriately, things go awry: Projects require overhauling, clients fall off rosters, and money is wasted. On the flip side, a deluge of undelegated, nonessential tasks splattered across leaders' desks amount to an albatross around their neck. Most times these outcomes can be avoided if the right tasks are simply delegated appropriately.

© The Author(s) 2018
K. Mariama-Arthur, *Poised for Excellence*, DOI 10.1007/978-3-319-64574-2_31

Of course, letting go does not mean stepping away completely. That would be reckless, or at the very least, negligent. And no leaders want to be derelict in their duty. It is important for leaders to hold their team accountable to ensure that the work is done well even after it has been delegated. Although focusing on accountability should not result in micromanaging, a good leader keeps an ear to the ground to make sure things are going smoothly and to see whether any adjustments need to be made. After assigning tasks, a system of checkpoints and deadlines should be established. This even helps those performing the tasks to successfully see them from start to finish. Trust must be balanced with prudence.

The benefits of delegating are many. Not only does it lighten a leader's workload, but also helps employees develop their abilities, which increases morale and self-esteem. Besides, it teaches the "next generation" of employees about leadership. Even though new hires and emerging leaders start with basic tasks, they reap the benefits of amassing new and varied professional experiences as they continue to expand their reach. They can use these skills and experiences later in their careers, as well as share the importance of delegating with others along the way. When practiced throughout the workplace, delegating can create a cooperative culture that prides itself on teamwork and the effective allocation of human capital resources.

Gratitude is an essential element of delegating. Acknowledging good work and rewarding effort ensure that the members of your team will stay committed and motivated when the next project rolls around. One way to reward excellence is to increase responsibility in the future or, perhaps when appropriate, even offer a promotion. A financial bonus is also a great way to recognize a job well done. Conversely, if the work was done unsatisfactorily, a leader should offer honest and useful feedback to help an employee improve performance in the future. Even though best efforts do not always result in the desired outcome, that should not discourage delegating whenever appropriate. Again, when leaders attempt to do all the work themselves, they place unnecessary burdens on themselves and put their projects in jeopardy. While it is true that delegating may not always be easy or executed with perfect results, it is a critical component of good governance that cannot be ignored.

Leaders who dismiss the necessity of delegating soon discover where they went wrong. When the ego is at play, leaders will proudly carry the weight of the world on their shoulders. While grappling with adversity, they may still attempt to tackle tasks solo, even if the most critical things do not get done, or done well. This can put a leader in a precarious situation that raises the specter of their competence and effectiveness. It can also cause added mental, emotional, and physical strain, resulting in health issues that can take a toll on their overall performance. Additionally, when there is no team assembled to execute tasks collaboratively, it can result in a daunting backlog that can wreak havoc on the integrity of the organization rather quickly.

The most effective leaders delegate because they know that maximizing resources is critical. They have no interest in taking on excess tasks gratuitously. They know that such choices almost always result in misery and regret. They celebrate diversity of expertise and appreciate how the power of focused synergies can enhance a project's outcome. They assemble "dream" teams and create masterminds to move projects forward expeditiously. No matter how bright or talented a person may be, vast and divergent responsibilities are often best managed among by a team of competent individuals who can work together to bring a vision into fruition. By identifying the right members for the team and assigning specific tasks based on their experience, expertise, and enthusiasm, leaders can delegate with dexterity and set even the most challenging projects up for extraordinary success.

I once worked with a team of experts on a high-profile event in a major metropolitan city. When we started, there were about 10 of us. By the time we got into the thick of it, the once whale of a group had been whittled down to about half that size. I vividly remember being about two months out from D-day and feeling the sting of overwhelm wash over me. I knew we could have really done the event justice with more time, but there was not any. We were crunched for the little time we had and our backs were up against the wall. Individually and collectively, we knew that we would need to reorient ourselves and redelegate duties, or lose face, income, and more. As one of the leaders within the group, I felt the need to step up to the plate and do more, even though I knew I was incapable of doing it all.

I realized that each of us could leverage our distinct skillsets to maximize results. In addition, I worked with each person to delegate additional tasks because, well, we were limited in capacity. We also reached outside the team to delegate some additional duties leading up to the event as well as on the day of it. It was hard work anyway, but it was made more difficult by the lack of available support. By the time the event rolled around, we were all mentally and emotionally exhausted. In the end, however, everything came to fruition in the best way that it could, although not perfectly. By effectively delegating during crunch time, we cut our losses exponentially and learned a great deal that could be used toward future collaborations and applied to brand-new opportunities to delegate.

# Core Strategies

The strategies outlined in the following sections offer guidance for cultivating your skill and insight in delegating. They are distilled from the lessons I have learned from exceptional leaders across various industries.

## Identify Potential Candidates

When deciding to whom you should delegate tasks, first take a hard look at those with above average abilities and top performers. They are all uniquely positioned to do good work, your job is to determine which ones are the best fit. If the task provides an opportunity to pursue an advanced leadership role, especially in the context of succession planning, it is probably best reserved for someone with high potential. On the other hand, if you simply need to complete a project with above-average results by leveraging the acumen of someone with a proven track record, you likely will assign it to a high performer.

There also may be other available employees who do not fit into either category, but whom you should still consider. Do not overlook anyone who may be able to add value to the project and who might benefit from the opportunity to improve his or her skillset and to gain experience. Additionally, if assembling a team may be necessary, consider how to best compile the team based on synergies and compatibility.

## Delegate!

Once you have identified potential candidates or in some cases an entire team, determine exactly how their expertise and experience match up to the various tasks at hand. Then take a good look at your deadlines, key benchmarks, and the scope of the duties to be shared. If you know someone is a great writer but obsesses over every word and would take three days to do what another teammate could do with excellence in only a day, choose the latter to perform the literary aspects of the project. Practical considerations must factor into every decision to delegate.

Once you have preassigned everyone to a specific task and given them a deadline, there is nothing left to do but delegate. Make sure, however, that before you send your team off to the races, you provide clear guidance on expectations, including deadlines and protocols, and how deliverables should be presented. There is nothing worse than having someone fail the expectations because of incomplete or ambiguous instructions.

## Actively Seek Out Opportunities to Empower the Team

Just because you have delegated the work, your job is not done yet. Look for regular opportunities to inspire the team to innovate and reach its goals, which will keep them focused and enthusiastic about their work. Rewarding the team at key benchmarks may be one idea. Another may be helping them leverage pivotal resources—for example, a certain technology to deliver cutting-edge results. If left to their own devices, energy and excitement can become stumbling blocks even for the most committed team members.

In addition, when you decide to praise someone, make sure you pull that person aside and explain exactly why you think he or she is doing well. Be specific in your accolades, but also underscore the importance of the person's role in completing the entire project. If you notice someone struggling, encourage him or her to find the motivation to continue and even help to modify the approach, if necessary.

## Evaluate Periodically and Offer Guidance

All collaborators need regular feedback, so conduct performance reviews at routine intervals. Offer honest, constructive feedback and explain how individual contributions are being incorporated into the grand scheme. Describing how the landscape architect's work contributes to comprehensive aesthetics, as well as advising on what reports to share with engineers at specific benchmarks, is relevant to understanding big picture dynamics.

Providing this kind of direction helps everyone better understand how to execute their responsibilities and, at the same time, allows you to take any steps necessary to correct mistakes and help them to forge ahead. The overall communication should be regular, open, and honest. There are fewer misunderstandings and less opportunities for bad habits to develop and persist if everyone receives ongoing feedback and appropriate guidance.

## Debrief After the Project Has Been Delivered

Even after you have given the charge and evaluated everyone's progress over the lifespan of the project, there is still a need to debrief once the project has been fully completed. Going over the process from start to finish is important to understand whether any substantive details or more efficient ways were overlooked. It is also important for leaders to receive feedback on their role to learn how to improve on delegating in the future.

This is the perfect time for every team member to receive more comprehensive feedback as well as to provide input and ask probing questions to determine the best ways to proceed during future collaborations. Make sure that someone is assigned the role of "scribe" and keeps a record of what transpires during the session. Committing the insights to paper and making them available for future reference is to everyone's advantage.

## Journal Questions

1. What is the value in delegating tasks to others?
2. How do you decide to whom you should delegate specific duties?
3. Have you ever been in a situation when you should have delegated tasks to others but failed to do so? What happened, and looking back, what specifically could you have done differently?
4. How did this principle help you better understand your role as a leader? How will its mastery enable you to cultivate greater effectiveness?
5. How will you use the preceding strategies to advance your commitment to delegating?

## Leadership Challenge

Identify two emerging leaders to mentor over the next three to six months. Help each to craft three specific performance outcomes for the mentoring relationship. Delegate two specific duties that could help them stretch and that would alleviate a burden on your current workload. Meet each mentee face-to-face once a month and email once a week. Track each person's progress individually and offer feedback. At the end of the selected time frame, evaluate how you have helped each emerging leader grow his or her leadership acumen? How did delegating impact your ability to govern?

# 32

# Master Effective Decision Making

*Good decisions require conscious thinking, conviction, and clarity of purpose, followed by prompt and resolute action.*

Decision making is a dynamic process involving the organization and analysis of infinite variables. It also involves taking a specific, timely course of action to achieve a particular outcome. If either of the steps are excluded from the process, it becomes difficult, if not impossible, to arrive at a sound decision or the desired result. Effective leaders learn how to traverse the process to improve their chances of success. They know that no matter what, good decisions are built on a rational process that impacts the efficacy of every endeavor. Therefore, they take the process seriously.

A "decision" represents change at a crossroads. Too often people make decisions based on whims, without fully considering what is at stake. They respond to what is urgent and take shortcuts. Such ill-informed choices can be devastating and, in some cases, even life altering. And the effects of a bad decision can easily spill over into your personal and professional circumstances. Although it is true that some decisions must be made in haste, all available options must still be considered seriously, even if only briefly, before adopting a determinative course of action. Those who fail to look before they leap are bound to feel great regret as they fall.

Even though leaders have the capacity to influence their own decisions, they also influence the decision-making processes of the organizations they serve. As the *Harvard Business Review* notes: "A company's value is [seen as] no more (and no less) than the sum of the decisions that it makes and executes."[1] Leaders who master the steps of decision making add real value to their organizations. That mastery has a butterfly effect that impacts culture, performance,

© The Author(s) 2018
K. Mariama-Arthur, *Poised for Excellence*, DOI 10.1007/978-3-319-64574-2_32

and even scalability. Decisions also establish a precedent, for better or for worse. Thus, learning to make prudent decisions is imperative for the person at the helm, especially since the results of their decisions will no doubt reverberate throughout the organization and impact individuals and processes in ways that are often unexpected.

Good decision making means taking a few steps back to consider how actions might affect lives. Most times that means being altruistic. Though it also means determining which paradigms are relevant and which options might have the greatest impact on those individuals who are most vulnerable to change, as well as on existing processes altered, any of these could potentially impact the organization's structure and flow. When leaders make decisions, they cut off all other possibilities, at least for the time being. Hence, they must think through the options prudently before reaching a final decision. More often than not, once you press "play," you must endure the melody that rings out, even when it is off key. Smart leaders know it is always better to make a well-reasoned decision, than to live with unintended consequences and regret.

A decision is meaningless unless followed by concrete action. It cannot be just any action, though. It must be purposeful, strategic and calculated to achieve the maximum impact. To execute a decision effectively, leaders first consult with themselves to conduct an independent examination of the facts and to brainstorm and consider how possible courses of action might yield certain results. However, they do not always stop there. Oftentimes, they solicit the advice and support of qualified experts who understand the importance of the decision, who are familiar with the nuances of a particular industry, and who can help achieve the best results. Whether they arrive at a decision alone, or with the help of others, they move forward and memorialize it by taking decisive action.

Once a decision has been made and specific action taken, a leader takes responsibility for the consequences, whatever they might be. They also recognize that with responsibility comes accountability. Saving face is not always possible and ego is not a badge that leaders wear well. Sometimes well-conceived decisions yield unwanted results. Even the best-laid plans can sometimes go awry. However, when a plan falls short, it may be time to head back to the drawing board to reexamine assumptions and strategies. There is almost always something that has been overlooked or that can be revised. Notwithstanding errors of judgment or unforeseen circumstances, a leader must get back out there and make more decisions, free from the burden of uncertainty. They do so by owning up to their decisions and then facing the unpredictable terrain with fortitude and a renewed perspective.

The most effective leaders take stock in making well-reasoned and well-executed decisions. They know that facing the unknown and navigating inherent challenges with courage and determination are necessary aspects of the overall process. Moreover, they know that being on the other side of an effective decision is one of the best places to be. That said, they do the groundwork and make the necessary adjustments to assure that their decisions are not arbitrary or capricious, but grounded in good thinking, clarity of purpose, and unbridled conviction.

Even though Napoléon Bonaparte is widely considered one of history's most revered and shrewd military tacticians, his decision to invade Russia in 1812 demonstrated the consequences of a leader's failure to master the decision-making process.[2] When Czar Alexander I stopped complying with the Continental System embargo because of its impact on Russian trade, Napoléon reacted and decided to invade Russia as retribution. That, however, was a knee-jerk decision and in making it in haste, he failed to establish a clear understanding of the overall landscape—that is, the *Grande Armée's* capacity to deal with what the Russian army had in store, and the variables at stake in the star-crossed conflict.

Napoléon's leadership style, including ignoring critical intelligence, further exacerbated the decision-making process. When his army arrived in Moscow, the city was deserted. There was no food and no supplies. There was not a single human to confront and wage war with. Fires were set to further sabotage any potential plans to pursue or pillage. In addition, Russia's bitter cold winter, a lack of shelter, and consummate starvation signaled the beginning of the end of this hapless invasion. The result was an unfortunate large-scale loss that nearly decimated the entire *Grand Armée* and eventually forced Napoléon into exile. His decision to invade Russia and the consequences that ensured, represent one of the most egregious examples of decision making gone wrong. It is one that should remind every leader of why making informed decisions is so crucial and why mastering the process is a nonnegotiable component of effective leadership.

## Core Strategies

The strategies outlined in the following sections offer guidance for cultivating your skill and insight in making effective decisions. They are distilled from the lessons I have learned from exceptional leaders across various industries.

## Do Your Research

Researching the lay of the land is critical to good decision making. What kind of information do you need to make the best decision possible? Is it scholarly research? Quantitative or qualitative analysis? Interviews? Whatever it is, gather it. Consider examining case studies or reviewing lessons learned from previous experiences. Whatever you need, make sure that you have the required resources at your disposal when you are ready to evaluate them. Comprehensive resources make for a competent and more complete view of the landscape. Relying on inadequate or irrelevant sources will only make for poor decisions. In addition, remember that where necessary, your research strategy should also include advice from experts who may bring unique perspectives and important evidence to the fore. This is particularly relevant when traversing unfamiliar territory.

## Assess the Attendant Risks

Before you make any decisions, assess the risks involved. The benefits may be obvious, but uncovering risks usually requires a closer examination. Do not skim the surface or assume the risks will be inconsequential. Instead, start by compiling a list of potential problems. Ask what you could stand to lose by moving forward. Play the devil's advocate, and then reexamine your research. Also review past decisions that you or your peers have made. Compare and contrast the risks in each instance. By studying the mistakes of the past and trying to determine how they could have been avoided, you can better understand potential risks in the current decision. Moreover, by assessing the attendant risks, you will be less likely to fall into traps that haste or other faulty decision-making mechanisms often produce.

## Brainstorm Available Options

Once you have pored over the potential risks, you must also consider the potential benefits of making the decision. After all, if there are none, it probably is not the best decision for you. Make a list of at least 5 to 10 reasons why you or the organization stands to benefit from the current decision. This will provide the most compelling rationale for making the decision. To understand the best way forward, you must then consider all available options. This is ultimately about strategy, so, do not self-censor. It is better to allow free-flowing thought to guide the process. You can always edit to a nub later. Make a list of at least 10 possible options. Describe them fully and then rank them according to plausibility. Eliminate the bottom half of the list, then determine the top five best options. Have a roundtable vote and distill the list down to the top three. Finally, pick one. This is more than likely the best choice on the list.

## Develop a Straightforward Strategy for Execution

Once you decide which option is the best, you must develop a straightforward strategy for execution. It should be comprehensive and include key details from start to finish, including a contingency plan for addressing unforeseen challenges. No matter how solid a plan you develop though, know that adversity can strike at a moment's notice. Being prepared with an alternative strategy is your best defense against floundering in the midst of uncertainty. Hence, "tie your camel," so to speak. Then, evaluate the respective strategies against the past performance of others who were similarly situated. Even though the final product should be airtight, it also should leave room for improvement or a course correction should you discover new information that might impact the outcome. Being nimble is also a core component of executing a sound strategy.

## Move Forward Decisively

A strategy is just words on paper without action to move it forward. Fear can paralyze even the most capable decision makers, so make sure you do not let it prevent you from acting. If preliminary steps are required prior to execution, address those in advance, making sure you have allocated sufficient time and resources to accomplish them. Adequate planning is a critical part of any execution strategy. You may even need to consult with others to ensure that the steps you are taking are sensible, given the outcome you seek. Once you have those details squared away, step forward decisively. You are now in the arena, and fighting to realize your primary objective, so maneuvering with conviction should be the only option.

## Journal Questions

1. Describe your internal decision-making process and how it assists you in arriving at important decisions.
2. In your experience, which factors make decision making difficult?
3. Are you risk-averse? Explain.
4. How did this principle help better understand your role as a leader? How will its mastery enable you to cultivate greater effectiveness?
5. How will you use the preceding strategies to advance your commitment to taking decisive action?

## Leadership Challenge

Identify one critical area of indecision currently impacting your life. Write down the top three reasons why you have not taken action. Next, write down three steps you will take immediately to move the decision forward. After taking them, write a letter to yourself about how quickly you were able to end the stagnation and how you can use these steps in the future when you are plagued by indecision.

## Notes

1. Blenko, M.W., Mankins, M. & Rogers, P. (2010 June). The Decision-Driven Organization. *Harvard Business Review* 88(3). Retrieved February 20, 2017 from https://hbr.org/2010/06/the-decision-driven-organization.
2. Asprey, R. B. (2000). The rise of Napoleon Bonaparte. New York: Basic Books.

# 33

## Pull Up Weeds By Their Roots

*A cursory review of a problem is not likely to lead to a solution. Because leaders are problem solvers, they take a deep dive to find the sources of their problems and work diligently to solve them.*

Problems are like weeds in a garden. They often crop up when we least expect them, and when they do, they have the potential to disorient our focus and frustrate our goals. If not properly addressed, they can easily choke out growth. Walking the path of least resistance does not help you with your weed problem. Unfortunately, it will only intensify it. To effectively tackle most problems, indeed, for all intents and purposes, you need to get on your "hands and knees" and dig for the root causes.

Sitting idly by as even the most mundane issues arise over the course of the day can prove troublesome. It is important to attend to those surface-level difficulties because they can quickly become a time sink and develop into more complex issues, if not taken care of expeditiously. Sometimes, though, when a leader solves one problem, he or she is then immediately confronted with another. These issues are often symptoms of more systemic problems—those with multiple layers that taint an overall organization, process, or system at its foundation and manifest like a virus throughout it. Consider, for example, the recent uptick in public outrage against police brutality and "lawlessness" in the United States. Fueled by a strong public policy against extrajudicial conduct, these concerns have emboldened the citizenry to expose the putative issues of implicit bias, institutional racism, and the abuse of authority that seem to rage at the department's core. This prominent example reinforces the idea that no organization or institution can afford to ignore root causes, especially when its integrity, competency, influence, and overall leadership success are at stake.

© The Author(s) 2018
K. Mariama-Arthur, *Poised for Excellence*, DOI 10.1007/978-3-319-64574-2_33

Because root causes usually are buried deep inside institutions, leaders must make a concerted effort to unearth them. The discovery process almost always starts with being observant and facing glaring truths, followed by a series of probing questions.

Why do these problems exist? When did they start? What happens if we do not solve them? How do we begin solving them? Is time of the essence? Who can I ask for help? Questions are asked and interviews are conducted until preliminary answers are found. However, a subsequent round of questions and interviews is usually necessary to help uncover any relevant information that may have been missed. Coordinating more in-depth research is often the next logical step, followed by qualitative and quantitative analyses. Getting to root causes clearly requires significant time and energy; but the most successful leaders readily commit to both. Consequently, they avoid having to put out persistent fires caused by conducting surface-level reviews and instituting prophylactic measures meant to "patch up" chronic issues.

The discovery process is so rigorous because important details often fall through the cracks and can be obscured by what appears to be well-manicured at first glance. Routine assessments help leaders to stay on top of potential issues and also place them in the best position to effectuate resolve when real problems arise. In addition, keeping meticulous records, performing annual and bi-annual inspections, purges, and other deep-dive analyses all ensure that challenges looming in the distance—or festering at the surface—can be dealt with effectively, or in some cases, kept entirely at bay. A proactive mindset helps to keep problems from reaching acute states due to negligence, laziness, or even the all-too-common antagonist, fear.

Smart leaders know that discovering root causes requires all hands on deck. Even the most dedicated, take-charge personalities—those who play full out and make it their business to systematically eradicate uncertainty—still require the assistance of key players to properly arrive at a satisfactory solution. While they understand the importance of doing their part to move the process along, smart leaders also value delegating. They know that spinning their wheels rarely results in resolution. Therefore, they pool their resources and redistribute duties among stakeholders to get things done efficiently. And once root causes are discovered, the parties can work together to devise feasible options, not only for solving problems currently on the table, but for addressing future problems as well.

Fatigue and bias often interfere with a leader's ability to arrive at root causes. Concluding that all avenues of approach have been exhausted—*because the individual is exhausted*—often results in prematurely suspending efforts to dig deeper or, alternatively, in postponing such efforts for a "later date." By the same token, when certain biases creep in to influence judgment and result in flawed thinking and in miscalculations, it becomes difficult to see the forest for the trees. In either case, there are always numerous, unexplored opportunities to rethink the process and uncover blind spots that mar one's ability to parse through the weeds. Leaders do well to enlarge the possibilities and assess where they went wrong. And, when they do, they minimize self-imposed crises and other situations requiring the compulsory depletion of financial, administrative, and other valuable resources. They also retain greater peace of mind, create a more congenial workplace environment, and secure the bottom line, all of which inures to their benefit.

The most effective leaders take seriously their roles in solving problems at the roots. They appreciate the fact that not all challenges are completely avoidable, so they pivot and adapt when necessary. They also know that given the diversity of tasks they juggle on a regular basis, getting caught in the crosshairs of an otherwise avoidable crisis—a situation that could have easily been averted by pulling up weeds by the roots—is a definite no-no. Hence they resist the urge to knuckle under when threats arise. Instead of ignoring the threats, covering them up, or skimming the surface of issues, the most effective leaders steady their minds and then get to work. They boldly navigate the mazelike paths that lead to risk, uncertainty, and the most menacing of challenges. Then, undeterred, they prepare for battle until the war against each is successfully waged.

I worked with a CEO who was having a difficult time understanding why he was experiencing trouble with stakeholders on a current project. At first glance, he thought that the issue stemmed from a misunderstanding about the workflow, but after digging a bit deeper he realized that the problem was more systemic and required an overhaul of the structure and internal policies to solve it. Although he was initially focused only on the surface issues, he soon recognized that a superficial review would yield only superficial results. He needed to get to the bottom of the situation but was unprepared to take on the work necessary to achieve it.

What this CEO found was that the extra bit of research, questions, and analysis were not as cumbersome as he imagined. More than that, though, he found that the additional efforts were critical in addressing the underlying issues and getting to the real source of the problems. Without getting to the root causes, he still would have been hovering around the surface and been uncertain about where the most problematic issues were. As a result of taking a "deep dive," he was able to successfully transform policies, overhaul his business structure, and solve the underlying problems with the stakeholders. "Pulling up weeds by the roots" allowed him not merely to complete the project successfully and maintain key relationships, but also to make necessary adjustments that would serve the group prior to the next collaboration.

# Core Strategies

The strategies outlined in the following sections offer guidance for cultivating your skill and insight to become an effective problem solver. They are distilled from the lessons I have learned from exceptional leaders across various industries.

## Take a "Deep Dive"

Begin by tracing surface-level problems down to their roots. While you may begin with "topsoil," stopping there will seldom provide you with the information or the context you need to find resolve. In preparing to take a deep dive, ready your mind for the work that lies ahead. Remember the point of the exercise is to find root causes, so accept that there may be some fits and starts. Investigating several leads before anything turns up is not uncommon. Expect that. As you journey through the maze of details, keep a journal of what you discover. Make note of anything that seems curious. If you come across any interesting insights, chronicle them, and notate any suspicions. Resist assuming that whatever you feel is wrong, or that any detail is irrelevant. Sift through the evidence first before making a determination. Ask a host of questions. When did this issue begin and what triggered it? What were the attendant circumstances? How might you have unknowingly contributed to the problem? Ask tough questions of yourself and other interested parties. Push past superficial data to get to the heart and soul of the matter.

## Brainstorm

Even after finding the source of any issue, your work has truly just begun. You must also brainstorm to determine potential courses of action: You need options when creating a strategy for attack. You need to have options when creating a strategy. Many of those options may be mediocre, some good, and a few great. Your job is to develop the best options so that you can resolve the problem with minimal damage to the organization and the people within it. Create a list of potential options that address specific root causes. While you brainstorm, remember not to self-censure. Let the ideas flow freely. From the most aggressive to the most conservative, just list whatever comes to mind. Consider creating categories where you can list options and aggregate ideas as they come, without interfering with their flow. For example, "Ideas requiring the assistance of third parties" or "Options under 10k". Once the ideas have been distilled, you should walk away from the session with at least three to five valid possibilities.

## Perform a Risk Assessment

After discovering the source of a problem and brainstorming possible solutions, you must also assess the risk involved with each potential course of action. The goal is to develop a course of action that addresses the problems but does not cause more problems than it solves. This is not to say that you should not take risks, but you should know what you are diving into before jumping in headfirst. Determine what is at stake, and what sacrifices you are willing to make, to achieve the results you seek. In performing your risk assessment, also consider the benefits of each potential option. There will be pros and cons associated with each. Your job is to uncover them through careful vetting. Challenge yourself to discover what may not be obvious on its face as you consider each idea. There is no doubt that an artful combination of honesty and creativity will serve you well at this juncture.

## Thoroughly Review Available Options

One you have gathered your options and assessed the risks and benefits involved, you should rank them in order of importance. Decide which ones stay and which ones go. What are the top three and how should they be executed? Take the time to vet each option thoroughly. Scrutinize each one ruthlessly. Do not simply select options that seem the quickest and least painful to resolve. Oftentimes the best way forward may be the most expensive, time-consuming, and most labor-intensive. Do not undermine your success by trying to take the easiest way out. However, if you find that the most feasible option also gives you greater peace of mind because it is cheaper, and takes less time and effort, then so be it. There is no need to put yourself through the wringer for the sake of the rigor. The most important part of your analysis is determining whether the solution you choose will effectively solve the problem at hand. If it does, you are clearly batting a thousand. So choose it and abandon the rest.

## Take Decisive Action

After you have selected the best option, you must write out a step-by-step plan of execution, detailing how you will proceed. Remember that a good decision is only good if there is follow-through and execution. Your plan of action must include a sound strategy along with specific tactics that will help you achieve the desired outcome. If you "decide" to buy a new home, but have not determined your budget, saved any money, managed your credit score, researched desirable neighborhoods or properties, you have done yourself no favors in the execution phase. Taking decisive action always seals the deal. Do not procrastinate or overthink. Do not second-guess the decision that you have elevated to the number one spot. Strike with confidence, knowing that you have prepared yourself for this important task and that you are up for the challenge. If you begin to waver, simply revisit your "why" and remember that it was the root cause that brought you here. Then close the gap between your current and future realities by taking decisive action.

## Journal Questions

1. Do you focus on the source of a problem when attempting to solve it? Explain.
2. How do you assess risks and benefits when considering possible solutions to a problem?
3. At what point do you determine how conservative or aggressive your strategy should be when problem-solving?
4. How did this principle help you better understand your role as a leader? How will its mastery enable you to cultivate greater effectiveness?
5. How will you use the preceding strategies to advance your commitment to solving problems at the foundational level?

## Leadership Challenge

Identify a problem that you currently face. Instead of doing a cursory review and trying to quickly dispose of it, take a deep dive. Focus on solving it at the foundational level. First, make a list of five key symptoms of the problem. Next, determine its source by carefully examining how each symptom manifests. What insight did you uncover by probing at the foundation?

# 34

## Say "No" and Own It

*Trying to please everyone is a tried-and-true recipe for disaster. The most effective leaders refuse to vacillate: They say "no" to the people and things that interfere with their ability to maintain peace of mind and to operate with excellence.*

Leaders are ambitious go-getters who welcome new and challenging opportunities with resourcefulness and enthusiasm. They enjoy contributing at a high level and collaborating with others to drive results. Because of their compelling instinct to serve, it is not surprising that they are often called on to share resources and add value to other people's projects. Although serving others is an important aspect of leadership, an incessant desire to please can be detrimental, resulting in guilt, dissatisfaction, and a lack of commitment to one's own mission. And when competing interests surface, acquiescing to outside appeals only makes matters worse.

To avoid falling into the people-pleasing trap, leaders must be selective about their commitments and determined about devoting resources to only the highest priorities. Clarity about their responsibilities and their capacity to extend finite resources beyond their immediate scope can determine the success or failure of an endeavor. Without question, success requires being true to one's self. And, being true to one's self requires candor, discipline, and a willingness to accept that others may react negatively to what they perceive as rejection incident to the exercise of free will. Anger, disappointment, and resentment are familiar responses to an emphatic "no." However, the most successful leaders learn to say it without equivocation.

Multitasking, a common deception, is another provocation to which leaders must say "no." First, multitasking is a myth. The human brain is programmed to focus on one thing at a time. Despite our futile attempts, our

© The Author(s) 2018
K. Mariama-Arthur, *Poised for Excellence*, DOI 10.1007/978-3-319-64574-2_34

brains are never actually doing two or more things at once. When numerous variables are thrown into the mix, the brain rapidly switches between them, rather than simultaneously processing them. Stringing together competing interests only compromises performance. Attempting to write that scientific memo while taking notes during an unrelated conference call is clearly counterproductive. Each of the two tasks will suffer an unfortunate casualty as a result of the clear lack of focus. A safer bet is to concentrate on a discrete task to move it forward and reduce the likelihood of making needless errors. For these reasons, saying "no" can truly be an excellent way to maximize brain power, as well as overall success. Sometimes, less really is more.

Even though there are plenty of good reasons to collaborate under the right set of circumstances, not every opportunity is worth pursuing. There are equally good reasons why a leader might choose to abstain: A proposal might not be a good fit, it could produce more harm than good, or there may simply be a lack of available resources to contribute. Early vetting always proves valuable and can, at the very least, prevent setbacks that often result from hasty decision making and shortsightedness. There are countless instances of partnerships gone awry because someone failed to do her or his due diligence or to say "no" when they saw the writing on the wall signifying an ill-fitted collaboration.

When leaders fail to say "no" and neglect their own priorities, they almost always face sobering consequences. Missed deadlines, a substandard work product, and harm to stakeholders and the organization at large; all these represent fallout from a leader's inability to say "no." By foreseeing the consequences of their involvement, leaders can avoid many of the negative outcomes associated with invariably deciding on a "yes." Even when the involvement amounts to a "favor," it still requires the same level of analysis. Good intentions often pave the way to unintended consequences and regret. A leader's hapless downfall is no exception.

Although seemingly counterintuitive, saying "no" can simultaneously serve the person or group doing the asking. Although it is true that leaders need to vet opportunities and conserve resources, they also are charged with empowering others to take charge of their own destinies. Leaders facilitate the process by encouraging individuals, teams, and even an entire organization to step up to the plate and take responsibility for their outcomes. As such, saying "no" can inspire greater self-reliance, promote creativity, and strengthen problem-solving skills. This newfound focus can also reenergize an entire project, producing unexpected innovations and potentially more advantageous results.

Leaders who learn to say "no" and own it exercise the freedom to create boundaries and, as a result, enjoy great peace of mind. They refuse to get bogged down in the muck and mire of others' impassioned undertakings, especially because most do not serve the greater good. Instead, they remain focused on their own relevant pursuits and work diligently to carve out time and space to create continued excellence. In the end, they realize that saying "no" can make the biggest difference between success and failure. For their part, they consistently choose success.

The benefits of being a "naysayer" are, without question, invaluable. I, however, learned it the hard way, through trial and error, over the course of my career. There have been numerous times when I mistakenly, albeit enthusiastically, volunteered my time and other resources for projects at the behest of individuals who were within my circle of influence, but whose purposes and missions were misaligned with my own. I justified my involvement by telling myself that I had the right motivations. I wanted to contribute and knew that my efforts inevitably would move the projects forward.

Here is the catch though: In retrospect, I can honestly admit that most of these projects could have easily moved forward successfully without my help. Nevertheless, I lost a little bit of myself each time I devoted my limited resources to the priorities of others. Often winding up with the short end of the stick, most times I had little to show for my efforts. As you might have imagined, my own projects suffered, too. Eventually, I realized that I had to get my priorities straight and learn to say "no" without apologizing if I was going to be successful. Initially trying to apply this newfound thinking felt a bit awkward and even counterintuitive. I am hard wired to serve (*Karima* means "generous"), so I had to work really hard on honing my self-talk. However, in the end, it all worked out. It was an important lesson to learn that has helped me to successfully navigate complex business situations, as well as everyday interpersonal interactions, purposefully and with tact. I only wish I had learned it sooner. Perhaps a lot sooner.

# Core Strategies

The strategies outlined in the following sections offer guidance for cultivating your skill and insight for saying "no." They are distilled from the lessons I have learned from exceptional leaders across various industries.

## Ruthlessly Prioritize Tasks

Being intensely focused on your obligations is the first step to begin the journey toward saying "no." Often, the reason people get distracted is that they do not pay enough attention to the items on their plates. Ruthlessly prioritize your tasks by being clear on deadlines and the substance of the deliverables.

Then, break them down into easily workable components by months, weeks, and even days, whenever applicable. For example, if you have an article due in a month, you may want to first set aside time to conduct relevant research during the current week. Then, create a detailed outline it the second week. Next, consider executing a draft during the third week, and finally editing during the last week.

You do not want to be overwhelmed, so execute tasks in small parts to inspire progress and feelings of accomplishment. Write down deadlines and time blocks where you can see them; they will serve as constant reminders. The most important tasks should, of course, be addressed first and given the most time to complete. The goal is to understand where the demands on your resources lie so that you can better organize your time and address any competing interests. By being proactive, you are in the best position to allocate your resources to where they matter the most.

## Identify and Eliminate Extraneous Activities

Any activity that does not align with your purpose and priorities is extraneous to it. Identify these activities early on so that they can be quickly dismissed. If, for example, you are leading an accounting team and are tasked with isolating actuarial data, make that your sole focus. If someone intervenes, asking you to compile data on crime statistics instead, you will quickly see why such a task might be extraneous. In such instances, you must compare the relevance of the proposed activity to the prevailing purpose. If they are divergent, you must discard the one that takes you off course. The same idea applies to random requests for assistance with unrelated projects or "emergency" interventions that will only serve to distract you. If you have laser-like vision and let nothing get in your way, you can be proactive and successfully identify and eliminate extraneous activities (i.e., "distractions") whenever they arise. This will allow you to devote your time and energy to the most pressing and relevant tasks at hand.

## Resist the Urge to Please Others

At first glance, it may seem natural to want to please others. The desire to be helpful and please others in the process is honorable; there is nothing wrong with doing good for good's sake. Yet, when people-pleasing becomes the leading motivation for your involvement in projects and other undertakings, you will find that resentment is not far behind. Instead of feeling guilty about asserting yourself, resist the "unjustifiable" urge to please others. Even though helping others to achieve their goals may be an important part of leaders' role, doing so to one's own detriment is unacceptable.

People assume that you choose to help them because you believe in their cause. Pandering to egos is disingenuous. If you do not believe in what a person or organization stands for, simply refuse to get involved. Remember that your "brand" is also at stake, and the risk to your reputation may not merit your involvement. Think twice before jumping on the bandwagon for causes that are out of alignment with what you truly believe in. Better for someone to feel momentary disappointment than to damage a brand, waste precious time, and mislead others.

## Avoid Making Unwarranted Apologies

Leaders must avoid making unwarranted apologies after asserting their right to say "no." As stated earlier, not all opportunities are a good fit. Some need to be declined, and when they do, there is no better response than an unequivocal "no." If you are not careful, apologizing can become second nature. You may even find yourself offering apologies in situations that are entirely inappropriate. Moreover, by making unwarranted apologies, you also demonstrate that you will do whatever it takes to please others, even if that means hurting yourself.

The best way to sidestep this behavior is to make well-reasoned decisions and then stick to them. There is no need to be stressed out over imagined reactions to your decision. You almost always are apologizing for no good reason, except for your own guilt. You can overcome it, however, by simply saying "no" and avoid the unnecessary apology in the first place.

## Own It and Move On

Leaders also must resist the urge to ruminate after saying "no." They must own it, be content with it, and move on. Having faith in your decision helps you remove any doubt associated with it. Nonetheless, there are better ways to own your decision than replaying the scenario in your head. Embracing the "why" behind your decision is usually the most helpful strategy because it helps you understand how you arrived at it. It is the motivation behind the decision, which is, of course, even clearer than the decision itself.

Once you have made a true decision, you must cut off any other possibility and move on. Burn the boats, as there is no turning back once you have drawn a hard line in the sand. Leaders who adopt this strategy find it far easier to move past hesitation, negate doubt, and assert themselves with confidence when they need to say "no."

## Journal Questions

1. Identify a time when you have said "no" to a request for your time and resources. Why did you say "no?" Do you feel you made a good decision? Explain.
2. Describe at least three negative consequences resulting from a previous decision to say "yes." How could a "no" have changed the outcomes mentioned earlier?
3. List three different ways that you can say "no" when it is necessary.
4. How did this principle help you better understand your role as a leader? How will its mastery enable you to cultivate greater effectiveness?
5. How will you use the preceding strategies to advance your personal commitment to saying "no" and owning it without apology?

## Leadership Challenge

More than likely, there is no shortage of requests for your time, attention, and other valuable resources. To best prepare yourself to handle these requests, list your current and most compelling priorities for the year. Break them down by their respective deadlines and note the essential resources required to complete each task successfully, and anticipate any periods of intense activity. Keep this information at the top of mind. Practice respectfully declining once a day over the next two weeks. This will help you say "no" when you need to. When you decline, ask yourself how you felt saying "no" and remaining committed to your own priorities. Then, write yourself a short letter explaining the importance of saying "no" when you need to, especially this year. Keep it handy and review it when the requests start to pour in.

# 35

# Distinguish Management from Leadership

*Leadership and management are complementary but distinct skillsets. Leaders must know the difference between the two not only to lead effectively, but also to teach others how to lead and manage with competence.*

Both management and leadership are critical skills for any organization, but they are not identical skills. "Management" is about processes. Managers examine organizational and administrative undertakings, execute procedures, evaluate performance, and enforce deadlines. They also use organizational resources to accomplish key objectives. The goal of management is to produce consistency that leads to quantifiable results. Management is about the development of hard skills and technical expertise; it is about implementing the mandates handed down by others.

"Leadership," on the other hand, focuses on the development of people through influence. Leaders create visions that call people to action. They inspire change and innovate, and they always are looking to the future to make new dreams a reality. Just like managers, leaders can exist anywhere within an organization's hierarchy. Titles do not matter much. However, while most leaders do have titles, titles are not required to effectuate the work: Generating influence is truly its own animal. That said, leadership is about the development of soft skills, challenging the status quo, and finding fresh perspectives. Leaders build relationships and align synergies.

Knowing the difference between the two is critical to the long-term health of any organization. Confusion contributes to serious inefficiencies and a lack of overall effectiveness throughout the organization. When managers do not manage and leaders do not lead, organizations experience a kind of schizophrenia that can have a lasting effect on their culture. A leader understands that an

© The Author(s) 2018
K. Mariama-Arthur, *Poised for Excellence*, DOI 10.1007/978-3-319-64574-2_35

artful combination of both visionary leadership and competent management is necessary to create value and to maintain it. While managers keep the ship's engines running, leaders steer it into the future. Both are essential and each of them must know their purpose and align their behaviors accordingly.

Regardless of the idiosyncrasies inherent in their roles, both leaders and managers must approach them with an overwhelming sense of purpose. Because of these idiosyncrasies, however, each actor's purpose is fundamentally distinct. Nonetheless, that purpose must drive their focus, behavior, and support their capacity to execute the extraordinary goals of their work. Not surprisingly, when leaders are clear on each actor's purpose, they not only execute their own work better, but help others to do the same. Their clarity helps both leaders and managers to effectively build capacity and avoid the common confusion that often thwarts their success. It also helps them to work more collaboratively, lessens adversarial tendencies, and helps them to achieve the overarching goals of the organization. When knowledge and understanding lead the way, both leaders and managers reap remarkable benefits.

Because leaders are driven by a strong desire to move visions forward in the name of guiding change, they must be flexible and willing to navigate uncertainty. A 2013 study by the American Psychological Association found that leaders often operate in dynamic and complex social environments that require them to possess strong perceptive and adaptive abilities in order to make good decisions and be effective.[1] Together, these abilities form the key components of what researchers have termed leadership complexity, "the process by which an individual achieves some degree of fit between his or her behaviors and the new work demands created by the novel and often ill-defined problems resulting from changing and uncertain work situations."[2] Make no mistake, change is a constant variable. Leaders must be equipped with the mindset and skill set that enable them to navigate it with clarity and confidence, even when it presents at a moment's notice and shakes them to the core. Leadership complexity gives them that edge.

Managers, like leaders, are energized by a clear purpose. Unlike leaders, however, they are not necessarily change-oriented. That said, any relevant changes they might make would be programmatic, incremental, and small scale.[3] As award winning business and management thought leader John P. Kotter notes in his seminal work, the early pioneers who invented management, "were trying to produce consistent results on key dimensions expected by customers, stockholders, employees, and other organizational constituencies, despite the complexity caused by large size, modern technologies and geographic dispersions. That has always been, and still is, its primary function."[4] This also suggests a heavy focus on maintaining the status quo to insure the integrity and stability of already established systems, rules, and regulations.

There is very little desire to "upset the apple cart;" in fact, to do so would likely be frowned upon for all the above reasons. To that end, their focused oversight is designed to produce a well-oiled and predictable machine, when executed properly. For them, the inspiration behind their work is simple: Consistency is a constant variable. Managers are catalysts for promoting best practices over innovation, technical expertise over soft skills, and the good decisions made by others, rather than leading the charge themselves.

The most effective leaders make it their business to distinguish leadership from management. While many make the unfortunate mistake of defaulting to pejorative comparisons between the two, smart leaders know that in reality leaders and managers are not rivals. To the contrary, they are the interdependent building blocks of effective organizations everywhere, regardless of industry or expertise. Therefore, they are eager to learn all they can about each of them, inclusive of their similarities and differences. They know that creating expectations in either will be difficult, if not impossible, without first having a fundamental understanding of both. They refuse to rely on outmoded definitions, superficial distinctions, or confusing analogies. Instead, they get down to brass tacks and learn to competently distinguish them.

One of my corporate clients had an executive team that grappled with distinguishing between management and leadership, which got them into a lot of trouble. There was serious confusion about what the objectives of each role were and how to properly execute them. From high churn rates to high turnover rates, poor performance, and lost profits, they were hemorrhaging assets and had no idea how to stop the constant flow. They asked me to work with the team and provide targeted professional development programming. I designed a series of workshops that provided insight on the differences as well as demonstrated how to effectively navigate each of their respective roles.

The workshops introduced fundamental distinctions, analyzed relevant case studies, provided reference materials specific to the company's industry, and encouraged role-play throughout; they all found the materials tremendously valuable. The team realized that the failure to identify and understand the principal differences in roles was the gravamen of their dilemma. It caused tremendous confusion. That confusion caused them to approach their work in the dark—they were unsure who should be doing what and how they should be doing it. It also prevented them from determining which objectives to pursue, as well as developing a relevant game plan for success.

In the end, the clarity and insights executive team gained from the workshops allowed the members to refocus and take on the newly defined roles with confidence. It also helped them to enjoy their work more and fostered camaraderie, which was welcome relief to the blatant resentment and hostility they lived with previously.

# Core Strategies

The strategies outlined in the following sections offer guidance for cultivating your skill and insight in understanding the key differences between management and leadership. They are distilled from the lessons I have learned from exceptional leaders across various industries.

## Know the Difference Between the Two

Management and leadership are complementary but fundamentally distinct skillsets. To get a better handle on the differences between the two, begin by reading one scholarly book on each topic. They should each review the topic in broad terms. While you read, take notes on the finer points; create a chart to compare and contrast the essential features of the two. Then read two or three relevant articles that focus on how to distinguish each concept in the workplace. Next, consider attending substantive workshops in each topical area to add an additional layer of value: An interactive experience would provide an opportunity to ask questions, receive feedback, and of course role-play a few skills in real time. Remember, your goal is to increase your understanding of each concept at a foundational level.

## Become Educated in Management

Now consider management by itself. Research the top five thought leaders in the management industry and extract the most compelling theories. Highlight their disruptive insights. Mine for the gold that can help you establish a firm grasp on the topic. Take a moment to reflect on how these concepts differ from those grounded in leadership. Then determine how you can use what you discover to enhance the management culture in your workplace. Identify at least three core areas that could be improved and three corresponding strategies to apply from your research. Then sit down with your managers to discuss. Additionally, determine how you can leverage a few key strategies to your advantage. No doubt that mastering relevant management concepts would serve you well. Break down the concepts and strategies so that you can increase your understanding and elevate your performance. Apply takeaways immediately.

## Become Educated in Leadership

After expanding your net understanding of management, consider taking a deeper dive solely on leadership. Research the top five thought leaders in leadership itself and delve into their most compelling theories. Highlight their disruptive insights. Mine for the gold that can help you establish a firm grasp on the topic. Then determine how you can use these newfound principles to enhance the leadership culture in your workplace. Identify at least three core areas that could be improved and three corresponding strategies to apply from your research. Then sit down with your team to discuss. Additionally, determine how you can leverage a few key theories to become more effective in your field. Break down the concepts and strategies so that you can increase your understanding and elevate your performance. Apply takeaways immediately.

## Determine the Best Outcome for Each

Once you have a handle on both management and leadership concepts, determine what the best outcomes for each should be. This, of course, will help you craft strategic and complementary goals for the workforce. Start by asking a few relevant questions: What objectives should a manager strive for? What about a leader? Why are the two so different, and how do these objectives complement each other? How can you help each to perform his or her roles more effectively? What do they need to know? Should their strategic objectives be evaluated yearly? Quarterly? Monthly? How should they identify stretch goals? Devote one whole day to analyzing these queries for each concept. Understanding the differences at a granular level will empower you to help your organization maximize its performance, competitive positioning, and its overall success.

## Empower Your Teams with Mutual Development Opportunities

One of the most transformative ways to help both the leadership and management reach their goals is through mutual development opportunities. Without a doubt, professional development is relevant for emerging, as well as seasoned, leaders and managers. To keep the process of learning ongoing, consider scheduling several programs throughout the the year based on relevant subject matter, as well as areas that others have expressed interest in. In addition, to keep things interesting, mix up the format and location of the various sessions. A workshop help outdoors, that includes a team-building hike, might inspire the group to think outside the box—or perhaps demonstrate how camaraderie can be instrumental in effectuating organizational goals. That said, consider organizing a session where the teams can cross-pollinate. The benefits of managers and leaders learning together, as well as challenging one another to put their best foot forward, are, invariably, worth their weight in gold.

## Journal Questions

1. Have you ever confused management with leadership? Discuss.
2. In what ways have you used these skillsets to increase your effectiveness within the workplace?
3. List three ways to explain the difference between management and leadership to your colleagues.
4. How did this principle help you better understand your role as a leader? How will its mastery enable you to cultivate greater effectiveness?
5. How will you use the preceding strategies to advance your commitment to managing and leading more effectively?

## Leadership Challenge

Encourage your organization to host a training session on the differences between management and leadership. Advise that the training should include interactive components so that participants can flesh out ideas and apply distinctions in real time. Ask participants to complete evaluations at the close of the training. Did they grasp the key takeaways?

## Notes

1. Hannah, S., Balthazard, P., Waldman, D., Jennings, P., & Thatcher, R. (2013). The Psychological and Neurological Bases of Leader Self-Complexity and Effects on Adaptive Decision-Making. Journal of Applied Psychology 98 (3), 393–411.
2. Bennis, W., & Thomas, R. (2002). Geeks & Geezer: How Era, Values, and Defining Moments Shape Leaders. Boston: Harvard Business School Press.
3. Kotter, J. (1990). A Force For Change: How Leadership Differs From Management. New York: The Free Press.
4. Kotter, J. (1990). A Force For Change: How Leadership Differs From Management. New York: The Free Press.

# 36

## Acknowledge the Elephant in the Room

*Elephants are pretty hard not to notice. Instead of pretending that they do not exist, be courageous and confront organizational challenges as quickly as possible.*

The truth can be difficult to accept, especially if it impacts you adversely: Bad news seldom goes down easy. Even still, it is important to acknowledge it; otherwise, the consequences might wreak havoc on your life or on the lives of others. In business, ignoring the elephant in the room can be costly. Not only can it ravage an organization's financial standing, but it can also destroy its reputation, competitive advantage, and in some cases its ability to exist at all. Even though the consequences of ignoring hard truths are rarely top of mind when they unfold, they definitely should be. Brushing them off is akin to flirting with disaster, which has never been a wise strategy. Still there are those willing to risk it all in favor of slim odds. Despite such brazenness, however, they soon find it was far easier to simply acknowledge the elephant in the room.

Despite the mounds of credible evidence pointing them in the opposite direction, sometimes leaders forget that avoidance is not a strategy. Turning a blind eye and a deaf ear to uncomfortable circumstances may be enticing, but it only delays the inevitable. Instead of running away from the inevitable, effective leaders must face the facts head-on. That may mean going it alone or involving stakeholders. It may also mean that the problem needs to be addressed in phases. A Strengths, Weaknesses, Opportunities and Threats (SWOT) analysis is often a good place to start. Consider the strengths and weaknesses as well as the opportunities and threats associated with the elephant. What could the organization gain? What could it lose? Could there be an opportunity to rebrand and restructure or increase scalability and bottom-line impact?

© The Author(s) 2018
K. Mariama-Arthur, *Poised for Excellence*, DOI 10.1007/978-3-319-64574-2_36

We have seen what happens when a leader fails to address the elephant in the room. Consider the role of Enron, the mortgage crisis, and the financial collapse of 2008. The common denominator in all these failures of leadership was an unwillingness to address the problems that many in the organization knew existed. Instead of addressing root causes and pulling the plug on bad behavior, they indulged in short-term gains, hoping that the chickens would not come home to roost. That thinking led to a vicious cycle of misconduct that was eventually discovered and punished in the end, but not without first damaging the integrity and corpus of the organizations, as well as the lives of many third parties who were directly affected by the fallout. The bottom line is this: When the downsides are too serious to ignore, then it is time to act.

There are significant upsides to addressing the elephant in the room. The first, and perhaps most advantageous, is getting ahead of the crisis. There is nothing like short-circuiting a disaster before it strikes. Whistleblowers can save organizations and even lives, especially when the wrongs committed are strikingly egregious. Such courageous actions sometimes even serve as deterrents for future bad actors. Whistleblower Lynn Szymoniak showed such courage when she stood alone to help the United States recover funds from the Bank of America during the subprime mortgage crisis in the late 2000s. In addition, even when the symptoms of a potential casualty have begun to rear their ugly heads, the financial losses and harm to an individual's or organization's reputation can be sufficiently diminished or entirely avoided when the elephant is swiftly confronted.

Leaders who take the initiative to confront the elephant in the room lessen the impact of the blow. Again, even though it may seem more comforting to ignore problems, hoping they will go away on their own, they rarely do. The longer you wait to address a problem, the more acute it usually becomes. Think for a moment about the lifecycle of any infection. Even if it is subclinical and difficult to detect, the invasion by the microorganisms is nonetheless ongoing. The longer the infection is disregarded and goes untreated, the more it grows in severity and impact. Crises brewing within organizations are no different. They may root in obscurity for a time, but in most cases the damage is mounting like a silent killer. That is why it is so imperative for leaders to be proactive and immediately confront the signs, symptoms, and manifestations of full-blown problems when they arise.

It may seem counterintuitive, but there are compelling reasons why someone might choose to avoid confronting a crisis or even refrain from acknowledging it all together. One is called *information avoidance*. Information that is perceived as painful, in conflict with present beliefs, or that requires taking some unwanted action, can cause someone to shrink from discovery or proactive engagement. Information avoidance is defined as "any behavior designed to prevent or delay the acquisition of available but potentially unwanted information," according to the American Psychological Association.[1] Moreover, in an insightful feature published by the *Journal of Economic Literature*, Carnegie Mellon University's George Loewenstein, Russell Golman, and David Hagmann discuss how and why people avoid information that might otherwise result in cognitive dissonance and instead create more favorable realities comprised of self-affirming data, even when such data is false and does not serve them.[2] Leaders who indulge in information avoidance do so at their own peril. They also do their organizations a grave disservice.

In the final analysis, the most effective leaders acknowledge the elephant in the room as a straightforward mechanism for avoiding crises. Even though mental discomfort and other hardships usually accompany the trek towards the proverbial elephant, those inconveniences are only minor nuisances in the grand scheme of things. Responsible leaders steady their hearts and minds, and then, continue to take two steps forward until they arrive face to face with adversity. No matter how dreaded, though, they do not capitulate. What they know for sure is that long-term gains outweigh any short-term discomfort. They find the courage to acknowledge the inevitable, and then deal with any blowback head on.

Fannie Mae and Freddie Mac were subprime elephants in the room that largely went unnoticed while numerous other mortgage funding industry giants, including countless investors, took the brunt of the public scrutiny and responsibility for their role in the subprime mortgage crisis.[3] As government-sponsored enterprises, they historically have been behind the clear majority of home loans offered to homebuyers in America, which means they also needed to stay competitive. To do so, they customarily took on risk to increase profitability, but that risk was softened because their losses were guaranteed by the government.

What made these two mortgage companies elephants in the room? Their sheer size and prominence within the industry made them hard not to notice (i.e., they are two of the world's largest financial institutions), as well as their major role of providing wholesale liquidity within the mortgage finance system, using various sophisticated mechanisms. These mechanisms historically had allowed them to act as vested intermediaries within the mortgage ecosystem. In the early 2000s when the housing bubble grew, however, loan originators found other ways to maneuver within the marketplace, sans Fannie Mae and Freddie Mac.

This activity caused Fannie Mae and Freddie Mac to lose market share, so they began investing in the subprime securities and credit agencies thought to be incredibly "low-risk" to recoup what they had lost. Unfortunately, these sources were not low-risk and these mortgage giants suffered colossal financial losses as a result. Even though their shareholders absorbed the bulk of these losses, they were deemed "too big to fail" by regulators and lawmakers. In September 2008, the entities were placed into conservatorship and will likely remain there for the foreseeable future, although there has been strong interest in having them operate independently again—a priority clearly expressed by the Trump administration. Not surprisingly, though, their current state of affairs have prompted questions about why the duo escaped initial scrutiny and were not held fully accountable for their role in the 2008 crisis—as unambiguous elephants in the room.

## Core Strategies

The strategies outlined in the following sections offer guidance for cultivating your skill and insight in acknowledging the proverbial elephant in the room. They are distilled from the lessons I learned from exceptional leaders across various industries.

### Keep Your Eyes and Ears Wide Open

Pay attention to what is going on around you—what you see, what you hear—all of it. Do not ignore the obvious or pretend things are not the way they seem out of convenience because it suits your sensibilities. Be willing to call a spade a spade. Hard truths, as mentioned time and again, must be faced with courage and conviction. As we have seen countless times before, disregarding your perceptions only results in delaying the inevitable and serving up bitter consequences for all involved. When you become privy to a problem or challenge, acknowledge it openly and honestly and encourage others to do the same. If in doubt, talk to someone you trust about your suspicions. Chances are a confirmation will clear up any doubt, or if you are off track, clarify why. It is far better to miss the mark and be accused of being a zealot, than to jeopardize the integrity of what is at stake by ignoring critical details. When you see a problem or a challenge, acknowledge it openly and honestly. Make sure others do as well. It is better if everyone is on the same page and moving through the issue together.

## Stick to the Facts

Hoopla is a drama multiplier. Avoid the hype. Stick to the facts and tune out other people's arbitrary interpretations. Remember that truthiness is not the same as the truth. Juggling misinformation and exaggeration will only get you riled up unnecessarily. Instead, rely on your own observations and firsthand accounts. Information has the tendency to become colored by individual opinions and biases. While you do not want to be swayed by spurious reasoning, it can happen fairly easily if you defer to others without first examining the facts yourself. Learn to develop informed opinions and resist the urge to draw conclusions and react based on hearsay or other unsubstantiated, indiscriminate information. Rumors and innuendo have a strange way of drawing people into the fold and snaring them to their detriment—refuse to be one of "those people." Refuse to be led astray or influenced by spurious reasoning.

## Evaluate Objectively

Resist being sidetracked by your own bias and other subterfuge when assessing any information before you. Evaluate the facts objectively. If you want to make a good decision, your sources must be high-quality, accurate, and unbiased. Use *your* judgment. Do not be swayed by others' opinions on how to interpret facts. Essentially, the facts must be observable, measurable, and easily verifiable by a disinterested third party. Even though it is critical to exercise good judgment, be careful to exclude personal feelings from the equation. A decision on the merits requires independent thinking, not the trappings of subjectivity, where emotions and arbitrary personal experiences play a determinative role in the evaluation process. In addition, clearing your mind of distractions and other emotional baggage is crucial when trying to make an objective evaluation. If you wake up on the wrong side of the bed, get yourself together before sitting down with a major decision. The people and the process deserve better. Determine in advance that you will show up with your best foot forward.

## Decide on the Way Forward

Once you have the lay of the land, you must then decide how to move forward. Which strategy makes the most sense? How do you fully acknowledge the elephant in the room? How will you accomplish what you need to accomplish in the allotted time? If the elephant is particularly egregious, your plan of attack may be more complex. It may require more time and energy, and a greater financial commitment. Likewise, it may require the assembly of a specialized team to execute. On the other hand, if the matter is smaller in scale, then your strategy may be more straightforward and succinct, and may not require the outlay of excessive resources. That said, the level of thought and preparation that goes into it should be no less significant. The considerations are the same as with any other decision: You must brainstorm, analyze possible courses of action, select a single one to guide the process, and then develop strategies and tactics that support it. Being intentional and strategic are key to successfully deciding on the way forward.

## Take Decisive Action

Once you have identified the problem, it is time to act. Challenge yourself to do whatever is necessary to address and fully resolve the challenge. Do not bargain with yourself or allow fear or procrastination to affect your ability to meet the deadlines to execute your crisis plan. The elephant may be big and hairy, but your charge is to proceed forward with clarity and conviction. Embrace the elephant. Taking the first step is usually the most important one, as it marks your commitment to seeing it through. If alerting key stakeholders is the bold move that will help you dig your heels in and get the ball rolling, do it. There is nothing like accountability once the alarm has been rung. That is also the beauty of taking decisive action: Once you are in the arena, you no longer have the option of "backing out" even if fears creeps in. Further, once you have determined a final course of action, focus on deliberately executing each component until complete. While acknowledging the elephant is vitally important, your efforts will be in vain if you do not also render it powerless by taking decisive action as the pièce de résistance of your overall strategy.

## Journal Questions

1. Discuss your strategy for handling highly charged situations at work.
2. Identify three possible strategies for initiating a difficult conversation that no one wants to have.
3. Are you comfortable confronting egregious behavior when necessary? Does it matter if you have to confront the situation by yourself?

4. How did this principle help you better understand your role as a leader? How will its mastery enable you to cultivate greater effectiveness?

5. How will you use the preceding strategies to advance your commitment to acknowledging the elephant in the room and not sweeping conspicuous issues under the rug?

## Leadership Challenge

The next time an awkward situation arises do not pretend it does not exist. Acknowledge it and deal with it swiftly. After you do this, notice how you feel. Is it not better to confront an elephant in the room than deny its existence?

## Notes

1. Sweeny, K., Melnyk, D., Miller, W., Shepperd, J. A. (2010). Information Avoidance: Who, What, When, and Why. *Review of General Psychology*, 14(4), 340–353.

2. Rea, S. (2017 March 13). Information Avoidance: How People Select Their Own Realities. *Carnegie Mellon University*. Retrieved March 15, 2017 from https://www.cmu.edu/news/stories/archives/2017/march/information-avoidance.html.

3. McDonald, O. (2012). Fannie Mae and Freddie Mac: Turning the American Dream Into a Nightmare. New York: Bloomsbury Academic.

# 37

# Leverage Your Professional Wheelhouse

*Experience is the best teacher. Leaders know how to harness their experiences to realize their expansive visions.*

Leaders are eager to apply what they know to improve the substance and process of worthwhile endeavors. They look for opportunities to use their specialized knowledge, skills, and abilities to add value: Without a doubt, they know how to leverage their professional "wheelhouses" (i.e., areas of one's expertise or interest). Their array of skills and accomplishments in their specific fields include academic degrees, certifications, specialized training, work experiences, and the lessons learned along the way. While each achievement may represent a different way of gathering knowledge, none of this means that leaders should be considered "polymaths," or jacks of all trades and masters of none. It is typical and even advantageous for someone to acquire knowledge from various sources to improve in their professional field. Moreover, people often change careers and the experiences gained early on can serve them well later in subsequent ventures. Professionals are no longer expected to remain in careers until receiving the stereotypical gold watch at retirement.

For example, an attorney-turned-doctor, who now owns a consulting firm that specializes in advising Fortune 500 companies, should not be accused of wishy-washiness. Given this varied background, he or she can usually draw from numerous knowledge sources to advise clients better than someone who has been only in the consulting business since college graduation. Almost every profession provides a core skill set and rich experiences that provide the foundation not only to perform well within it, but also to be applied in other relevant instances. When leaders recognize their ability to leverage

© The Author(s) 2018
K. Mariama-Arthur, *Poised for Excellence*, DOI 10.1007/978-3-319-64574-2_37

unique tools of the trade is unlimited, they take nothing for granted and avail themselves of a myriad of compelling opportunities to add value.

A well-rounded professional wheelhouse gives leaders more flexibility to do their work well, and when the knowledge and skills are complementary, their value compounds. Even if the knowledge and skills do not appear to be complementary, they may still work in the leader's favor. It is important that leaders look for that edge, something that sets them apart from other people; this is why you should never dismiss professional experiences without first analyzing their potential impact on your career. For example, individuals who have enjoyed successful careers as public speakers often find success leveraging it as a complementary skill set. This is true even when a new career may require the mastery of a distinct, substantive expertise.

Leveraging a professional wheelhouse has numerous advantages, including expert status, an easier path to promotion, adding value to situations that demand resolution, and guiding someone through challenging situations by applying unique insights. It also increases opportunities outside your primary focus, which is the key to expanding professional circles and growing your ability to lead. It also fosters lifelong learning in a way that is both useful and enjoyable and puts a person in the driver's seat when making well-reasoned career choices. When all is said and done, it allows an individual to operate from a strategic position of power, which is an enviable position to hold.

Leaders who fail to use their abilities to their maximum potential are doing themselves and their organizations a disservice. Leaders should never sell themselves short and should take the time to understand their professional reach. They must take advantage of what they know and not take for granted any of the skills they have amassed because they can add value in most circumstances. "Smart" leaders know that you do not discount knowledge and skills or leave them behind to atrophy. All skills can be applied to add value in some way, shape, or form, and for better or worse, have taken you to where you are today. That said, they incorporate their diverse knowledge, skills, and abilities into all that they do.

The choice to leverage one's professional wheelhouses can make or break an opportunity that is brewing on the horizon. Depending on the nature of the opportunity, the unique combination of skills and experience must be selected and framed to highlight and extract those components that can best advance the goals of an endeavor. The most effective leaders take the time to thoroughly understand the ins and outs of a potential opportunity, as well as how they can add the most value to it. When they do both, they put themselves in the best position to wield influence and create more advantageous outcomes for others.

Sir Richard Branson is someone who knows how to leverage his professional wheelhouse and has created multiple opportunities and a multibillion-dollar empire as a result.[1] He enjoys finding solutions to problems using creativity and innovation. That being said, very early on in his career, he realized that he did not have to limit himself to any one particular industry or focus. Reaching deep into his entrepreneurial mindset, Branson was able to identify a variety of solutions to common challenges by leveraging diverse skill sets and pooling valuable resources to his advantage. He is a master collaborator. He knows how to maximize synergies: He has revolutionized ways to define new and more valuable ways to capture cutting-edge opportunities within both the goods and services industries.

Applying these ideas, Branson has used the Virgin brand to bring him enormous success, as well as developed countless other brands that have yielded similar successes. From cosmetics to record deals, and vodka to airlines, Branson is one smart cookie who knows that the possibilities are limitless when you think big and "leverage" the power of your professional wheelhouse.

# Core Strategies

The strategies outlined in the following sections offer guidance for cultivating your skill and insight in leveraging your diverse skills and experience to add value. They are distilled from the lessons I have learned from exceptional leaders across various industries.

## Know Your Worth

If you do not recognize your worth, you really can hardly expect others to do so. What knowledge, skills, and experiences do you have that distinguish you from the crowd? What are your deep smarts, and how can you use them to do extraordinary work in the marketplace? How have people and processes been improved by deploying your unique skills and experience? Do not sit idly hoping that someone will recognize your worth. Develop your own, intimate understanding of it and give yourself the credit that you deserve. Then bring it to the attention of the world by owning it. Above all, you must have the confidence to express it to stakeholders in your circle of influence and beyond, without reservation.

## Do Not Second-Guess Yourself

Once you have identified your unique value, do not second-guess it. Also, do not compare yourself to others. Stand firm in your knowledge of self and let your light shine without qualification or hesitation. Ignore haters, naysayers, and anyone offering gratuitous commentary. Everyone has an opinion about something, and there is often little you can do to change those opinions. More often than not, though, they are without merit and have more to do with them than you. Attempts to discredit leaders at every level are nothing new. Your predecessors know this all too well, and your successors will know it, too. The bottom line is that you should know better than anyone else who you are and what you are capable of doing. Disregard extraneous commentary by anyone trying to adversely influence the way you think about yourself or discredit you. Adopt a mindset that allows you to filter out negativity and one-off assertions about your potential by others.

## Ignore the So-Called Competition

What other people are doing to leverage their unique skills and experience is none of your business. Again, resist the urge to compare and contrast your experience and outcomes with theirs. Run in your own lane and remain narrowly focused on the best way to make use of your own toolbox. If you often get distracted by the so-called shiny objects, remind yourself that no one can do what you do in the way that you do it. Commodities are fungible; you are not a commodity. By definition, the exclusive combination of your education, skills, experience, and perspectives make you uniquely positioned to deliver value. Do not make the mistake of measuring your worth against another; you will either do yourself a grave injustice or inflate your own ego unnecessarily. In either case, the so-called competition should never be your focus. However, your own growth and consummate success should.

## Connect the Dots for Yourself and Others

Take a hard look at who you are, what you bring to your organization, your industry, and any new opportunities on which to collaborate. Let others know how you can help based on what you know. By the same token, be proactive and take the initiative to create opportunities where none exist. Do not fail to highlight key experiences and insights that can help current and potential partners achieve goals. Get crystal clear on your unique value proposition. An individual or organization may be in desperate need of a strong collaborator but is unaware that it is you who can bridge the gap. As they say, "A closed mouth does not get fed." Do not starve your ambition; feed it and it will thrive. If it is opportunity that you seek, be willing to boldly navigate the landscape within and across industries to capture it.

## Cash in on Prime Opportunities

Sometimes opportunities fall in your lap; other times you need to create them. Whatever the case, do not fail to seize an opportunity once it is within your sights. By the same token, do not waste time with opportunities that do not serve you, or enable you to leverage your wheelhouse advantageously. Too often, precious time is wasted chasing unicorns. Determine early on whether a seemingly attractive opportunity is really an appropriate one. Then, once you have successfully captured a golden egg, move quickly and do not fail to follow up. Return calls and carry out tasks in a timely fashion. There is probably nothing worse than being in the precipice of success, and then allowing it to slip through your fingers due to negligence. Be careful not to find yourself asleep at the wheel when duty calls.

# Journal Questions

1. Do you have a strong sense of your professional strengths and weaknesses?
2. Have you ever evaluated your professional wheelhouse? If so, what is inside? If not, do it now.
3. How have you showcased the talents that have driven your success?
4. How did this principle help you better understand your role as a leader? How will its mastery enable you to cultivate greater effectiveness?
5. How will you use the preceding strategies to advance your commitment to leveraging your diverse experience and expertise?

# Leadership Challenge

Make a list of your top 10 talents. Connect each talent to an industry and a problem that you can solve. How can you add greater value by leveraging your talents and expertise in these core areas?

# Note

1. Branson, R. (1998). Losing My Virginity: The Autobiography. London: Virgin Pub.

# 38

# Come Down from the Ivory Tower

*Leaders are the most effective when they subordinate their ego and become a visible, visceral, and accessible part of the organizations they serve. Creating artificial divisions by insulating and elevating themselves defeats this objective.*

Being holed up in an "ivory tower" is no place for a leader. To effectively influence anyone, a leader must be approachable and willing to establish an emotional link to others. Emotional links are developed by having real dialogues, rather than delivering canned speeches; rewarding good behavior with face-to-face praise, or providing other constructive feedback when needed; and speaking to all employees with respect. The "links" include establishing authentic connections with senior management as well as the various employees located throughout an organizational pyramid. Without question, high-touch experiences are critical to leaders' success.

A leader who views people from a perch is almost always out of touch. The view from up top, though sweeping, is far from complete. Even though it is important to have a big-picture vision that addresses global issues, it is more essential to have "native" context for matters affecting subordinates, clients, and other key stakeholders. Being on the ground and interacting with people on a close level provides leaders with a better understanding of the problems facing an organization and increases opportunities for collaborative success.

The ivory tower is an enticing place to retreat, a sanctuary of sorts. It is a comfortable shield against the burdens and challenges that most of the rest of an organization faces. Besides, it can make a leader feel a bit invincible, pulling all the levers of control from above, handling all the big, important jobs that no one else is qualified or trusted to do. It is, however, also a place that gives a false sense of security, often masking incompetence and inexperience.

© The Author(s) 2018
K. Mariama-Arthur, *Poised for Excellence*, DOI 10.1007/978-3-319-64574-2_38

In addition, because there is not always a sense of urgency or palpable oversight in the ivory tower, it often becomes a place where vision and ambition die and autonomy and privilege rule the day.

Although obviously enticing, the ivory tower is also a potentially dangerous place to be. If leaders spend too much time thinking about big-picture issues, especially in isolation, they risk becoming disconnected from the group, developing "blinders," or a skewed vision about what else is at stake. Leaders who are devoted to eradicating childhood hunger, but are unaware that many of their own employees' children go to bed hungry every night is tragic. The more removed leaders are from the whole, the less likely they can appreciate its challenges. If an us-versus-them culture develops, morale suffers, making it more likely that misinformation and misunderstandings will proliferate, thereby making leaders' jobs even more difficult.

If you find yourself stuck in the ivory tower, do not fret. There are plenty of ways to disembark. Being more visible is a good start. Attending social functions and spending quality time with colleagues outside of work are great ways to show engagement. Thoughtful leaders also will make themselves accessible and approachable in other ways. For instance, sending out personal emails, speaking at company events, making their opinions heard, and humanizing their role as a leader rather than being a detached figurehead.

Random acts of kindness also go a long way in helping a leader withdraw from the ivory tower. Being friendly, considerate, open, and sociable make leaders appear more accessible and less insular. As the flesh-and-blood harbingers of change, their influence is only as strong as their capacity to connect with others. Even though they may have different titles and work in bigger, fancy offices, they are only human and should be treated as such. By the same token, leaders who are receptive to the kindness of others leave a lasting impression and further affirms the genuineness of their humanity.

The most effective leaders, however, ignore the guise of the ivory tower. They refuse to submit to its beguiling enchantments, realizing that it only serves one purpose: To unjustifiably alienate leaders from the inner workings of the organizations and institutions that they serve. Just like the mavericks who tear down the walls of injustice, audacious leaders tear down the artificial walls of the so-called ivory tower. They avoid working in silos. They know that interaction, collaboration, and accessibility are all crucial to developing an interdependent culture that thrives. For them, there is no such thing as categorical exclusivity; they reject any thinking or behavior that proves incompatible with the tenets of sound leadership.

Canadian Prime Minister Justin Trudeau's leadership style demonstrates the value of coming down from the ivory tower. According to Lisa Kimmel, president and CEO of the PR firm Edelman Canada: "Trudeau's leadership style is characterized by transparency, accessibility, openness, and a willingness to collaborate."[1]

"These are the very traits that Edelman's most recent 'Trust Barometer' shows are most admired and valued by the mass population in public and private sector roles."[2] By all accounts, Trudeau's leadership style has endeared the public to him and has made them feel that he cares about and is interested in what they think. He does not take an insular approach to governance. Instead, he is transparent and authentic. Trudeau does not consider himself above reproach and admits to being fallible.

Case in point: The infamous "Elbowgate" controversy in which Trudeau was said to have roughed up a member of Parliament. He apologized and took full responsibility for the incident. What he knows for sure is that the way to create community is through active and authentic engagement. His clear views on integrating his leadership role and the function of government to create a bridge to the people rather than away from them is evidence that Trudeau is a leader who is in touch and in sync with the issues facing the community-at-large. His incredible influence, throughout Canada and around the world, is evidence of his refusal to be holed up in an ivory tower.

## Core Strategies

The strategies outlined in the following sections offer guidance on cultivating your skill and insight on how to avoid the allure of the ivory tower. They are distilled from the lessons I have learned from exceptional leaders across various industries.

### Check Your Ego at the Door

Is your ego preventing you from connecting with others? If so, closely examine your persistent craving for praise and the need to feel self-important. An egotistical attitude will only limit personal and professional growth. As leaders, we are first and foremost human beings, flaws and all. We are no better than the flock, and they are no worse than us. When misplaced feelings of superiority start creeping in, or a compelling desire to separate from others persists, remind yourself of the previous statements.

As individuals, we are independently important because we are integral parts of the whole. Each separate individual only adds value to the group. Dismount your high horse. Resolve to interact with individuals outside of your immediate circle. No leader can exist as an island. The best way to truly connect with others is by subordinating your ego and embracing the inclusive goals of effective leadership.

## Acknowledge the Benefits of Community

Community is important to building culture. To further cement this idea, ask yourself a few basic questions. How can interacting with others help you be a better person or professional? How can you collaborate with others and help them to become better? Acknowledge that you can achieve more with others than you can alone. Whether it is simply bouncing an important idea off someone or working together to complete a tedious project, community matters.

Community, as a collaborative unit, makes any organization an effectual entity. Without the unit working in sync, and the individuals within it propping one another up, it can be difficult to address the cross-functional and sometimes overwhelming demands of the business cycle, as well as the complex goals of the organization.

## Lead with Your Humanity

It takes more energy to reject someone than it does to embrace the person. Love people. Smile. Hug when you can. Accept appropriate displays of affection from others with enthusiasm. Do not be a curmudgeon. Every now and again, check in to see how people are doing; see what you can do to brighten up someone's day. A kind word can go a long way and can come at a time when someone really needs it. Perhaps at a time when someone is feeling dejected or uninspired.

Think about those instances when you felt less than your best and someone said or did something nice for you. It probably made a world of difference, right? Seek out opportunities to recreate those experiences for others on a regular basis. No doubt all that goodness will make its way back to you when you least expect it, but need it the most.

## Make a Concerted Effort to Get Know Others

There is so much to discover about those you work with so closely, day in, day out. Learning more about them, their successes, and even their challenges will help you to develop a greater appreciation for their unique contributions to the workplace. Shift the focus away from yourself and get curious about others and what they bring to the table. Remember, when people know that you care and they feel appreciated, they are happy to commit their hearts and minds to a vision that inspires. So "go first."

Start meaningful conversations. Inspire others to be open and share their stories. In turn, they will encourage you to share yours. Reciprocity is key. If you are there for others, others will be there for you. If you view your community as valuable in its diversity and unique contributions, it will view yours in the same way and be more inclined to support your efforts.

## Cooperate to Create a Culture that you Love

Work with others to bring communal principles to fruition. It is too monumental a task to go it alone—plus, it requires the input of others to get it right. Start the conversation and get people excited about sharing their values and what matters the most in creating a cohesive culture that thrives. Discuss substance and structure. Ask how the various aspects of culture and community affect their mindset and performance. In terms of perks and policies, ask what they want and why they want it. A few days per month to telecommute? Gym benefits? A safe space to share workplace issues in confidence?

Whatever they suggest, the underlying rationale is the most important to capture. It exposes true concerns, helps you to move beyond superficial appeals, and puts you in the best position to create an organizational environment that supports the needs of its most precious resources. Brainstorm and review a few case studies on successful cultures to get an idea of what others have done and why it worked. Determine how you can apply lessons learned and modify them to fit the unique goals that you are trying to achieve. Together you can come up with several brilliant strategies to create a culture that you love, can continually improve on, and all be proud of. In the end, that is exactly point.

## Journal Questions

1. Do you distinguish and separate yourself from others at work based on socioeconomic status, gender, title, or position? Discuss.
2. Are you tuned into the issues facing your organization and its workforce at both the macro and micro levels? Explain.

3. How often do you network and mingle with others outside of the workplace environment?
4. How did this principle help you better understand your role as a leader? How will its mastery enable you to cultivate greater effectiveness?
5. How will you use the preceding strategies to advance your commitment to engaging the larger community and not be so insular?

## Leadership Challenge

Think about how often you connect with the people inside your organization or professional community. Identify three opportunities to be more visible and connect more meaningfully within the next 30 days. Actively participate and challenge yourself to engage in more one-on-one interactions with new people. How does it feel to be more visible and to interact with the community at large?

## Notes

1. Deutschendorf, H. (2015 October). Why Emotionally Intelligent People Are More Successful. *Fast Company*. Retrieved October 14, 2016 from https://www.fastcompany.com/3047455/why-emotionally-intelligent-people-are-more-successful.
2. Deutschendorf, H. (2015 October). Why Emotionally Intelligent People Are More Successful. *Fast Company*. Retrieved October 14, 2016 from https://www.fastcompany.com/3047455/why-emotionally-intelligent-people-are-more-successful.

# 39

# Sharpen Your Communication Skills

*Leaders must master the art and science of communication because it is the lifeblood of every human interaction.*

Communication is a high-priority skillset that every leader, without exception, must master. The fundamental building blocks of their success rely on the prudent execution of this premise. In its most basic sense, "communication" is the ability to convey and capture information in context to expand understanding and influence. Undoubtedly, these subcomponents guide every single interaction. Although developing this skill takes time and effort, considerable results can be realized in a relatively short period with focus and consistent practice.

We communicate in several ways, though we typically view verbal communication as the primary method. Words—or silence—convey much of our intended meaning. The way we utter words also tells the listener a great deal about us, including our intentions. The speed with which we speak, the tone, and the pitch all communicate the significance of our underlying emotions. The content of our narratives and the organization of our thoughts also send the world a message about our intellect, capabilities, and motives.

We also reveal much about ourselves through nonverbal communication. Gestures, facial expressions, and body language each express substantial meaning to others. When there is inconsistency between verbal and nonverbal communication, listeners often derive more meaning from the nonverbal cues than from the words that we actually speak. Slumped shoulders or tapping fingers can turn a beautifully spoken speech into a liability. The goal is to convey a cohesive message by synchronizing the verbal and nonverbal dialogue

© The Author(s) 2018
K. Mariama-Arthur, *Poised for Excellence*, DOI 10.1007/978-3-319-64574-2_39

into a single, harmonious expression. When this is accomplished successfully, the listener receives the complete message that the speaker intends.

The ability to communicate a vision, to deliver a speech, to participate in a debate, and to handle conflict all factor into the perception of a leader. Those who can communicate well often are perceived as more intelligent and trustworthy than those who struggle with communication. This holds true even if the less-skilled communicators are actually more intelligent and trustworthy than their silver-tongued counterparts. Effective communicators command greater respect and admiration and encounter less resistance to change. They also understand that we humans are often easily swayed by a master communicator and avail themselves of this distinction.

Leaders who do not take the time to learn this skill are at a severe disadvantage, which unfortunately extends to the organization as well. Not only do they lack the ability to inspire others, effectively negotiate deals, and leverage diplomacy, but sometimes lose team members to competitors who communicate visions with greater competence and impact. When a crisis occurs, the world looks to its leaders to shape the defining narrative and ease fears through a well-organized and compelling speech. In the competitive arena, the leader without well-developed communication skills often fades into obscurity.

Historically, the most admired leaders have all been extraordinary communicators. Look at the clear majority of U.S. presidents and the most successful CEOs around the world irrespective of industry. They all have been silver-tongued speakers; all have the gift of gab. Put them in any situation and they could each talk their way in or out of it. Remarkable communicators are trusted assets to a committed base and formidable forces to the unlucky adversary found on the rough edges of their prowess. Without question, they reap the uncommon benefits of marshaling competence and confidence at a high level.

The most effective leaders know that exceptional communication skills are essential to wielding influence, building and maintaining rapport, and securing the bottom line. Without exceptional communication skills, leaders can bang the gavel, but it will only fall on deaf ears. Leaders who understand how to meaningfully connect, to deliver core messages that spur others to action, and to resolve conflict with finesse are among the most compelling and revered. Ask any accomplished leader and she or he will affirm that superlative communication skills are the fire and ice of a robust and enduring leadership platform. They know that channeling excellence simply demands it.

British Prime Minister Winston Churchill was known for his phenomenal speeches and overall remarkable communication skills. He practiced incessantly before every speech, in front of the mirror, and for up to one hour for every minute that he was to speak. He won the Nobel Prize in Literature for both his historical writings and his prolific speeches.[1] A talented writer, Churchill wrote a multivolume history of World War I and a memoir after World War II. His public speaking skills earned him great respect in government and around the world, even long after his death. His legacy will forever represent his poise and ability to not only articulate compelling values but also to deliver them with impact and influence.

Churchill knew that the key to his success turned on his ability to become an effective communicator—although he was not always one. In fact, he had a speech impediment and had difficulty pronouncing the letter "s." Like most great leaders, however, he recognized that this shortcoming would impact his professional trajectory and, sooner rather than later, took the necessary and arduous steps to improve it daily. As a result, he developed an impeccable work ethic at an early age. Churchill took the bull by the horns and made sharpening his communication skills a priority, which changed his professional trajectory. He will forever be hailed as an oratory genius for his remarkable ability to stand and deliver with excellence.

## Core Strategies

The strategies outlined in the following sections offer guidance for cultivating your skill and insight as a skilled communicator. They are distilled from the lessons I have learned from exceptional leaders across various industries.

### Assess Current Skill Level

To understand which communication skill you need to develop further, first take stock of where you are now. That means performing an honest self-assessment and then having a third party provide one after. Record yourself giving a short talk of no more than five minutes and then one of up to 30 minutes. Identify three areas where you are strong and three areas that require improvement. Examine content, organization, and verbal as well as nonverbal delivery. Have the other party examine these aspects as well. In rounding out your evaluation, explain why some forms of communication are easier than others for you. Compare your own evaluation with the one provided by the third party. Note any similarities and differences.

## Seek Appropriate Development

Once you know where your strengths lie and which areas require more attention, begin working to turn your weak areas into strengths. Start by incorporating daily practice into your routine based on the feedback you received from your assessments. Next, research professional development programs available in your immediate area or region. Begin with Toastmasters. After you complete the program or determine you need additional enrichment, seek more advanced resources.

There are numerous programs around the country (or perhaps outside of it) of varying scales and prices. Next, find out if any online opportunities may be appropriate to help you supplement your overall learning plan. If you discover an excellent program that requires travel or a financial investment, plan for it. Be open to learning from people who can offer a more advanced exploration of communication, even when the cost seems prohibitive. Sometimes you should "pay the cost to be the boss." In addition, scout out seasoned presenters with a proven track record who can act as mentors so that you can maximize your efforts.

## Practice

There is no more tried-and-tested method of becoming a better communicator than practice. Churchill said that he practiced an hour for every minute he spoke. Most people balk at this. If you are serious about improving, however, you must practice tirelessly to perfect your delivery. Although the ratio may look slightly different than Churchill's, it should reflect a concerted effort. I teach my clients to stand up and deliver their full presentation as if the audience were right in front of them. No stopping. No do-overs. I ask them to focus and treat every practice session like game day.

You should do the same. Practice like you *mean it*. How you perform in private will inevitably spill over into how you show up in public. No matter how tired you get or no matter how redundant the rehearsals may seem, keep going. Incessant practice brings out the best thinking, structure, and delivery. It also ensures that you will be the most relaxed and confident on game day, which will help you to give your best performance.

## Get Expert-Level Feedback

Once you begin to practice and speak more regularly, make sure to get feedback from seasoned speakers. They will have both the skill and perspective to evaluate your talks at a higher level. Let them know that you are on a mission to become a better orator and that you would appreciate any insights they are able to provide. To make the most effective use of their time, ask them to consider specific areas that you are targeting for improvement. They also may have some of their own suggestions depending on what you are trying to achieve. In addition, you may want to consider working with them more intensely as you prepare for major talks.

In some cases, you may want them present in the audience, or alternatively, to at least review a recording afterward to provide targeted feedback once you have delivered a speech. Keep a journal of your progress while working with experts so that you can reference their insights time and again while you continue to grow your acumen.

## Do Not Get Overconfident

Even if you are improving, you will discover that you still have blind spots, which means that there is always room for more improvement. For better or worse, this will be where you find yourself most of the time. Do not let your progress lull you into complacency. You can always do more and be better. One proven way to avoid becoming complacent or overconfident is by giving more speeches, practicing daily, and continuing to seek feedback from more seasoned speakers. Each time you practice, give a new speech, or review your feedback, you will discover a new level of excellence.

You may have thought you mastered your body language, but then realize that you tug at your jewelry when you get nervous. Only with persistent practice and exploration can you make these kinds of key discoveries. Commit to improving not only each and every time you make a presentation or give a speech, but also daily. Incremental improvements will compound over time, and you will become more polished with every effort.

## Journal Questions

1. Have your communication skills ever been evaluated? Why or why not?
2. Name two key components of communication that you would like to improve. Explain why improving them will make an impact on how you lead.
3. Would you be willing to practice as diligently as Churchill to develop greater skill and comfort as a communicator? Discuss.

4. How did this principle help you better understand your role as a leader? How will its mastery enable you to cultivate greater effectiveness?
5. How will you use the preceding strategies to advance your commitment to becoming a skilled communicator?

## Leadership Challenge

Research three professional development opportunities in the public speaking and communication arenas. Compare and contrast each program. Pick one to enroll in during the next month. Note your progress after three months. Did your communication skills improve after the program? If so, describe in what way(s).

## Note

1. Nobel Media AB. (2014). The Nobel Prize in Literature 1953. *The Nobel Prize Org.* Retrieved February 15, 2017 from http://www.nobelprize.org/nobel_prizes/literature/laureates/1953/.

# 40

## Encourage Leading at All Levels

*Leadership is not reserved for the select few who operate at the top of organizational hierarchies. It is a clarion call to anyone willing to heed the principles and to do the work, which can be done at all levels.*

The best leaders do not produce followers; they produce competent leaders who can function independently and are committed to creating successive and robust leadership pipelines. When the proper systems are in place, this idea is successfully promoted throughout an organization's hierarchy, not merely within its upper echelons.

Although it is true that organizations often rely on leaders in the C-Suite to represent an idealized version of leadership, it is not the only place or way that individuals within it can lead. To achieve growth, scalability, and competitive advantage, individuals within organizations must lead at all levels. This means instilling the core principles of leadership from top to bottom and everywhere in between.

The process is brought to fruition by introducing leadership at all levels as an intrinsic component of an organization's mission and culture. As a practical matter, each individual employee must understand how his or her work creates value and be reminded that everyone is an asset to the organization. Titles and positions are irrelevant for this purpose. Neither would necessarily increase an employee's commitment to doing the work or performing it better. It is, however, an innate desire to serve, along with the recognition of being a valued member of a team doing the work, that matters.

Treating leadership and culture as complementary concepts drive collaboration, shared responsibility, and competitive advantage. The goal is always to increase employee engagement and to build greater trust among the group,

© The Author(s) 2018
K. Mariama-Arthur, *Poised for Excellence*, DOI 10.1007/978-3-319-64574-2_40

**251**

which further helps an organization achieve profitable business outcomes. This results in expanded capabilities of each employee, establishment of a leadership culture, cross-functional collaboration, confidence to learn and do more, effective team-building, self-policing, and giving and welcoming honest feedback, with an eye toward growth.

How do organizations facilitate leading at all levels? The most successful organizations do so by concentrating on education and employee development. Increasing employees' competencies across the board, regardless of their positions, is critical. Nevertheless, this must be done with an additional goal in mind: succession planning. Formulating the next generation of leaders is always an important aspect of the dialogue. Nonetheless, to be clear, facilitating leading at all levels in not simply about training. It is, however, about prioritizing the organizational goals and encouraging everyone to take personal responsibility for creating improved outcomes.

Ownership is a key element in this overall strategy. Organizations should not hide the ball, though. It is practical to include employees in the discussion and planning phases. Beyond creating buy-in and enthusiasm, understanding why this undertaking matters to organizational success also can drive employee performance.

One of the extraordinary benefits of succession planning is that it helps an organization strategically build its talent pipeline. Companies that properly develop "bench strength" are more successful overall. Of particular interest are those who show an above average potential (i.e., high potentials) to lead, who have the "potential, ability, and aspiration for successive leadership within a company."[1] When high potentials are groomed for successive leadership, organizations experience an enhanced workplace culture, creation of a robust leadership pipeline, increased employee retention, competitive advantage, and even considerable shareholder returns. These benefits increase when high performers—"key contributors who demonstrate high performance and are capable of a lateral move,"[2] though are not necessarily motivated to garner a leadership position—as well as other uniquely positioned employees, expand their roles to lead within their respective areas of expertise and functionality.

When this principle is ignored and leadership becomes a top-heavy concept, organizations do not perform well. Power concentrated at the crown is often lopsided. No one person or small group can effectively drive change. When this does happen, however, human capital gets left behind, and so do the efforts needed to propel the vision forward. There is also an unfortunate disconnect and chasm that occurs, further dividing the organization, its goals, and the pathway to unified ownership of success by the collective.

Leaders who instill the value of leading at all levels create cultures that align with and promote strategic goals by encouraging active participation at every echelon. This creates ownership, which is critical to gaining commitment from others to perform effectively. Individuals who feel they can contribute to the big picture and have something at stake are more enthusiastic about their work and encourage peers to commit and perfect their performance as well. It is this shared sense of responsibility, accountability, and collective commitment that makes leading at all levels such a fundamental leadership principle.

Leaders who get this right flourish and their organizations thrive because, together, they have created the next generation of auspicious leaders within a continuous pipeline. They know that the glory of leadership is not in personal accolades; it is in passing along a lifetime of acquired knowledge to those who will eventually take the reins of leadership at various levels throughout an organization's hierarchy. When repeated time and again, this concept becomes part of an organization's cultural anatomy and fosters unqualified excellence throughout it. Empowering others to lead is like teaching them how to fish. Once you have taught them that skill, they will never go hungry.

President Barack Obama is an excellent example of a leader who encouraged leading at all levels. As the 44th President of the United States, he had extraordinary vision and courage to make tough decisions when it mattered most. An exceptional leader in his own right, he was never satisfied simply being the only one. His tip-of-the-spear message to every American was to take responsibility for their own destinies as well as our shared destiny as citizens of the United States of America. Through activism, awareness, personal and professional development, outreach, organization, and a great deal of straightforward, bona fide strategies, President Obama ushered in a new generation of leaders at every level. For him, it did not matter where you existed in an organizational hierarchy or administration.

Obama firmly believed in empowering everyone with a voice and the commitment to champion new ways of thinking and behaving and to lead auspiciously from the front. Because his tremendous leadership message was so compelling and even visceral, it has reverberated far beyond his presidency and resulted in legions of socially conscious advocates who have led stunningly disruptive movements, including the legendary January 2017 "Women's March on Washington" that simultaneously took place around the world.

## Core Strategies

The strategies outlined in the following sections offer guidance for cultivating your skill and insight into embracing leadership at all levels. They are distilled from the lessons I have learned from exceptional leaders across various industries.

## Challenge the Status Quo

A top-heavy leadership structure is a concept of the past. For organizations to operate in the most effective manner, the ways of the old guard must be reevaluated. To encourage leading at all levels, challenging the status quo is a must. The first order of business is to take a good look at how things have been done previously throughout an organization. Remember, just because a policy is still in place does not mean that it is a good one. Give every department a thorough vetting.

Are there opportunities to improve on substance and procedure? Brainstorm with a team about ways in which you can improve them. If you discover that the critical administrative functions in the payroll department all could be done electronically, it is probably time for an overhaul. Similarly, if you find that there is no accountability with staff on the overnight shift, consider introducing a new system of checks and balances. Finally, examine how delegating leadership can improve form and function throughout the organization.

## Empower Employees to Lead at All Levels

If an organization's employees are not used to leading at all levels, there of course will be some hesitation. Be proactive by introducing leadership as a cultural imperative that exists along the full spectrum of roles and responsibilities throughout the organization. Provide examples of how employees functioning in nontraditional leadership roles have distinct opportunities to lead and move the company's vision forward. The janitor. The night auditor. The secretary. The front desk assistant. The list will be as long and as unique as the diversity of roles within your organization.

In addition, urge those in traditional leadership roles to delegate functional responsibilities and to encourage nontraditional leaders to expand their reach. By providing direction and support for employees to step up to the leadership table and exercise their potential, you set a new expectation for excellence and collaboration. When leading at all levels is reinforced by the foundations with of the organization, it creates momentum and helps people move forward with enthusiasm and confidence.

## Organize Leadership Development Programs

Continuous development is a key component of leading at every level. When you engage in transitions at the organizational level, it is important to be mindful of helping individuals make the transition at the departmental and functional levels as well. Leadership development programs address this need. To maximize the outcomes of development programs, first determine which skills need to be addressed and in what order for each segment of the organization's population.

For example, members of the C-Suite may need to focus first on enhancing emotional intelligence before delving into the strategic methodologies for engaging international stakeholders. The front desk assistant may begin with a communication module and advance to conflict-resolution segments thereafter. Once the framework and rationale have been established, you can decide the best kinds of programs to institute initially and which to address in the future, subsequent to onboarding.

## Follow-Up and Evaluate

The success of any transition cannot be fully examined unless there is follow-up and some form of meaningful evaluation. Developing an innovative leadership culture is no exception. It must still be analyzed at a granular level. To determine how these newly minted leaders are performing, take a closer look at the net returns during relevant time periods. The intervals will vary depending on the rigor of the transition, the programming, and the projected outcomes.

Begin by asking every employee to describe their experience. What feedback did they provide? Are there better ways to approach this goal that have been overlooked? Were any portions poorly executed? Then observe the outcomes objectively. Assign an impartial task force to evaluate key metrics and report back on its findings. What results have employees produced? What gaps have been observed and how can they be addressed? What gains and losses has the overall organization experienced as a result?

If one goal was for the COO to develop greater conflict-resolution skills, but her temper tantrums persist and she refuses to accept constructive feedback, it is a clear indication that the strategies designed to address this issue have not worked. Determining why and what steps to take next are critical to finding a resolution. Remember that whatever system is used to evaluate this process must be clear and able to address the agreed-on metrics comprehensively.

## Fine-Tune the Way Forward

Once you have evaluated the results of an endeavor, you are in the best position to determine how to proceed in the future. Reshaping an organization's culture to include the concept of leading at all levels is no small feat. No doubt you will experience some pushback and missteps along the way. Perhaps not all employees were receptive to the idea. Maybe others were too aggressive in taking the leadership reigns, which resulted in a few rough patches here and there.

Review any miscalculations as well as the successes to strengthen the overall process. You may discover that evaluations should take place monthly rather than quarterly, or that leadership development programs on Monday mornings was a great idea. Even though you can always continue to make improvements incrementally, you should also develop a clear plan for immediately incorporating the collective observations into the plan's expansive framework. This way you can continue to improve on the process in an organic and purposeful manner.

## Journal Questions

1. Have you ever empowered someone to do something they were afraid to do? How did it make you feel afterward?
2. Has someone ever empowered you to take the lead when you were afraid to? What made you decide to step forward?
3. What professional development opportunities have you provided to your team in the past? Which ones are under consideration for the future?
4. How did this principle help you better understand your role as a leader? How will its mastery enable you to cultivate greater effectiveness?
5. How will you use the preceding strategies to advance your commitment to promoting leading at all levels?

## Leadership Challenge

Identify three ways to infuse the concept of "leading at all levels" into your leadership culture. Explain who and what would be involved, and why. Outline and assign responsibilities. After 30 days of observing the process, evaluate the results. How do you feel knowing you are empowering your most valuable resources?

# Notes

1. Bersin by Deloitte. (n.d.). High Potential/HiPo (and Maturity Model). *Bersin by Deloitte*. Retrieved February 6, 2016 from http://www.bersin.com/Lexicon/details.aspx?id=12845.
2. Bersin by Deloitte. (n.d.). High Performer. *Bersin by Deloitte*. Retrieved February 6, 2016 from http://www.bersin.com/Lexicon/Details.aspx?id=12844.

# 41

# Conclusion

*Excellence is a powerful exemplar—a universal symbol of distinction, achievement, and mastery. It is the unequivocal driving force behind world-class brand performers, irrespective of industry or expertise. As far as standards go, excellence is the best place to begin any effort of consequence.*

This book has introduced 40 fundamental principles to help leaders effectively navigate performance challenges and maximize their success across industries. Together, they represent 360 degrees of leadership excellence and take a "deep dive" into the granular aspects of leadership mastery, integrating them into a holistic process.

The principles have been divided into four distinct categories and represent concepts that:

1. Foster leadership excellence
2. Cultivate excellence through disruptive paradigm shifts
3. Nurture excellence through collaboration, benevolence, and valued-based service to others
4. Promote excellence through fundamental calls to action

Each category also embodies a corresponding idea that further clarifies its purpose. Effective leaders must:

1. Take personal responsibility for advancing their leadership ethos
2. Develop a mindset that craves innovation

© The Author(s) 2018
K. Mariama-Arthur, *Poised for Excellence*, DOI 10.1007/978-3-319-64574-2_41

3. Ground their efforts in service to others
4. Take strong actions that lead to measurable results

Leaders who refuse to just dabble and instead commit to mastering the fundamental principles that drive results experience profound success. In the pages that follow, each principle is synthesized, underscoring its broader implications and highlighting its unique value. Each micro-brief (i.e., chapter) also includes a provocative query challenging the reader to dig a bit deeper to master it. It is a last look—if you will—encouraging you to further consider the application of each principle in context. The idea is that as you read and reread this book, you will continue to extract beneficial insights and use them to transform the organizations and institutions you serve.

# Part I: Principles that Foster Leadership Excellence Through Focused Introspection

## Chapter 1: Exceptional Leaders Are Lifelong Learners

Because leading is a rigorous undertaking, it is also an extraordinary privilege. Leaders who fail to commit to learning as a lifelong vocation can easily forfeit this privilege. Extraneous contributions fast become irrelevant. Continuing to strategically expand one's knowledge base is a nonnegotiable leadership imperative. It adds perpetual value to a leader's insights, inspires trust, and encourages others to follow.

*How can you visualize learning to honor the privilege of leading?*

## Chapter 2: Emotional Intelligence Drives Leadership Success

Emotional intelligence is the lifeblood of effective leadership. Mastering this soft skill is not only pragmatic but also improves the success of every human interaction. Leaders who choose to forgo this "secret sauce" and rely solely on cognitive intelligence and technical ability to govern will miss key opportunities to successfully influence the complex dynamics of intrapersonal and interpersonal interactions.

*How can you approach emotional intelligence as a strategic priority?*

## Chapter 3: Get Out of Your Way and Stop Sabotaging Your Success

External opinions abound. The beliefs leaders holds about themselves, however, are the most important in influencing their thinking, behavior, and project outcomes. Because self-limiting beliefs are among the most common and formidable challenges to effective leadership, leaders must discard them or risk being controlled and crippled by them.

*How can you decisively confront self-sabotage?*

## Chapter 4: You Are Your Own Best Barometer

Relying on one's thinking and decision-making ability is critical to becoming an effective leader. Even though seeking wise counsel is an important component of competent leadership, listening to the wisdom of one's gut increases gumption, cultivates resourcefulness, and encourages self-reliance. Leaders are expected to exercise good judgment, but they also must have the courage to trust it.

*How can you develop greater self-reliance without indulging arrogance?*

## Chapter 5: You Are Your Competition

Competition usually is understood as a contest between rival externalities. When leaders are properly focused on delivering value and operating in excellence, however, the idea of external competition becomes irrelevant. This realization liberates the soul and invites leaders to see themselves as their sole competition.

*What is your motivation to become better for your own sake?*

## Chapter 6: Integrity, Transparency, and Ethical Behavior Always Matter

Prioritizing candor and principled conduct is fundamental to ethical leadership. The stakes are always high and aberrations generally are frowned on. Because the potential for an unfortunate scandal always exists, "smart" leaders must rely on sensory acuity, moral rectitude, and compliance guidelines to avoid the appearance and occurrence of impropriety.

*How can you amplify your commitment to integrity and transparency?*

## Chapter 7: Leaders Create the Best Version of Themselves Without Apology

For leaders, image and reputation are everything. The impressions that others have fuel, or quell, leaders' influence. These impressions are based on a number of key factors that leaders must curate conscientiously. To create the best versions of themselves, leaders must do what is necessary to build and maintain a compelling personal and professional brand.

*How can you create the best version of yourself by elevating your brand?*

## Chapter 8: World-Class Leaders Lead by Example

What leaders do, rather than say, is the biggest determinant of how they are perceived and whether they can successfully influence others. Lip service falls flat. Effective leaders leverage their behavior to make their case. Where words matter, though, they are bolstered by congruent behavior.

*Does your behavior position you to lead by example?*

## Chapter 9: Leaders Own Their Mistakes and Embrace Constructive Criticism

No one is perfect. Every leader makes mistakes, has knowledge gaps, and struggles with blind spots. When leaders accept this reality, they can willingly subordinate their egos and welcome constructive feedback. It is through this important process that they evolve and become their best self.

*Do you have the courage to acknowledge your frailties?*

## Chapter 10: Visionary Leaders Eliminate "the Box"

Leaders have big ideas and reach for the impossible. Preconceived notions of success and failure do not constrain them. As visionaries, they create, rather than rehabilitate, ideas and cultivate new ways to be and to do. Without unlimited vision, progress and potential are not available, so they graciously break the mold.

*How can you enlarge your vision of possibilities?*

# Part II: Principles that Cultivate Leadership Excellence Through Disruptive Paradigm Shifts

## Chapter 11: Strive for Progress, Not Perfection

Progress, rather than perfection, is the optimal benchmark for determining success. Moving forward with a purpose, and acknowledging any improvements along the way, provides an objective measure of growth. Perfection is an abstraction—a subjective idea that does not exist. Smart leaders stay away from the notion of perfection.

*How can you achieve S.M.A.R.T. goals without pining for perfection?*

## Chapter 12: "True Grit" Beats Passion

Passion is a great initial motivator, but insufficient to sustain the long-term energy and focus needed to accomplish most goals. An individual's ability to successfully maneuver during tough times is a testament to intestinal fortitude. For leaders, grit is an indispensable component of every endeavor and creates a greater sense of fire in the belly than passion alone.

*How can you leverage grit to strengthen your mindset and appetite for achievement?*

## Chapter 13: Work Smarter, Not Harder

Even though producing high-quality work is a must, long hours and extensive labor do not automatically guarantee it. For leaders, transforming outcomes is about the effective use of resources rather than the rigor of the pursuit. Thoughtfully calibrating resources and priorities is a more productive way to achieve premium results.

*How can you marshal your resources to work smarter?*

## Chapter 14: Prepare for War in Times of Peace

Change can happen at a moment's notice. Advanced preparation is a judicious way to avoid reactive strategies, especially during a crisis. Hoping that a situation will not occur, or waiting until it evolves to confront it, usually results in stress and poor decision making. Being proactive is the key to responding with a level head to resolve a situation prudently.

*How can you get ahead of challenges and create proactive strategies?*

## Chapter 15: Turn "Shoulds" into "Musts"

Important goals are approached with an unmitigated sense of urgency. Only "musts" get done. "Shoulds" are discretionary—not priorities. They do not merit the same commitment as their life-and-death counterparts. Leaders who raise the bar on achievement set novel expectations about what must get done and govern themselves accordingly to reach goals of substance.

*How can you transform empty longings into "musts"?*

## Chapter 16: Lead with Influence, Not Authority

Titles are not the best evidence of professional authority, or an individual's ability to lead. The most effective leaders prefer to lead with influence, not authority; they know that is where real power resides. Because the magnitude of a leader's influence determines whether others will follow, smart leaders rely on their native ability to shape hearts and minds, rather than on the symbolism of authority.

*How can you leverage influence to expand the reach of your leadership?*

## Chapter 17: Reboot and Relax

All work and no play will make Jack and Jill dull. Perpetual drive and commitment require equal intervals of rest and relaxation. To consistently put their best foot forward, leaders must identify and prioritize constructive ways to step away from the busyness of schedules and the demands of workloads. Mental, physical, and emotional renewals are each fundamental to this result.

*How can you incorporate rest and relaxation into your regular routine?*

## Chapter 18: Always Look for the Silver Lining

Maintaining an optimistic outlook, regardless of the circumstances, is a pivotal strategy of effective leaders. They understand the power of perspective and look for the silver lining, a lesson, or a bright spot, despite the enormity of a situation. Not surprisingly, they usually find it. The bottom line? There is always a diamond hidden in a rough exterior. The most effective leaders seek it out and seize control of their destiny.

*How can you adjust your perspective to discover the silver lining?*

## Chapter 19: See the Forest *and* the Trees

Leaders need to home in on the details, while also seeing the big picture, to capture the complexity of the leadership landscape. Adaptable vision, allowing them to focus on what is the most important in the moment, makes this possible. Fixating exclusively on one or the other, though, is a luxury that conscientious leaders simply cannot afford.

*How can you expand and contract your vision to see the forest and the trees when necessary?*

## Chapter 20: Think of Fear as an Ally

Fear gets a bad rap. Albeit well-known for its remarkable ability to arouse feelings of doubt and disillusionment, it is also a powerful indicator. The most effective leaders reframe fear, transforming it from a foreboding and paralyzing force into one that offers a relevant lesson in every experience.

*How can you transform fear into an affirmative force?*

# Part III: Principles that Nurture Leadership Excellence Through Benevolence, Collaboration, and Value-Based Service to Others

## Chapter 21: Honor Human Relationships

As human engineers, leaders cannot escape the certainty of human interaction. Their work is focused on making authentic connections and building and honoring human relationships. Failure to honor relationships diminishes leaders' credibility and hinders their potential to successfully lead and influence others.

*How will you preserve the sanctity of human relationships?*

## Chapter 22: Use "Honey" to Catch Flies, Not Vinegar

Some leaders believe that "being nice" may cost them their professional credibility. This, however, is not the case, per se. Understanding the important connection between demeanor, behavior, and boundaries increases the likelihood of leadership success and provides guidance on how leaders can use "honey" rather than "vinegar" to strengthen every relationship.

*How can you use "honey" to develop more valuable relationships?*

## Chapter 23: Give Credit Where It Is Due

Self-assured leaders freely praise excellence in others. They enjoy supporting and inspiring greatness; they know that doing so will not diminish their own self-worth. An unwillingness to celebrate others reflects emotional immaturity and robs a leader of important opportunities to boost self-esteem, dignity in one's work, and the motivation to achieve continuous accomplishments.

*How can you be more intentional about acknowledging excellence in others?*

## Chapter 24: Promote Fairness and Consistency

Leaders must promote fairness and exercise good judgment to earn the trust of a committed base. When the rules are interpreted fairly and applied consistently, it is easy for individuals to submit to a leader's influence and authority. On the other hand, when they are not, the damage to a leader's credibility and the organizational culture can be devastating.

*How can you encourage fairness and consistency daily?*

## Chapter 25: Confront Workplace Bullies

An often painfully familiar pastime, bullying usually evokes memories of elementary school, fitting in, and rituals of intimidation. Unfortunately, eighth-grade graduation is not where the story ends. Bullying continues to plague many adults and has become a painful part of their professional life. Leaders must confront this workplace tragedy and urge others to confront it, too.

*How can you be a force for good and effectively confront workplace bullies?*

## Chapter 26: Collaborate with Experts to Maximize Results

Leveraging the know-how of highly skilled professionals can help leaders navigate industry complexities with ease. The value of assembling a team of shrewd advisors, especially at a project's inception, cannot be discounted. Going it alone and churning out substandard work is never worth the sacrifice. Discerning leaders welcome the wisdom of qualified experts who add value to the substance of their work.

*How can you collaborate with experts to produce high-quality work?*

## Chapter 27: Challenge the Status Quo

Leaders cannot afford to cling to "best practices" or the comfort of institutional mores. These conveniences hold organizations back. Being open-minded about change is necessary to lead as well as encourage buy-in from others. Instead of acquiescing, leaders must challenge the prevailing norms to transform the status quo successfully.

*How can you tackle age-old ideas and practices to create new possibilities?*

## Chapter 28: Leverage Leadership Ethos to Shape Culture

Human resource challenges can pose a serious threat to workplace culture and interfere with an organization's forward momentum. Unhappy employees do not perform well and that discontent spills over into the fiber of the organization. Leaders who leverage ethos to shape culture can help an organization steer clear of these challenges as well as create meaningful opportunities for growth, enhanced governance, and successful collaboration among stakeholders.

*How can you use ethos to influence the organizational culture?*

## Chapter 29: Practice Tolerance

Today's global workforce amplifies the need for cultural awareness. Diversity and inclusion are key targets of this effort. Prejudice, bias, and stereotypes can all affect perception. Even still, leaders must learn to connect and communicate with others in spite of differences. Without tolerance, it is difficult, if not impossible, to create a cohesive and collaborative workforce or an amiable workplace environment.

*How can you practice tolerance within the workplace?*

## Chapter 30: Create a Vision that Inspires

Creating a compelling vision that inspires others is the primary objective for every leader. Of course, it encourages buy-in and can fuel an unassailable campaign for change. Beyond garnering endorsements or creating consensus, though, it also must spur others to action. When individuals and organizations are invigorated to implement a compelling vision, magic happens.

*How can you create a dynamic, big-picture vision that inspires others and spurs them to action?*

# Part IV: Principles that Promote Leadership Excellence Through Fundamental Calls to Action

## Chapter 31: Delegate!

Leaders often assume more than their fair share of work. However, delegating responsibilities can help maximize resources and minimize stress. Claiming that "no one else can accomplish the task" is merely an excuse. It also deprives a leader of the freedom and opportunity to duly transfer the workload elsewhere. The most effective leaders relinquish control and thrive by delegating.

*How can you relinquish control and delegate to be more effective?*

## Chapter 32: Master Effective Decision Making

Decision making is a comprehensive process that takes focus and skill to execute. Leaders make critical decisions all the time and, therefore, need to master that skill. Considerably more than simply reaching a random conclusion, good decision making requires organization, clear thinking, and a thorough vetting of possible outcomes and alternatives.

*How can you master the decision-making process to facilitate better outcomes?*

## Chapter 33: Pull Up Weeds by Their Roots

Superficial probing rarely results in the discovery or resolution of a problem. Leaders must dig deep to discover root causes and eradicate them. Unresolved issues only resurface later and create a persistent cycle of confusion and dissatisfaction until they are addressed. Leaders must take a "deep dive" and pull up weeds by their roots.

*How can you dig deeper to solve problems at their roots?*

## Chapter 34: Say "No" and Own It

Agreeing to take on a project solely to please someone else is a leadership faux pas. It causes stress, frustration, and interferes with leaders' ability to execute their own priorities. Effective leaders say "no" and own it without apology. They know that piling on other people's priorities is a recipe for disaster and, therefore, avoid it at all cost.

*How can you learn to say "no" with confidence and focus on your own mission?*

## Chapter 35: Distinguish Management from Leadership

Managers and leaders perform two distinct but complementary roles. Leaders need to understand the fundamental differences to avoid confusion and navigate failed expectations within the workforce. When this distinction is prioritized and shared throughout an organization, both managers and leaders perform at optimal levels.

*How can you remain clear on the key differences between management and leadership?*

## Chapter 36: Acknowledge the Elephant in the Room

Much like elephants, issues that negatively affect an organization are often glaring—even when people pretend not to notice. No matter what, though, leaders must face the most difficult and obvious organizational challenges head on, or risk escalating the negative consequences associated with them.

*How can you confront the proverbial elephant in the room?*

## Chapter 37: Leverage Your Professional Wheelhouse

Leaders can maximize their capacity and add value by drawing on a diverse reservoir of skillsets developed over time. This unique combination of knowledge, skills, and experience can be leveraged independently as well collectively. By spreading their wings and marshaling their professional wheelhouse, leaders amplify the length and breadth of their contributions.

*How can you use your diverse skillset to add value to your organization?*

## Chapter 38: Come Down from the Ivory Tower

Leadership can be demanding. Nonstop requests and a never-ending work-load can make isolation attractive. Leaders who disconnect from the world around them, though, soon find that they are out of touch with what matters the most. Remaining well-informed, engaged, and accessible are each critical to effective leadership.

*How can you remain accessible and engaged with others?*

## Chapter 39: Sharpen Your Communication Skills

Effective leadership demands the ability to communicate with competence. Because leaders consistently engage with others, both individually and in groups, they must learn to master this critical skillset. Without the ability to maneuver competently through basic and complex social interactions, leaders will have a difficult time executing the essential functions of their role.

*How can you improve your communication skills to reinforce your leadership acumen?*

## Chapter 40: Encourage Leading at All Levels

Leadership is not reserved for those who operate in the upper echelons of an organization. Titles and apparent authority, by themselves, do not reflect the measure of able leadership; however, drive and a good-faith commitment to serve do. When the idea of leading at all levels is empowered throughout an organization, the benefits reverberate inside and outside of it.

*How can you encourage leading at all levels to strengthen the leadership pipeline?*

## Final Thoughts

Leadership is not for the faint of heart. Success requires a true commitment to service, along with humility, vulnerability, grit, and an unquenchable desire to learn and improve. Take this charge seriously. Sink your teeth into each principle. Grow your acumen and embark on an unconventional journey that transcends legacy.

Remember, we all are works in progress. At our best, though, we are poised for excellence.

*To your success in the organization, the boardroom, and beyond!*

# Bibliography

3M. (n.d.). *3M US Company History*. Retrieved September 2, 2017, from http://solutions.3m.com/wps/portal/3M/en_US/3M-Company/Information/Resources/History/?MDR=true

Abbatiello, A., Knight, M., Philpot, S., & Roy, I. (2017, February 28). Leadership Disrupted: Pushing the Boundaries. *Global Human Capital Trends*. Retrieved March 3, 2017, from https://dupress.deloitte.com/dup-us-en/focus/human-capital-trends/2017/developing-digital-leaders.html?id=us:2el:3dc:dup3822:awa:cons:hct17

Adichie, C. N. (2012, December). *We Should All Be Feminists* [Video File]. Retrieved December 20, 2013, from https://www.ted.com/talks/chimamanda_ngozi_adichie_we_should_all_be_feminists/transcript?language=en

Asprey, R. B. (2000). *The Rise of Napoleon Bonaparte*. New York: Basic Books.

Bandura, A., & Adams, N. E. (1977). Analysis of Self-efficacy Theory of Behavioral Change. *Cognitive Therapy and Research, 1*(4), 287. https://doi.org/10.1007/BF01663995.

Bennis, W., & Thomas, R. (2002). *Geeks & Geezer: How Era, Values, and Defining Moments Shape Leaders*. Boston: Harvard Business School Press.

Berger, L. (2014, December 30). The Hard Truth About the Current State of Soft Skills in the U.S. *Huffington Post*. Retrieved November 30, 2014, from http://m.huffpost.com/us/entry/6133618

Bernard, B. (1985). *Leadership and Performance Beyond Expectations*. New York: The Free Press.

Bersin by Deloitte. (n.d.-a). High Potential/HiPo (and Maturity Model). *Bersin by Deloitte*. Retrieved February 6, 2016, from http://www.bersin.com/Lexicon/details.aspx?id=12845

Bersin by Deloitte. (n.d.-b). High Performer. *Bersin by Deloitte*. Retrieved February 6, 2016, from http://www.bersin.com/Lexicon/Details.aspx?id=12844

© The Author(s) 2018                                                    **271**
K. Mariama-Arthur, *Poised for Excellence*, DOI 10.1007/978-3-319-64574-2

Blenko, M.W., Mankins, M., & Rogers, P. (2010, June). The Decision-Driven Organization. *Harvard Business Review, 88*(3). Retrieved February 20, 2017, from https://hbr.org/2010/06/the-decision-driven-organization

Bort, C., & Blappo, B. (2015, September 22). CNN Does Not Get to Cherry-Pick the Rules of Journalism. *Esquire*. Retrieved September 9, 2017, from https://www.google.com/amp/www.esquire.com/news-politics/news/amp30076/cnn-rules-of-journalism/

Branson, R. (1998). *Losing my Virginity: The Autobiography*. London: Virgin Pub.

Canwell, A., Dongrie, V., Neveras, N., & Stockton, H. (2014). *Leaders at All Levels: Closing the Gap Between Hype and Readiness*. Deloitte University Press: A Report by Deloitte Consulting and Bersin by Deloitte.

Chan, D. (2000). Understanding Adaptation to Changes in the Work Environment: Integrating Individual Difference and Learning Perspectives. *Research in Personnel and Human Resources Management, 18*, 1–42.

Chowdry, A. (2014, October 10). Microsoft CEO Satya Nadella Apologizes for Comments on Women's Raises. *Forbes*. Retrieved February 9, 2017, from https://www.forbes.com/sites/amitchowdhry/2014/10/10/microsoft-ceo-satya-nadella-apologizes-for-comments-on-womens-pay/#113c0c646d2b

Copeland, M. (2014). *Life in Motion: An Unlikely Ballerina*. New York: Touchstone.

Damasio, A. R. (2003). *Looking for Spinoza: Joy, Sorrow, and the Feeling Brain*. Orlando: Harcourt.

Damasio, A. R. (2005). *Descartes' Error: Emotion, Reason, and the Human Brain*. New York: Penguin Books.

Deutschendorf, H. (2015, October). *Why Emotionally Intelligent People Are More Successful*. Fast Company. Retrieved October 14, 2016, from https://www.fastcompany.com/3047455/why-emotionally-intelligent-people-are-more-successful

Dixon, T. (2015). *Money: The Life and Fast Times of Floyd Mayweather*. Endinburgh: Birlinn Publishers.

Duckworth, A. (2016). *Grit: The Power of Passion and Perseverance* (Unabridged). New York, NY: Audioworks, an Imprint of Simon & Schuster Audio Division.

Duckworth A. (2016, November 11). *Spotlight with Angela Duckworth*. INBOUND 2016, Boston, MA.

Gardner, H. (2006). *Multiple Intelligences: New Horizons* (Completely rev. and updated). New York: Basic Books.

Goleman, D. (1995). *Emotional Intelligence: Why It Can Matter More than IQ*. New York: Bantam Books.

Hampton, D. (2015, January 12). What's the Difference Between Feelings and Emotions. *The Best Brain Possible*. Retrieved September 12, 2016, from https://www.thebestbrainpossible.com/whats-the-difference-between-feelings-and-emotions/

Hannah, S., Balthazard, P., Waldman, D., Jennings, P., & Thatcher, R. (2013). The Psychological and Neurological Bases of Leader Self-Complexity and Effects on Adaptive Decision-Making. *Journal of Applied Psychology, 98*(3), 393–411.

Jack, D. (2014, March 8). *Address: If You Want Peace, Prepare for War—U.S. Military Pre-Eminence and Why it Matters*. Hudson Institute. Retrieved January 25, 2017, from https://www.hudson.org/research/10155-address-if-you-want-peace-prepare-for-war-u-s-military-pre-eminence-and-why-it-matters

Kotter, J. (1990). *A Force for Change: How Leadership Differs from Management*. New York: The Free Press.

Leonard, D., Barton, G., & Barton, M. (2013). Make Yourself an Expert. *Harvard Business Review, 91*(4), 127–132.

Livermore, D. A. (2015). *Leading with Cultural Intelligence: The New Secret to Success*. New York: American Management Association.

Mariama-Arthur, K. (2014, December 2). The Star of 'Million Dollar Listing Miami' on Working Smarter, Not Harder. *Success*. Retrieved February 27, 2017, from http://www.success.com/article/the-star-of-million-dollar-listing-miami-the-star-of-million-dollar-listing-miami-

Mariama-Arthur, K. (2016, July 22). *The Number one Reason Leaders Need Feedback: The Value of Feedback in a Professional Environment, Especially for Those in Leadership Positions*. Black Enterprise. Retrieved September 8, 2017, from http://www.blackenterprise.com/career/career-advice/the-number-one-reason-leaders-need-feedback/

Maslow, A. (1943). *A Theory of Human Motivation. Psychological Review*. Princeton University.

McDonald, O. (2012). *Fannie Mae and Freddie Mac: Turning the American Dream into a Nightmare*. New York: Bloomsbury Academic.

McLean, B., & Elkind, P. (2003). *The Smartest Guys in the Room: The Amazing Rise and Scandalous Fall of Enron*. New York: Portfolio.

Microsoft. (n.d.). *What Empowerment Means to us*. Microsoft. Retrieved January 20, 2017, from https://news.microsoft.com/empowerment/

Mikkelsen. K., & Jarche, H. (2015, October 16). The Best Leaders Are Constant Learners. *Harvard Business Review* 93 (10). Retrieved June 10, 2016 from https://hbr.org/2015/10/the-best-leaders-are-constant-learners

Morgenson, G. (2010, May 8). Ignoring the Elephant in the Bailout. *The New York Times*. Retrieved February 3, 2017, from https://mobile.nytimes.com/2010/05/09/business/09gret.html

Namie, G. (2014). *The WBI Definition of Workplace Bullying*. The Workplace Bullying Institute. Retrieved September 12, 2014, from http://www.workplacebullying.org/individuals/problem/definition

Namie, G. (2017). *2017 Workplace Bullying Institute U.S. Workplace Bullying Survey*. San Francisco: Workplace Bullying Institute.

Nobel Media AB. (2014). *The Nobel Prize in Literature 1953*. The Nobel Prize Org. Retrieved February 15, 2017, from http://www.nobelprize.org/nobel_prizes/literature/laureates/1953/

Northouse, G. (2007). *Leadership Theory and Practice* (3rd ed.). Thousand Oaks: Sage Publications.

Powell, C. L., & Kotlz, T. (2012). *It Worked for Me: In Life and Leadership* (1st HarperLuxe ed.). New York: HarperLuxe.

Rea, S. (2017, March 13). *Information Avoidance: How People Select Their Own Realities*. Carnegie Mellon University. Retrieved March 15, 2017, from https://www.cmu.edu/news/stories/archives/2017/march/information-avoidance.html

Ricketts, K. (2009). *Say Hello to Leadership*. University of Kentucky College of Agriculture. ELK1-100.

Salovey, P., Bracket, M. A., & Mayer, J. (2006). *Emotional Intelligence: Key Readings on the Mayer and Salovey Model*. New York: National Professional Resources.

Seth, R. (2016, June 29). *Five Leadership Lessons from Canadian Prime Minister Justin Trudeau*. Fast Company. Retrieved March 5, 2017, from https://www.fastcompany.com/3061046/5-leadership-lessons-from-canadian-prime-minister-justin-trudeau

Simmons, E. (1998). *The Marines*. Triangle: The Marine Corps Heritage Foundation.

Smith, L. (2007). *The Few and the Proud: Marine Corps Drill Instructors in Their Own Words*. New York: W. W. North & Company.

Stephen, M., Vahdat, H., Walkinshaw, H., Walsh, B., Canwell, A., Dongrie, V., & Volini, E. (2014). *Global Human Capital Trends: Engaging the 21st Century Workforce*. Deloitte University Press: A Report by Deloitte Consulting LLP and Bersin by Deloitte.

Sweeny, K., Melnyk, D., Miller, W., & Shepperd, J. A. (2010). Information Avoidance: Who, What, When, and Why. *Review of General Psychology, 14*(4), 340–353.

The Henry Ford. (n.d.). *Elin Musk: Founder PayPal, SpaceX, Tesla Motors & Solar City*. The Henry Ford. Retrieved February 16, 2017, from https://www.thehenryford.org/explore/stories-of-innovation/visionaries/elon-musk/

Tunca, D. (2016). The Chimamanda Ngozi Adichie Website. [online] L3.ulg.ac.be. Retrieved February 23, 2017, from http://www.l3.ulg.ac.be/adichie/cnabio.html

Wegmans. (n.d.). *Company Overview*. Retrieved July 6, 2017, from https://www.wegmans.com/about

Wilson Burns, E., Smith, L., & Ulrich, D. (2012). Competency Models with Impact Research Findings from the Top Companies for Leaders. *People & Strategy, 35*(3), 16–60.

# Index[1]

---

[1] Note: Page number followed by 'n' refers to note.

© The Author(s) 2018
K. Mariama-Arthur, *Poised for Excellence*, DOI 10.1007/978-3-319-64574-2

CPSIA information can be obtained
at www.ICGtesting.com
Printed in the USA
LVHW080133090819
627060LV00005B/14/P

AUG 2 7 2019